PHP by Example

A Practical Guide to Creating
Web Applications with PHP

Alex Vasilev

Apress®

PHP by Example: A Practical Guide to Creating Web Applications with PHP

Alex Vasilev
Department of Software Systems and Technologies,
Taras Shevchenko National University of Kyiv, Kyiv, Ukraine

ISBN-13 (pbk): 979-8-8688-0257-7   ISBN-13 (electronic): 979-8-8688-0258-4
https://doi.org/10.1007/979-8-8688-0258-4

Managing Director, Apress Media LLC: Welmoed Spahr
Acquisitions Editor: James Robinson-Prior
Development Editor: James Markham
Editorial Assistant: Gryffin Winkler
Copyeditor: Kim Burton

Cover designed by eStudioCalamar
Cover image designed by Barbara A Lane from Pixabay

Distributed to the book trade worldwide by Springer Science+Business Media New York, 1 New York Plaza, Suite 4600, New York, NY 10004-1562, USA. Phone 1-800-SPRINGER, fax (201) 348-4505, e-mail orders-ny@springer-sbm.com, or visit www.springeronline.com. Apress Media, LLC is a California LLC and the sole member (owner) is Springer Science + Business Media Finance Inc (SSBM Finance Inc). SSBM Finance Inc is a **Delaware** corporation.

For information on translations, please e-mail booktranslations@springernature.com; for reprint, paperback, or audio rights, please e-mail bookpermissions@springernature.com.

Apress titles may be purchased in bulk for academic, corporate, or promotional use. eBook versions and licenses are also available for most titles. For more information, reference our Print and eBook Bulk Sales web page at http://www.apress.com/bulk-sales.

Any source code or other supplementary material referenced by the author in this book is available to readers on GitHub. For more detailed information, please visit https://www.apress.com/gp/services/source-code.

"All Rights are reserved by the Publisher except for Russian, Ukrainian and Bulgarian rights".

Translated into the English from the Ukrainian.

Previously published in Russian as "Программирование на PHP в примерах и задачах" (2021) by Eksmo Publishing

Previously Published in Ukrainian as "Програмування мовою PHP" (2022) by LIRA-K Publishing

If disposing of this product, please recycle the paper

In memory of my dad. Thank you for all you gave, and sorry for all I didn't return.

Table of Contents

About the Author

Alex Vasilev is a software systems and technologies professor at the Faculty of Information Technology, Taras Shevchenko National University of Kyiv in Ukraine. He has taught programming (C++, C#, Java, JavaScript, Python, and PHP) for 20 years. To date, he has written over 30 programming books in his native Ukraine. This is his first book directly published in English.

About the Technical Reviewer

 **Vadim Atamanenko** is an experienced software engineer and technical reviewer with over 25 years of expertise in software development. His professional journey includes a leadership role in the analytical reporting department of Freedom Holding Corp. Throughout his career, he has actively contributed to the scientific community, publishing articles on the application of artificial intelligence in the financial sector.

Vadim's technical expertise has been internationally recognized, evidenced by membership in two prestigious associations: IEEE (Institute of Electrical and Electronics Engineers) and Leaders Excellence at Harvard Square. His scientific papers have been published in various scholarly journals, including *Modern Science: Current Issues in Theory and Practice*.

Acknowledgments

To my dear children Anastasia and Bohdan, and all my family. Thank you for your support and love. You give meaning to my life and encourage me to move on.

I sincerely thank the great and professional Apress team for the outstanding support and dedication provided throughout the process of bringing the book to fruition. Their collective efforts have undoubtedly played a pivotal role in making the book better.

Introduction

There are many things in this universe you are not meant to understand. Now, that does not mean they are not real.

—*ALF* (TV series)

This book discusses the PHP programming language. PHP is a simple, beautiful, and elegant language. Moreover, it is special in some sense. PHP is designed to execute code on the server side. In other words, it is not enough to know PHP. It is also necessary to understand how and for what it is used. That is important since understanding the possibilities of a language is the key to using it effectively.

Note   PHP is a language designed for programming and web programming.

About PHP

The PHP language is used for creating sites and web applications. It has a long story, is popular among developers, and is supported by most host servers.

Details

Hosting is a service for providing resources and space on a server to host data and information (for example, web pages). The host server is a server that hosts the information. For the sake of simplicity, this means the host server is a computer (server) that hosts the user's web page (that is, the page where PHP is supposed to be used).

The author of PHP is Rasmus Lerdorf. The project started as writing scripts to support a personal web page and was initially titled Personal Homepages Tools or PHP Tools. Then, it was transformed into an independent and influential software product. Today, the name PHP is usually associated with the phrase *Hypertext Preprocessor*, which is not far from the truth.

Note   When writing this book, the current version is PHP 8. On the other hand, in practice, the latest version of the language does not immediately start to be used. There is some inertia here due to both objective and subjective factors. Therefore, universal approaches relevant to the last few language versions are considered. Notably, there is no sixth version: the seventh version follows after the fifth. The reason is that the attempt to release the sixth version was highly unsuccessful.

PHP is a scripted and interpreted language. Interpretability means that a program is executed under the control of a particular program called an *interpreter*. The interpreter reads the code line by line and executes the corresponding instructions.

🔔 **The PHP 8 Standard**   PHP 8 introduced a JIT compiler (short for *Just in Time*) for compiling PHP code to speed up program execution. When compiled, the program instructions are translated into processor-level instructions.

Scripting languages are usually high-level ones. Unlike conventional programs, scripts usually contain instructions for controlling ready-made software components. In other words, a scripting language is a straightforward language. Although, of course, not everything is always so rosy.

Details

The C language has influenced the syntax of the PHP language. Therefore, if you know languages such as C, C++, C#, or Java, you will find many familiar syntax constructions.

Of course, PHP is a programming language, among many others. But it has an essential feature in how PHP codes are used.

If you are dealing with any conventional programming language, the process of writing and using programs looks like follows. First, you create the program code—in other words, you write a program. Then, that program must be executed. How to do that depends on the language, but the most crucial question is whether the program is *compiled* or *interpreted*. If the program is compiled, a particular compiler program translates your program into machine instructions (or something similar to them), and then those instructions are executed. If the program is interpreted, a special interpreter program reads your program and executes statements from the code. But whatever happens, the important thing here is that you do all the operations on the same computer. You run the program on the computer and get a result. You can do anything you want with the result of the program execution, but the critical point is that it is enough to have only one computer.

With the PHP language, things are somewhat different. To understand the problem, let's consider what happens when you access a web page and how PHP is involved in that case.

A Client and a Server

In general terms, here is the scheme according to which the site is viewed on the network. In this case, the main acting "characters" are the computer on which you want to view the web page and the computer on which that page is located. The first computer (on which you are trying to view the web page) is called a *client*, and the computer on which the web page is located is called a *server*.

There is a connection between these computers through the global network; therefore, the computers can send information to each other. You work on a client computer and want to view a web page. To do that, you run a special program designed to view web pages. The program is called a *browser*. You open a browser (for example, Chrome, Opera, or Edge), and in the address bar, you enter the site address you want to view. The browser initiates a request to the server. The server receives the request, processes it, and returns a response to the client. The response contains the document's code; the browser should display it on the client screen. The general scheme of the "interaction" is illustrated in Figure I-1.

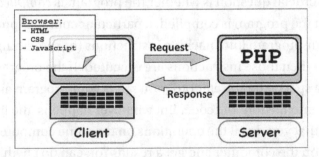

Figure I-1. *The scheme of the interaction between a client and a server*

The browser processes the document in HTML format (the abbreviation comes from Hypertext Markup Language). The text contains a special markup. The browser "understands" that markup and renders the document following the instructions embedded in the document. In addition to the actual HTML markup, the document displayed by the browser can contain additional instructions. For example, CSS (Cascading Style Sheets) formatting can be used in the document. The document may also contain JavaScript scripts. In the latter case, the browser executes these scripts. So, the server sends a set of commands, and the browser executes them. The important thing is that the commands are executed on the same computer that made the request.

Note   The server tells what to do, and the client's browser performs the necessary operations. Convenient but not always safe.

So, where is the place for PHP in this scheme? The answer is at the stage of processing the request by the server. When the server receives a request from a client, it processes the request, and while processing it, scripts can be executed—in this case, PHP scripts.

Details

Often, the script's output is a generated HTML code passed to the client.

But that is not all. Many programs try to exchange information over the network. Processes on a client send signals to processes on a server and back, and you need to know which signal is for which process. For that purpose, you use ports. Ports are unique integer identifiers the processes use to identify the signals sent to them. Therefore, requests from the client's browser and server responses must be synchronized by ports. That is, to work effectively with PHP, you need to solve quite a few technical problems. All that is considered step by step, as necessary.

How to Execute the PHP Code

Let's take the next step in studying PHP. Namely, focusing on how to execute a program written in PHP. If you are talking about the "natural" way of using PHP code, you would need a server and a client. That is two computers. The script (the program) is hosted on the server, and you can view the result of the program execution by accessing the web page on the server through the client browser. But even if all these resources are available, the described strategy is not very convenient since you need to edit the program on one computer (the server) and check the result on another computer (the client). So, it is clear that you would like to have a more reliable strategy.

An alternative way is to "trick" the browser. Namely, you can create an illusion that the server is a client itself. It's about using a *local server*. It is easy to switch to that mode. The advantage of the approach is that the program and its result are localized within the same computer.

On the other hand, PHP code can be executed using an interpreter—that is, approximately the same as in the case of other interpreted languages. That is probably the easiest way to see what the result of running a program is. Nevertheless, you should not forget that PHP programs are not written to be executed by the interpreter on the client's computer. So, there will be some tricks, too.

The Software

The book contains many examples, and in the process of studying them, it is desirable to disassemble the program and examine the result of its execution. That requires special software.

First of all, you have to install the software that supports PHP. To do that, go to `www.php.net`, as shown in Figure I-2.

Figure I-2. *The window for PHP support at* `www.php.net`

You should find the software download section in that window and download the necessary files.

Note In the simplest case, the installation comes down to unpacking the archive downloaded from `www.php.net`. That will likely be enough for using the PHP interpreter (`php.exe` file) in command-line mode. You may need to perform additional settings for a more "comfortable" work regime involving special software. If so, refer to the help information on the `www.php.net` page and use the help for the relevant software product (for example, a code editor).

Details

You can use the `php -v` command-line instructions to check the PHP version. To get PHP help, use the `php -h` command. Additional information about PHP can be obtained with the `php -i` command.

If you use the Windows operating system, you can enter the `cmd` instruction into the address bar of Windows Explorer to switch to the terminal mode. Then, you must change to the PHP directory in the terminal window. For example, if PHP is in the `C:\PHP` folder, the appropriate command would be `cd C:\PHP`. An alternative is to navigate to the PHP directory first and then enter the `cmd` instruction in the Explorer address bar.

Many operating systems of the Linux family have PHP pre-installed. But if this is not the case, you can use the `sudo apt install php` command to install PHP.

In general, to have a PHP interpreter that allows you to execute programs written in PHP is enough. However, you also need to type and edit your programs somewhere. In principle, a regular text editor could be the choice. But it's much better to install something more advanced, with support for PHP syntax (an editor that "understands" PHP special instructions).

Note It is easy to find a suitable editor for processing PHP code if necessary. However, such a strategy is mainly aimed at advanced users. That is why it is beyond your attention.

There are other options as well. For example, the Visual Studio Code development environment (the address is `https://code.visualstudio.com`) is quite convenient. The browser opened on the project page is shown in Figure I-3.

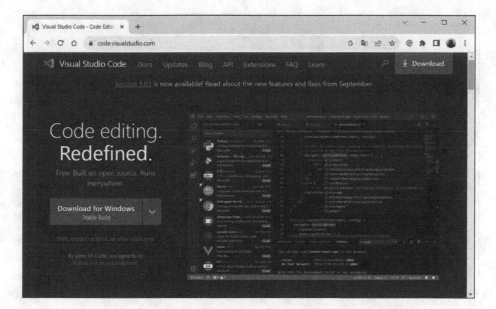

Figure I-3. *The Visual Studio Code project support page*

Details

The first time you run the Visual Studio Code application, you must confirm the installation of the PHP support in the Customize section.

Another good option for developing PHP programs is the NetBeans IDE. The installation files can be downloaded from `http://netbeans.apache.org`. Figure I-4 shows a browser open on the NetBeans project support page.

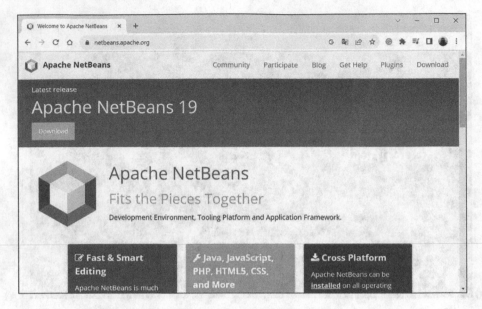

Figure I-4. *The NetBeans project support page*

Details

You may need the Java Development Kit (JDK) pre-installed on your computer to use NetBeans.

There are other helpful software products, including commercial ones. But once again, it is enough to install PHP and select a suitable code editor.

Note You will learn how to use the software (at the primary level) through examples.

About This Book

This book is entirely devoted to the PHP language, focusing on why it is needed and its features. It investigates the main constructions of the language, as well as the approaches and mechanisms used in PHP. In the book, considerable attention is paid to examples. The range of topics discussed in the book is enough for writing effective PHP codes. The main part of the book consists of twelve chapters.

- Chapter 1 contains simple programs, and it discusses how to use the software and analyzes the general principles of creating PHP programs there.

- Chapter 2 discusses variables and data types. There, you will learn how to create variables, perform operations with them, and use data of different types.

- Chapter 3 is devoted to the control statements. You will get a notion of the conditional statement, selection statement, and loop statements, as well as the goto instruction. All those are critical for creating efficient PHP programs.

- Chapter 4 contains information about arrays. In PHP, arrays have several unique features and will be the study's subject. This chapter discusses one-dimensional and multi-dimensional arrays, describes the iteration over a collection statement, and provides an overview of the basic operations performed on arrays.

- Chapter 5 describes functions. You will learn how they are created, discuss the mechanisms for passing arguments, consider how a result is returned, learn how to set default values for arguments, and how to create functions with an arbitrary number of arguments. You will consider ways for passing arguments by name. The chapter also focuses on recursion, anonymous functions, and some other topics related to functions.

- Chapter 6 deals with links, constants, global and statistic variables, file handling, and methods for working with multi-line text.

- Chapter 7 discusses the principles of object-oriented programming (OOP) and considers how PHP implements these principles. You will learn how to create classes and objects and what to do with methods. You will also meet constructors, destructors, and static class members. The chapter deals with the problem of copying objects and illustrates how to use private fields and methods. Some special methods are also described in the chapter.

- Chapter 8 is devoted to such an important OOP mechanism as inheritance. You will learn how a child's class is created and how methods are overridden. You will consider the features of constructors, private and protected members of a class in the context of the inheritance. The chapter also discusses the virtuality of methods, describes multi-level inheritance and contains some other information.

- Chapter 9 describes abstract classes and interfaces (including their implementation and inheritance). You will learn what traits are, how an interface can control the type of an object, what a namespace is, and how it is used.

- The principles of error and exception handling are discussed in Chapter 10. You become familiar with the main exception classes and learn how exceptions are generated. In addition, the chapter describes methods for creating classes for user-defined exceptions. Some other issues related to error and exception handling are also covered.

- Chapter 11 is devoted to generators and iterators. You will learn to use and apply the generator functions in different situations. You will also learn what iterators are and how they are created.

- Chapter 12 contains examples of using PHP programs in practice. The chapter discusses several subjects that give an idea of the role PHP codes play in creating web documents.

At the end of each chapter, for convenience, a summary lists all the main points discussed in the chapter.

Note This book is primarily for those with minimal programming experience, so the content is presented as simply as possible.

CHAPTER 1

The First Program

—I demand to restore the Earth's ozone layer.
—Alf, we won't make it by Saturday.

—ALF (TV series)

In this chapter, you will create your first PHP program. Namely, you will examine some simple code and determine how it can be executed. There is not much programming in the chapter, but a lot of information is essential for using PHP.

The Program's Code

A program in PHP is a set of instructions that an interpreter executes. These instructions must be appropriately formatted and passed to the interpreter for execution. The plans are focused on solving the following two tasks.

- Writing the code of a program

- Launching the program for execution

The second task is much more complex than the first one.

So, let's create your first PHP program. Namely, let's define what your program should do. Traditionally, the first program displays a message. You will do the same. Your program displays a welcome message in the output window (terminal). The program is shown in Listing 1-1.

© Alex Vasilev 2024
A. Vasilev, *PHP by Example*, https://doi.org/10.1007/979-8-8688-0258-4_1

Listing 1-1. The First Program

```php
<?php
   print("Hello, PHP!");
?>
```

The program begins with the <?php statement and ends with the ?> statement. That is a standard situation for all programs in PHP. The commands to be executed in the program are placed between these instructions. In this case, there is a single command. It calls the print() built-in function with "Hello, PHP!" passed as an argument.

Details

A function is a named block of code (command block) that can be executed by calling the function (by specifying its name with arguments, if necessary). Functions can be created in a program, or you can use built-in functions. Among the built-in functions, there is the print() function.

Text values are enclosed in double quotes. Also, text values can be enclosed in single quotes. Both styles are almost equivalent, but there are essential differences, which are discussed a little later.

It is also worth noting that every command in PHP ends with a semicolon.

(i) **Note**   Frankly speaking, print() is not exactly a function but rather a special syntax construction of the PHP language. But since its properties are similar to a function, consider it a function. And you proceed in the same way in all such cases.

As you might guess, the command displays a message in the terminal. The message's text is passed to the print() function as an argument. The following shows the result of running the program.

The output of the program (from Listing 1-1)
```
Hello, PHP!
```

There is nothing complicated in this program. It remains only to figure out how to run the program for execution.

Details

The argument can be specified without parentheses when calling the print() function. That means that instead of the print("Hello, PHP!") command, you can use the print "Hello, PHP!" statement. Another alternative to the print() function is the echo statement. Namely, the echo "Hello, PHP!" command could display the message.

The Interpreter Regime

Let's explore several options, and you can choose the one you like the best.

 Note   There are two regimes of the PHP program execution. The first one is the execution of a program using an interpreter on a client computer. The second regime means encapsulating PHP code in a document with HTML markup. In that case, you must use an external or local server. Implementing this is a little more complicated than executing the code with an interpreter, but it is more "natural" and related to practical PHP usage.

So, the first thing to do is to create a file with the program, as in Listing 1-1, and save that file with the .php extension. For example, name the file hello.php, located in the D:\Books\php\codes folder. Next, execute the file. At this stage, you need an interpreter, the php.exe file located in the folder where PHP was installed. Let's assume that PHP is installed in the C:\PHP folder. The recipe for launching the program is simple: in the terminal's command line, you must execute php.exe, passing the hello. php file to it (the file with the program) as a parameter. You can make that simple. You need to specify the full path to the php.exe file in the command line and, separated by a space, the full path to the file with the hello.php program. The corresponding command would look as follows.

```
C:\PHP\php.exe D:\Books\php\codes\hello.php
```

Nevertheless, specifying the full path to the files is not very convenient. In principle, you can move to the directory with the php.exe file installed and save the files with the PHP code in the same place. So, if PHP is installed in the C:\PHP folder, then to move to it, run the following command in the command line.

```
cd C:\PHP
```

Details

If you need to change a directory and a disk, use the /d option. For example, if you need to move from the D:\ drive to the C:\ drive, the command looks like cd /d C:\.

If the hello.php file is located in the same folder as the php.exe file, then you use the following command to run the program for execution.

```
php hello.php
```

The same command can be used under the Windows operating system if you add the path to the PHP folder to the Path environment variable and then move to the folder with the program file.

Details

Select the **Advanced** system settings item in the computer properties to get the Path environment variable. In the **System Properties** window, select the **Environment Variables** icon. In the **Environment Variables** window, select the **Path** position and change the contents of the corresponding variable.

The use of development environments simplifies testing and executing codes. Let's look at the Visual Studio Code environment as an example. Figure 1-1 shows the environment's window with the hello.php file open.

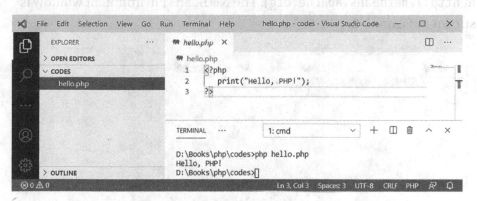

Figure 1-1. *The Visual Studio Code development environment window with the hello.php program file open*

In the environment window, open the folder with the program file. (You can use the **Open Folder** command from the **File** menu.) The files from this folder should appear in the **Explorer** section on the left side of the development environment window. In this case, select the file with the program. The file's contents are displayed in the central part of the window. You can run the program in the terminal, which is opened using the **New Terminal** command from the **Terminal** menu. In the example, you enter the following command in the terminal command line.

```
php hello.php
```

If you use the Windows operating system, the Path environment variable must contain the path to the php.exe file. If not, you must specify the full path to that file, and the command looks as follows.

```
C:\PHP\php.exe hello.php
```

If everything goes well, then the message displayed by the program should appear in the terminal.

However, the most comfortable and free way to develop is to use the NetBeans development environment (the site with the installation files is at http://netbeans.apache.org). The NetBeans environment window is shown in Figure 1-2.

Figure 1-2. *The NetBeans window*

To create a new project in this environment, select the **New Project** command from the **File** menu, as shown in Figure 1-3.

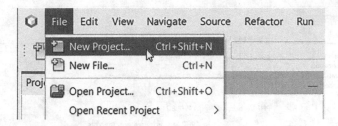

Figure 1-3. *Creating a new project*

The **New Project** window opens, as shown in Figure 1-4.

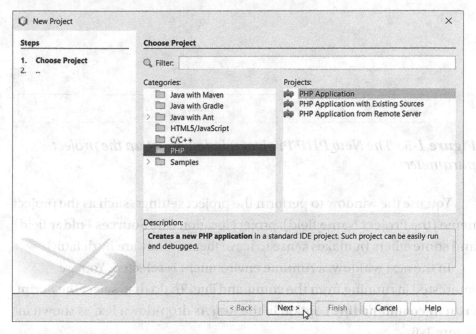

Figure 1-4. *The window **New Project** for creating a new project*

In the window, you select the type of application (a PHP project must be created). The following **New PHP Project** window appears, as shown in Figure 1-5.

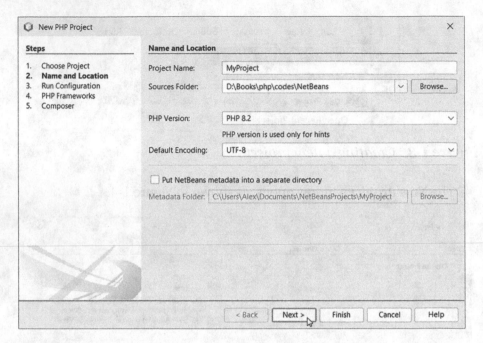

Figure 1-5. *The **New PHP Project** window to set up the project parameters*

You use the window to perform the project settings, such as the project name (the **Project Name** field), project location (the **Sources Folder** field), and some others (it makes sense to leave them as they are by default).

In the next window, a runtime environment is selected. You are interested in running from the command line. To do that, select the **Script (run in command line)** option in the **Run As** drop-down list, as shown in Figure 1-6.

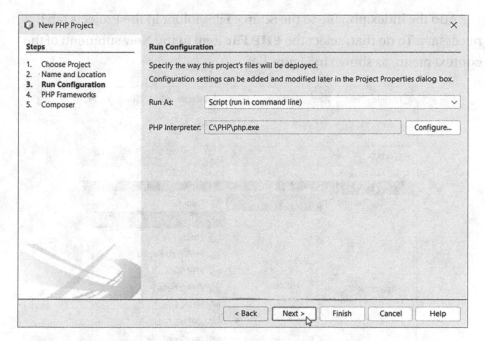

Figure 1-6. Selecting a runtime environment

The **PHP Interpreter** field specifies the location of the PHP interpreter (in this case, C:\PHP\php.exe). The settings in other windows should be left unchanged. Figure 1-7 shows the window of the newly created project.

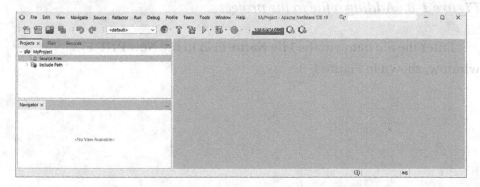

Figure 1-7. The window of the newly created project

Add the index.php file to the Source Files folder in the Projects tab if necessary. To do that, select the **PHP File** item in the **New** submenu of the context menu, as shown in Figure 1-8.

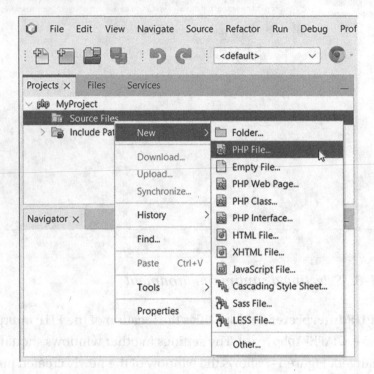

Figure 1-8. *Adding a file to the project*

Enter the file name in the **File Name** field in the **New PHP File** window, shown in Figure 1-9.

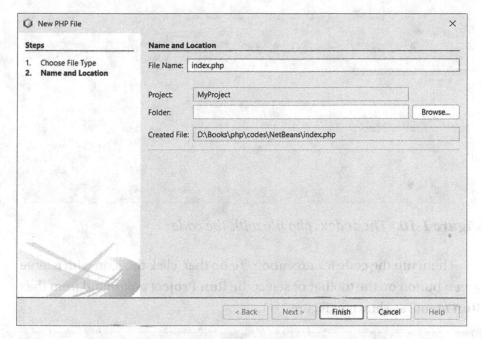

*Figure 1-9. The **File Name** field with the name of the file*

ℹ Note   In some NetBeans versions, the `index.php` file is automatically created in the project folder.

The code of the `index.php` file is entered in the editor window. Figure 1-10 illustrates the situation.

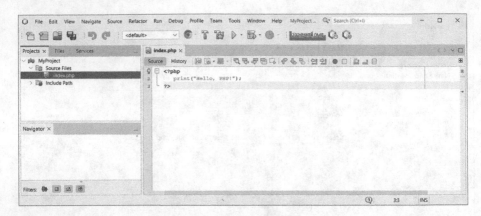

Figure 1-10. *The index.php file with the code*

Then, run the code for execution. To do that, click the icon with a large green button on the toolbar or select the **Run Project** command from the **Run** menu, as shown in Figure 1-11.

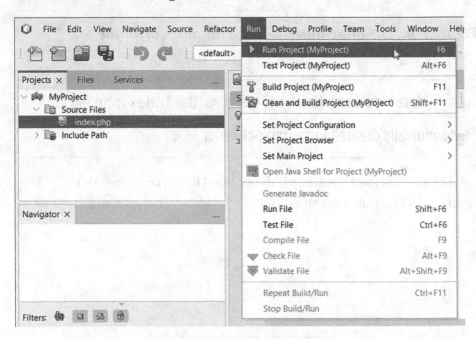

Figure 1-11. *Running a PHP program for execution*

The result of executing the code is displayed in the output area at the bottom of the NetBeans IDE window (see Figure 1-12).

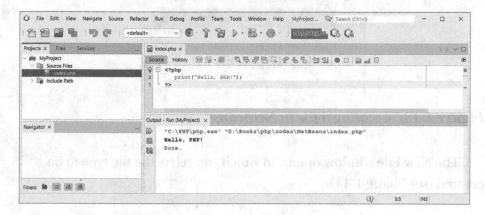

Figure 1-12. *The result of the program execution*

Thus, you can edit the program code conveniently and run it for execution.

ⓘ Note   The NetBeans environment has a simple and user-friendly configuration system. Its description is beyond the scope of the book. At the same time, if necessary, you can deal with related technical issues on your own.

It is also worth noting that some settings related to working with PHP are performed in a special window, which can be accessed using the **Options** command from the **Tools** menu.

In NetBeans, you can create a single file with PHP code instead of creating a project. To do that, in the NetBeans development environment window, select the **New File** command from the **File** menu (see Figure 1-13).

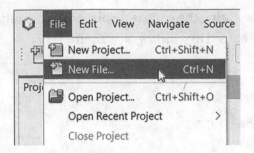

Figure 1-13. *Creating a file in NetBeans*

The **New File** window opens, in which you select the file type to be created (see Figure 1-14).

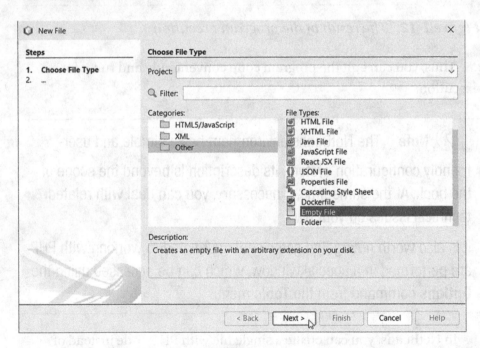

Figure 1-14. *Selecting the file type*

In particular, select **Other** in the **Categories** section and **Empty File** in the **File Types** section. Then, the **New Empty File** window appears (see Figure 1-15).

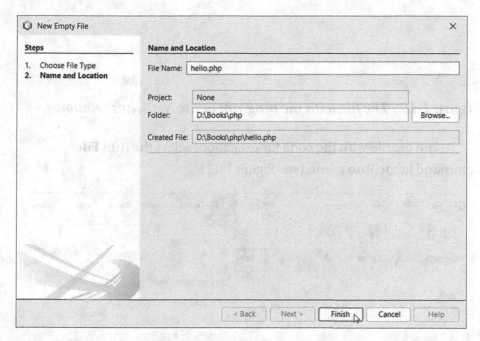

Figure 1-15. *The window to determine the file name*

In this window, you set the file name (hello.php in the **File Name** field). The **Folder** field specifies the file location (in this case, D:\Books\ php). As a result, an empty file is created into which you enter the program, as shown in Figure 1-16.

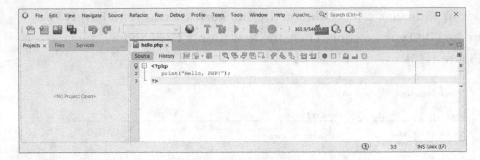

Figure 1-16. *The file with the program in the NetBeans window*

To run the file with the code for execution, select the **Run File** command in the **Run** menu (see Figure 1-17).

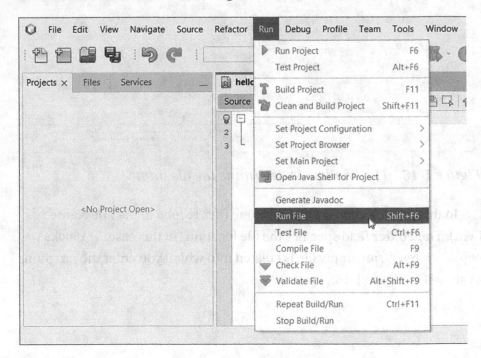

Figure 1-17. *Running the file with code for execution*

After you run the program for execution, the result appears in the output area at the bottom of the development environment window, as shown in Figure 1-18.

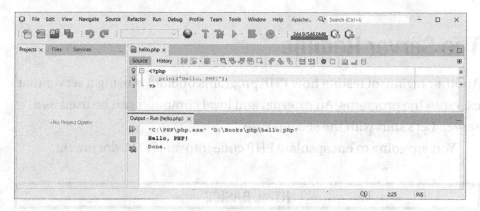

Figure 1-18. *The result of executing the program from the file*

Note   When you run the file for execution, the **Run File** window appears, in which you just need to click the **OK** button.

Details

Sometimes, it is vital to ensure that the encoding of the development environment editor matches the encoding in which the file is written and the encoding of the output area. You can change the default encoding of the NetBeans Environment Editor. To do that, open the `netbeans.conf` file (located in the `etc` subfolder of the folder where the NetBeans environment is installed). Then, find the `netbeans_default_options` parameter and append the value `-J-Dfile.encoding=UTF-8` (UTF-8 encoding is used) by the space. If there are any problems, it is recommended to consult the NetBeans IDE Help.

What software to use depends on taste, personal preferences, and technical capabilities. The main thing is to check the performance of the program codes from the book.

The Server Regime

Another regime of testing how PHP programs operate is using a server that executes the programs. An external and local computer can be used as a server. Let's start with the second case.

You are going to encapsulate PHP code into an HTML document.

HTML BASICS

To create web pages, a special document markup is used. That markup defines the document's structure and how its separate blocks are formatted— namely, the declarative language HTML (short for Hypertext Markup Language). The corresponding document contains plain text and special instructions called tags or descriptors. The instructions are for the browser that displays the document according to those instructions.

Let's use the HTML code shown in Listing 1-2.

Listing 1-2. The HTML Code of the First Project

```
<!DOCTYPE html>
<html>
    <head>
        <title>The First Program</title>
    </head>
    <body>
        <?php
```

```
    print("Hello, PHP!");
  ?>
</body>
</html>
```

This code must be saved in a `.php` file. It is the `hi.php` file located in the `D:\Books\php\codes` directory.

HTML BASICS

An HTML document begins with the `<!DOCTYPE html>` statement that defines the specification of the document. The document's contents are placed between the `<html>` and `</html>` tags. Metadata for the document is placed in the block defined by the `<head>` and `</head>` tags. In this case, there is only one element, separated by the `<title>` and `</title>` tags (the title element). The text `The First Program` contained in that element serves as the title for the web page (displayed on the document tab in the browser). The document's contents rendered by a browser are placed in a block marked with the `<body>` and `</body>` tags. There is only one snippet of PHP code similar to that from Listing 1-1. When the server executes that code, the text is added to the web document at the appropriate place. The `print("Hello, PHP!")` command prints the text. In other words, the text `"Hello, PHP!"` is added to the web page, and all that can be seen when you open the document with a browser. But how to open the web page is another question.

If you try to open the `hi.php` file with a browser, the result is not quite what you might expect. Namely, the file code is displayed in the browser window, as shown in Figure 1-19.

19

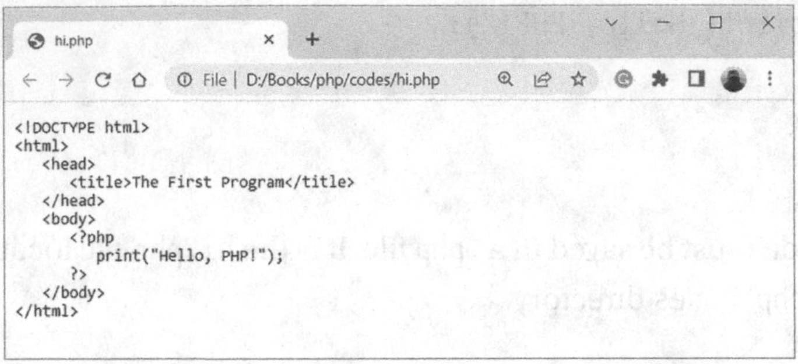

Figure 1-19. *Trying to open the* `hi.php` *file in a browser*

To get a different result, you need to run a local server. To do that, run `php.exe` with the `-S` option, followed by the `localhost` keyword, and, separated by a colon, a port number for the local server. In principle, the port number is arbitrary, but making it greater than 5000 is reasonable.

Details

In general, a port number is a number between 1 and 65535. The system processes use primary numbers for the ports.

After that, in the command line, specify the `-t` option and a link to the folder you want to identify with the root directory of the local server. More specifically, let's say the command looks as follows.

```
php -S localhost:6789 -t D:\Books\php\codes
```

The instruction runs the local server using port 6789. The server's root directory is identified with the `D:\Books\php\codes` folder. Such a command is correct if the `Path` environment variable contains the path to the `php.exe` file or if it is executed from the folder where the `php.exe` file is located. In general, the command might look as follows.

```
C:\PHP\php.exe -S localhost:6789 -t D:\Books\php\codes
```

Here, the full path to the `php.exe` file is specified.

If everything is done correctly, the local server is started. Now, open the browser and enter the following instructions in the address bar.

```
localhost:6789/hi.php
```

As a result, when opening the `hi.php` file, your computer emulates a server job. The result should look like what's shown in Figure 1-20.

Figure 1-20. *Displaying the `hi.php` file in the local server regime*

Note   The path to the displayed file begins from the folder specified when starting the local server. In this case, it is the `D:\Books\php\codes` folder.

You can use the mentioned NetBeans development environment to debug an HTML code with a PHP script encapsulated in it. Creating a new project is similar to the one discussed. However, when choosing a runtime environment (see Figure 1-6), select **PHP Built-in Web Server (running on built-in web server)** in the **Run As** drop-down list, as shown in Figure 1-21.

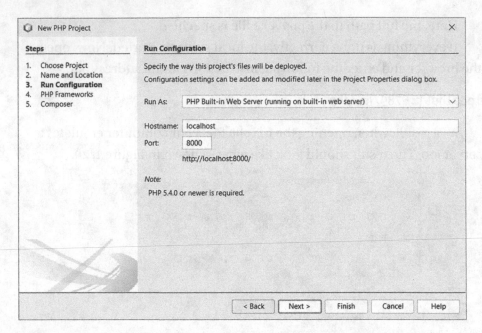

Figure 1-21. *Setting up the runtime environment for an HTML document*

The **Hostname** field contains the local host's name, and the **Port** field contains the port number. You can leave the default values there.

As a result, you should create a new project with the index.php file. Enter the HTML code (with the PHP script) in that file, as shown in Figure 1-22.

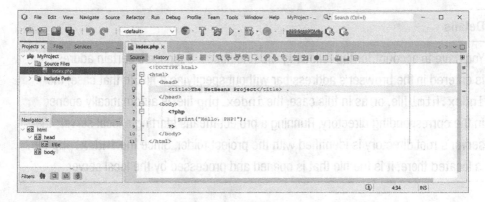

Figure 1-22. *The project window with the HTML code and the PHP script*

> **(i) Note**   Except for the page name, the code is the same as in Listing 1-2.

When you run the project, the browser opened on the local host is automatically launched. The result is shown in Figure 1-23.

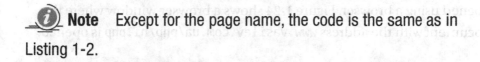

Figure 1-23. *The browser is opened on the local host*

Details

You have to account for the following circumstances. Suppose a certain address is entered in the browser's address bar without specifying a file. In that case, the `index.html` file, or, as in this case, the `index.php` file, is automatically opened in the corresponding directory. Running a project means starting a local server; the server's root directory is identified with the project folder. Since the `index.php` file is located there, it is the file that is opened and processed by the local server.

Finally, another way to test the PHP code is to host the corresponding file on an external server. That is the most reliable way of testing, but it has a significant drawback since not everyone has such an opportunity. But in general, the idea is simple. The file is uploaded to the server and then opened using a browser. Figure 1-24 shows a browser window where the document with the address `www.vasilev.com.ua/php/hi.php` is opened.

Figure 1-24. *The page* `www.vasilev.com.ua/php/hi.php` *is opened in the browser window*

Another inconvenience of using the external server is that you need to change a file not located on the local computer.

> *(i)* **Note**   Of the many options offered, it is necessary to choose
> one. In principle, running program codes from the command line using
> the PHP interpreter is more than an acceptable option. It is suitable for
> testing examples from all chapters except the last one. You have to
> use the local server regime to see the result of the PHP scripts.

Summary

- The upcoming chapters discuss the features of the
  PHP language. The functionality of the code covered
  in them can be tested in the interpreter regime. To do
  that, save the program in a file with the .php extension
  and execute the corresponding instruction in the
  command line.

- A good choice for developing PHP projects is the
  NetBeans development environment. It allows you to
  create projects for testing both in the interpreter regime
  and using a local server.

- To test the correctness of the program execution in the
  server regime, you can use the following template (the
  PHP code is placed in the block between the <?php and
  ?> instructions).

```
<!DOCTYPE html>
<html>
    <head>
        <title>The title of the page</title>
    </head>
```

```
<body>
    <?php
        // The PHP code
    ?>
</body>
</html>
```

CHAPTER 2

Variables and Data Types

We can't throw these things away. These are a part of who we are.

—*ALF* (TV series)

As usual, programs operate with data. And the data needs to be stored somewhere. If you deal with small blocks of information, variables are a good place to store it, which is the focus of this chapter. The chapter also discusses the main data types used in programs and the basic operations performed with variables.

Introduction to Variables

In its "classical" sense, a variable is a named block of memory that can be accessed through the name to read a value from memory or write a new value there. In PHP, creating variables is quite simple: you just need to assign a value to the variable. In other words, the variable appears in a program when a value is assigned to it.

There is a rule in PHP: the name of a variable begins with the $ symbol (this symbol is part of the variable name). To assign a value to a variable, you specify the variable's name, then put the assignment operator (equal

© Alex Vasilev 2024
A. Vasilev, *PHP by Example*, https://doi.org/10.1007/979-8-8688-0258-4_2

sign =) and the value to be assigned to it. For example, the $number=123
command assigns the integer 123 to the $number variable, and the
$text="Hello, PHP" command assigns the text value "Hello, PHP" to the
$text variable.

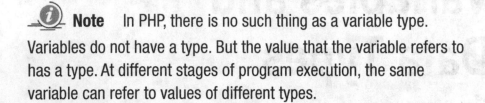

Note   In PHP, there is no such thing as a variable type.
Variables do not have a type. But the value that the variable refers to
has a type. At different stages of program execution, the same
variable can refer to values of different types.

First, let's look at Listing 2-1, a small example that uses a variable.

Listing 2-1. Creating a Variable

```php
<?php
    // Creating a variable:
    $number=123;
    #  A message that contains the name of the variable:
    print 'The variable $number: ';
    /*
        A message that contains the name of the variable:
    */
    print "the value is $number";
?>
```

The result of the program execution is as follows.

The output of the program (from Listing 2-1)
The variable $number: the value is 123

In the program, you also meet three types of comments
allowed in PHP.

Note   A comment is a text in a program destined for the programmer and ignored when the program is executed. In other words, comments explain the purpose of commands but do not affect the program execution.

There are single-line comments. A single-line comment begins with the double slash // or the # character. Anything to the right of the // or # characters is a comment. In addition to single-line comments, there are multi-line comments. Such comments can span multiple lines. A multi-line comment begins with /* and ends with */. Everything between these characters is a comment. The program used all three types of comments, although there was no need for that.

In addition to comments, the program contains several noteworthy commands. The first is the $number=123 instruction, which creates the $number variable with the value 123. In addition to that, there are two more commands for displaying messages in the terminal. Although both commands use the print() function, they are different.

 Note   This time, you pass an argument to the print() function without parentheses.

The difference between the commands is as follows. In the first case, the text to be displayed is enclosed in single quotes. In the second case, the text is in double quotes. In principle, in both cases, you get text. That means single and double quotes are two different ways to create a text. They are almost equal. But some differences also exist. In this case, both text values ('The variable $number: ' and "the value $number") contain the name of the $number variable. So, if the variable's name occurs in the text enclosed in single quotes, then when the text is displayed in the terminal, the variable's name is displayed. If the variable's name is placed in the text enclosed in double quotes, then when displayed in the output window, its value is substituted instead of the variable's name. Therefore, when executing the print 'The variable $number: ' command, exactly the text in single quotes is displayed. But when executing the print "the value $number" command, then, instead of the name of the $number variable, its value 123 is substituted in the text.

 Note   As a result of calling the print() function, the value of the argument passed to the function is displayed in the output window. But there is no line break in the output area. Therefore, two messages are displayed sequentially in the program discussed, one after the other in the same line.

Notably, many common tasks in PHP can be performed in different ways. The examples are several types of comments, several ways to create text literals, several instructions for displaying messages, and the list is not complete. The situation is typical for PHP. In this sense, the language is very convenient and "comfortable" if such a definition is suitable for a programming language.

Details

Along with variables, you can also use constants. A constant differs from a variable in a way that the value of the constant cannot be changed. To create a constant, use the define() function, the first argument of which is the name of the constant, and the second argument is the value of the constant. The dollar symbol $ is not used in the constant name. Constant names usually consist of capital letters. For example, the define("NUMBER",123) command defines the NUMBER constant with the value 123. You can check the existence of a constant with a specific name using the defined() function. The function argument is the name of the constant (in quotes).

Basic Data Types

As noted, variables have no type. Nevertheless, the value referred to by a
variable has a type. You can use the gettype() function to determine the
value type that the variable refers to. The variable is passed as an argument
to the function. The result of the function is a text with the name of the
type. In particular, integer numbers are of the integer type. Real numbers
(floating point numbers) are of the double type. Text is of the string type.
There is also the boolean type (logical values true or false), array (an
array), object (an object), resource (a reference to an external resource),
and NULL (which means no value for the variable). A small example that
illustrates the situation is shown in Listing 2-2.

Listing 2-2. The Type of Value

```php
<?php
    // An integer number:
    $value=123;
    echo $value," => type ",gettype($value),"\n";
    // A text:
    $value="text";
    echo $value," => type ",gettype($value),"\n";
    // A real number:
    $value=12.3;
    echo $value," => type ",gettype($value),"\n";
    // The null reference:
    echo $VALUE," => type ",gettype($VALUE),"\n";
?>
```

The result of the program execution is as follows.

The output of the program (from Listing 2-2)
```
123 => type integer
text => type string
12.3 => type double
 => type NULL
```

🔔 **The PHP 8 Standard**   When using PHP 8 and higher, you get a warning about the unknown variable $VALUE, which appears between the `type` and NULL tokens.

Here, you deal with a simple program. The $value variable gets consequently different values, and its type is determined for each value. To determine the type, use the gettype() function, the argument of which is the $value variable.

ⓘ **Note**   The last command is remarkable. It uses the $VALUE variable. That is far from being the same as the $value variable since variable names are case-sensitive (it matters whether the variable name contains capitalized letters or small ones). Therefore, $value and $VALUE are different variables.

To display values, an instruction based on the echo keyword is used. To the right of the instruction, comma-separated values are listed. They are displayed in the output area. In particular, these are the current value of the $value variable, the " => type " string, the name for the value type of the $value variable, which is calculated by the gettype($value) statement, and the escape sequence "\n".

Details

The \n instruction is a so-called escape sequence. If such an instruction is placed in a text enclosed in double quotes (this is important!), a line break is performed at the appropriate place when the text is displayed. Therefore, one should "print" the text "\n" to break a line. The \n escape sequence is not the only one in PHP. For example, the \t instruction inserts a tab character into a text.

The last statement echo $VALUE," => type ",gettype($VALUE),"\n" requires special explanation. As noted, PHP interprets uppercase and lowercase letters in the variable names (as opposed to the function names) as different characters. Therefore, the $VALUE variable has nothing to do with the $value variable.

In the preceding statement, try to display the value of the $VALUE variable in the output area, although the value has not been assigned yet to the variable. The variable has no value; in other words, the value of the variable is the NULL reference. That confirms the call of the gettype() function with $VALUE as an argument. When trying to display the value of the $VALUE variable, since it is missing, nothing is displayed in the output area. In this sense, the PHP language is more than "liberal" when a variable has no value.

ⓘ Note   There are quite a few functions designed to manipulate data types. An example is the settype() function used to apply a type. The get_class() function allows you to determine the class of an object. You can check the existence of a function using the function_exists() function. The existence of a method is checked using the method_exists() function. You can check if a variable refers to a callable object using the is_callable() function. There is a group of functions that allow you to check if data belongs to a specific type: is_array() (whether the variable refers to an array), `is_bool()` (whether the variable refers to a boolean value), `is_float()` (whether the variable refers to a real number), `is_int()` (whether the variable refers to an integer), `is_null()` (whether the value of the variable is the null reference), `is_numeric()` (whether the variable refers to a number or a string with a text representation of a number), `is_object()` (whether the variable refers to an object), `is_resource()` (whether the variable refers to a resource), `is_scalar()` (whether the variable refers to a scalar value), `is_string()` (whether the variable refers to a text).

Details

In addition to using the `settype()` function to change the type of a value explicitly, you can use the (`type_name`) instruction (a type name in parentheses) that precedes the value whose type is to be converted. For example, the (`int`) or (`integer`) instructions are used to cast to the integer type, the (`bool`) and (`boolean`) instructions are used to cast to the boolean type, the (`string`) instruction is used to cast to the text type, and the cast of a value to the real numeric type can be performed with the (`float`), (`double`), or (`real`) instructions (the last instruction has been deprecated in PHP 8). Also, there are other options.

The Arithmetic Operations

Some basic operations can be performed on variables and values of different types. Conventionally, all operations can be divided into arithmetic, logical, comparison, and bitwise. Let's also examine operations with text, assignment operations, and the ternary operator.

Details

Sometimes, you need to check if a value is assigned to some variable. In that case, you can use the `isset()` function (the name of the variable to check is passed as a function argument). To remove a variable, use the `unset()` function.

It is worth mentioning that the arithmetic operators +, -, *, and / are used to calculate the sum, difference, product, and quotient of two numbers, respectively. You use the ** operator (or the `pow()` function) to exponentiate. The % operator calculates the remainder of a division.

In addition to these binary operators, you can use the unary increment ++ and decrement -- operators. Moreover, they have the prefix and the postfix form.

Details

Binary operators have two operands. Unary operators have one operand. The prefix and postfix forms of the increment and decrement operators differ in whether the operator is placed before the operand (the prefix form) or after the operand (the postfix form).

Regarding "action" on the operand, the postfix and prefix forms are equivalent. The increment operator ++ increases the value of the operand by one, and the decrement operator -- decreases the value of the operand by one. For example, if the value of the $number variable is 100, then after executing the $number++ statement, the variable's value will be 101. The result will be the same if you use ++$number instead of the $number++ statement: the $number variable gets the new value 101. However, there is a difference between the postfix and prefix forms. The value of the expression with the postfix form of the increment/decrement operator is the "old" (which was before applying the operator) value of the operand. The value of the expression with the prefix form of the increment/ decrement operator is the "new" (calculated after applying the operator) value of the operand.

Details

Let's say there are commands $A=100 and $B=100. After executing the $a=$A++
and $b=++$B commands, $a has the value 100, and $b, $A, and $B have the value
101. That is because after executing the $A++ and ++$B statements, the $A and $B
variables increase their values by one (and get the value 101), but the value of the
$A++ expression is 100, and the value of the ++$B expression is 101. So, the $a
variable gets 100 as its value, and $b gets 101 as its value.

Examples of arithmetic operations are collected in Listing 2-3.

Listing 2-3. The Arithmetic Operations

```php
<?php
    // Variables:
    $A=5;
    echo '[1] $A = ',$A,"\n";
    $B=3;
    // Arithmetic operations:
    echo '[2] $B = ',$B,"\n";
    echo '[3] $A + $B = ',$A+$B,"\n";
    echo '[4] $A - $B = ',$A-$B,"\n";
    echo '[5] $A * $B = ',$A*$B,"\n";
    echo '[6] $A / $B = ',$A/$B,"\n";
    echo '[7] $A ** $B = ',$A**$B,"\n";
    echo '[8] $A % $B = ',$A%$B,"\n";
    $A++;
    echo '[9] $A = ',$A,"\n";
    --$B;
    echo '[10] $B = ',$B,"\n";
?>
```

The result of the program execution is as follows.

```
The output of the program (from Listing 2-3)
[1] $A = 5
[2] $B = 3
[3] $A + $B = 8
[4] $A - $B = 2
[5] $A * $B = 15
[6] $A / $B = 1.6666666666667
[7] $A ** $B = 125
[8] $A % $B = 2
[9] $A = 6
[10] $B = 2
```

Here, everything is quite simple, and it is believed that the result of the program execution does not require comments.

The Comparison Operations

In addition to the arithmetic operations, there are also the comparison operations. Those operations are implemented through the following operators: < (*less than*), <= (*less than or equal to*), > (*greater than*), >= (*greater than or equal to*), == (*equal to*), != (*not equal to*), === (*identically equal to*), !== (*identically not equal to*), and the <=> comparison operator. Most of the operators in the list are traditional and easy to understand. Maybe the exceptions are the <=> operator, *equal/not equal to* operators, and *identically equal/identically not equal to* operators.

It is important to know that when using the operators (including comparison ones) with operands of different types, automatic type conversion is performed. That means that to execute a statement, certain algorithms are automatically applied to transform the values of the operands in the statement. With the == and != operators, the comparison involves automatic type conversion. For example, you get true if you use the == operator to compare the boolean value true and the integer value 1 (the true==1 statement). The reason is that non-zero values are interpreted as true, and zero values are interpreted as false. Therefore, not only the true==1 statement gives true but also the true==2, true==-10, and false==0 statements.

Details

If you try to print the boolean value true, the 1 value is printed. Moreover, the boolean value false is not displayed at all. Instead of this value, the empty text is printed (that is, the text without characters).

But there are also more exotic options. For example, the 123=="123" statement, where you compare the 123 number and the "123" text for equality, gives true. That is because, here, the automatic conversion of the textual representation of the number "123" into the integer value 123 comes into play.

The comparison mode described may or may not be convenient. It depends on the context of the problem being solved. If you want the comparison to be performed without automatic type conversion, the === and !== operators should be used. For example, the true===1, false===0, and 123==="123" expressions give false.

🔔 **The PHP 8 Standard**   In PHP 8, the rules for comparing values have changed somewhat. The main innovation is that an empty text value is not interpreted as equal to zero. For example, in PHP 8, the value of the 0=="" expression is false, while the value of the 0=="" expression in previous versions of PHP is true.

Regarding the comparison operation <=>, it is performed as follows. Let's say you have an expression like $A<=>$B. The result of such an expression is -1, provided that the value of $A is less than that of $B. If the value of the $A variable is greater than that of the $B variable, then the $A<=>$B expression evaluates to 1. Finally, if the $A and $B variables have the same value, the $A<=>$B expression gives the value 0.

Details

An operation of the form $A<=>$B can be thought of as one that returns the sign of the difference between the values of $A and $B. Moreover, keep in mind that the operation involves automatic type casting. Therefore, for example, the "123"<=>123 expression gives 0 since the text "123" is automatically converted to the number 123. Accordingly, the value of "123"<=>12 equals 1. The true<=>123 expression has the value 0 because the non-zero integer value 123 is automatically converted to the boolean value true.

The Logical Operations

The logical operators are designed to perform operations on values of the boolean type (here, you also must keep in mind automatic type casting). To perform the logical operations, you use the binary operators && (*logical and*) and || (*logical or*), as well as the unary *logical negation* operator !.

The value of an expression of the form $A&&$B is true if the operands $A and $B, accounting for automatic type casting, both are equal to true. If at least one of the operands is false (or is interpreted after automatic type casting as one with the false value), then the $A&&$B expression gives false.

Note   Simply speaking, the $A&&$B expression is `true` only if both operands $A and $B in the expression are `true`.

The value of an expression of the form $A||$B is `true` if at least one of the operands $A or $B is `true` or its value is cast to `true` due to automatic type casting. If both operands are `false`, then the value of the entire expression is `false`.

 Note   It turns out that the value of the $A||$B expression is `true` if at least one of the operands in the expression is `true`.

It is worth mentioning that expressions based on the operators && and || are calculated from left to right according to the simplified scheme. Namely, if it is possible to determine the result of the entire expression after evaluating the first operand, then the second operand is not evaluated.

Details

If in an expression of the form $A&&$B, the first operand $A turns out to be `false`, then the value of the entire expression is equal to `false`, regardless of the value of the second operand $B.

In an expression of the form $A||$B, if the first operand $A is `true`, the value of the entire expression is `true`, regardless of the second operand $B value. Therefore, in these cases, the value of the second operand is not calculated.

The logical negation operator ! is a unary one. The value of an expression of the form !$A is `true` if the value of the operand $A is `false` (or is converted to `false` due to automatic type conversion). If the value of the operand $A is `true` (or is reduced to that value), then the !$A expression is `false`.

Details

There exist "twins" for the operators && and ||. They are, respectively, the and and or operators. These operators have lower precedence than the && and || operators. In some cases, it could be convenient to use them.

The Bitwise Operations

The bitwise operations are performed at the level of the binary (bitwise) representation of a number. Therefore, to understand the consequences of performing such operations, it is necessary to have at least an elementary idea of how numbers are encoded in the binary system.

Details

In the binary representation, a number is written as a sequence of zeros and ones. Formally, that can be represented as $\underline{a_n a_{n-1} \ldots a_2 a_1 a_0}$, where the parameters a_0, a_1, ..., a_n can take the value 0 or 1.

To convert a positive number from the binary to the decimal system, you can use the formula $\underline{a_n a_{n-1} \ldots a_2 a_1 a_0} = a_0 2^0 + a_1 2^1 + a_2 2^2 + \ldots + a_{n-1} 2^{n-1} + a_n 2^n$.

Let's take a look at the basic bitwise operators, starting with the *bitwise and* operator &. Suppose an expression like $A&$B is evaluated. Its result is a number. The binary code of that number is calculated following such a rule. The binary codes of the operands $A and $B are compared. Namely, in those binary codes, the corresponding bits are compared. The comparison result gives a bit for the expression value number.

Details

A computer uses a certain fixed count of bits to remember a number. Therefore, whatever the values are, they are implemented by the same count of bits, and there is a one-to-one correspondence between those bits.

With the & operator, you get bit 1 if both bits being compared are 1. If at least one bit is 0, the result is a zero bit. For example, the value of the 13&21 expression is the number 5. The explanation is as follows. The binary code of the number 21 is 10101. The binary code of the number 13 is 01101. The result of the 13&21 expression is calculated in such a way: the codes 01101 and 10101 are compared bit by bit, and if two bits are 1, then the output is 1. In all other cases (if at least one bit is 1), you get 0 as the output.

```
&  01101
   10101
   00101
```

As a result, you get the 00101 code, which corresponds to the number 5.

 Note   The binary representation of numbers used only five positions (bits). All other (previous) bits are assumed to be zero.

Using the *bitwise operator or* | when comparing bits in numbers, you get 1 if at least one of the bits is 1. In other words, the result of an expression like $A|$B is a number whose binary code is obtained by comparing the binary codes of the numbers $A and $B. In the number you get, a bit at a particular position is 1 if at least one of the compared bits at the same position in $A and $B is 1. If both compared bits are 0, the result is a bit with the value 0. Thus, the result of the 13|21 expression is 29 (the binary code 11101).

```
|  01101
   10101
   11101
```

The *bitwise exclusive or* operator ^ is different from the *bitwise or* | in that the output is 1 if one and only one of the bits being compared is 1. In all other cases (two bits are 1 or two bits are 0), the result is a bit with the value 0. For example, the result of the 13^21 expression is calculated as follows.

```
^ 01101
  10101
  11000
```

The code 11000 corresponds to 24. That is the value of the 13^21 expression.

The *bitwise inversion* operator ~ is a unary one. The result of an expression of the form ~$A is a number whose binary code is obtained from the code of the number $A by replacing zeros with ones and ones with zeros. In that case, the code of the number $A does not change, and a new value is calculated.

ⓘ **Note**   As you will see later, the value of the ~$A expression is the number -($A+1). For example, the value of the ~5 expression is the number -6.

The *bitwise shift operations* (when the bit representation of a number is shifted several positions to the right or left) are performed using the << (*shift to the left*) and >> (*shift to the right*) operators. The value of an expression of the form $A<<$n is a number whose binary code is obtained by shifting the binary code of the number $A by $n positions to the left. The left bits are lost, and the right bits are filled with zeros. The value of an expression of the form $A>>$n is a number whose binary code is obtained from the binary code of the number $A by shifting $n positions to the right. The right bits are lost, and the left bits are filled with the sign bit's value (the first bit, which is 0 for positive numbers and 1 for negative numbers).

Details

Coding negative numbers has its peculiarities. To understand the coding principle, imagine that numbers are stored using 8 bits. Let's say you have some code. For example, let it be the code 00010011 (number 19). Let's perform a bitwise inversion of that code (replace 1 with 0 and 0 with 1). You get the code 11101100. Now, add these two codes. The addition rules in the binary system are simple: 0+0=0, 1+0=1, 0+1=1, and 1+1=10. The last statement is 2+2=4, but only written in the binary code. So, if you add the codes 00010011 and 11101100, you get the code 11111111, consisting of ones.

Next, add one (the code 00000001) to that code. You get 100000000. But here, you must remember that you are dealing with a computer, assuming it stores numbers using 8 bits. But there are nine digits in the code 100000000. Therefore, there is simply no bit at the beginning of the number to remember the 1, which is lost. You get the code 00000000, which consists of zeros. That number is 0.

The result will be the same if you take a different source code and a different number of bits to remember the number. What did you get? If you take some positive number $X, invert its code (the ~$X expression), add these codes, and then add 1, you get 0 as a result. In other words, whatever the value of $X is, there is the relation $X+(~$X)+1=0. It is easy to see that the (~$X)+1 expression can be identified with the code of the number -$X (the number opposite to the value of $X).

Thus, if you need to get the binary code of a negative number, you should take the code of the opposite positive number, invert that code, and add 1. The first bit in the binary code of a number is used to determine a sign: for positive numbers, that bit is 0, and for negative numbers, that bit is 1.

The binary representation is converted to a decimal value for positive numbers according to the standard mathematical rules.

If you need to convert the binary code of a negative number into decimal representation, then you should follow these next steps. First, you invert the code. Then add 1 to it. The resulting value is converted to decimal representation according to the rules applied for positive numbers. The last step is to place a minus sign before the calculated number.

Let's assume that 8 bits are used to write numbers. Then, the result of the 41<<1 expression is the number 82. The explanation is as follows. The code of the number 41 is 00101001. After shifting by one position to the left, you get the code 01010010, corresponding to 82. If you shift the code 00101001 by two positions to the left (the 41<<2 statement), you get the code 10100100. Here, the first sign bit is 1. Therefore, the number is negative. You perform a bitwise inversion to determine that number and get the code 01011011. Then you add 1 and get the code 01011100. That is the code for the number 92. So, the result of the 41<<2 expression is the number -92 with the code 10100100. The result of the 41<<3 expression is the number 72 with the code 01001000.

Note   It is important to understand that such results will be if exactly 8 bits are used to store numbers. If the count of bits is different (for example, 32), then the result of the 41<<1 is 82 expression, the value of the 41<<2 expression is 164, and when calculating the value of the 41<<3 expression, you get 328.

When the 41>>1 expression is evaluated, the code 00101001 of the number 41 is shifted by one position to the right, which gives the code 00010100. It corresponds to the number 20. The 41>>2 expression value is 10 with the binary code 00001010. The result of the -69>>2 expression is the number -18. Here, you should consider that the code of the number -69 (when encoded using 8 bits) is 10111011. Shifting it by two positions to the right, you get the code 11101110. That is the code of the number -18.

Note   Once again, all these calculations are given for the case if the number is stored using 8 bits. A different count of bits means different (in general) results.

The Operations with Strings

Working with text is a vast theme to discuss. Here, let's focus only on the basic operations with text and the features of the text that you will need in the foreseeable future.

(i) Note   You already know that text literals can be enclosed in single or double quotes. In the latter case, if the text contains a variable's name, its value is substituted instead of its name. You can also insert escape sequences into such text, consisting of a backslash \ and a character that defines some operation. For example, \n is a break-line instruction, and \t is a tab. You can use \\, \$, \', and \" to insert backslash \, dollar sign $, single ', and double " quotes, respectively.

One of the basic operations often performed with text is the concatenation of strings. In PHP, the concatenation of strings can be done by using the . operator "dot". For example, the result of the "Learning"." PHP" expression is the string "Learning PHP". The same operation can be done with variables: the value of an expression of the form $A.$B is the text calculated by combining the text values of the $A and $B variables.

Details

If the $A and $B variables have non-text values, the $A.$B statement is calculated
by trying to convert those values to the text type and then concatenate them.
It is also worth mentioning that, unlike many other programming languages, PHP
does not use the + operator to concatenate text values. Moreover, applying this
operator to concatenate text values may lead to an error or unexpected result. For
example, the "1"+"2" expression does not give the text "12", as you might expect,
but the numeric value 3. The reason is that the + operator is an arithmetic one, so
the operands "1" and "2" are automatically converted to the integers 1 and 2,
respectively. After that, the numbers are added. Therefore, to get the text "12", you
should use the "1"."2" statement.

Another simple string operation is determining the length of a string.
In that case, use the strlen() function. You can compare strings for
equality/nonequality using the == and != operators. But here, you should
remember automatic type casting. Therefore, using the === and !==
operators sometimes makes more sense.

(i) **Note**   You can also use the strcmp() (the case-sensitive

comparison) and strcasecmp() (the case-insensitive comparison)
functions to compare strings.

There are several other essential operations performed with text.
Among them, one of the main ones is extracting a substring from a string.
To do that, use the substr() function. The function arguments are a
string (from which the substring is extracted), the index of the character
from which the substring is extracted, and, if necessary, the length of the
substring. If you do not specify the last argument, the substring is extracted
to the end of the string.

The str_replace() function is used to replace a substring in a string. The function replaces the substring specified by the first argument with the substring specified by the second argument in the string specified by the third argument.

---

i **Note**   You can access a single character in a string by specifying the character index in square brackets after the text value. For example, if the $A variable has a text value, then the $A[$n] expression is a reference to the character with the $n index. Character indexing starts from zero.

Assigning Values

In PHP, the assignment operator returns a value. That means an expression with the assignment operator can be an operand in another expression. In particular, the value of an expression of the form variable=value is the value of the variable on the left side of the expression. For example, after executing the $A=($B=100)+1, $A instruction has the value 101, and $B has the value 100.

Details

The $A=($B=100)+1 command assigns the ($B=100)+1 expression to the $A variable. That is the sum of two terms: ($B=100) and 1. When the $B=100 is expression evaluated, the $B variable gets the value 100, and the ($B=100) expression has the same value. Therefore, the $A variable is assigned the sum of 100 and 1, that is, the number 101.

There also exist simplified forms of assignment operators. They allow you to simplify the process of executing assignment statements of the

form $A=$A ◔ $B, where ◔ is a binary arithmetic or bitwise operator or the
string concatenation operator. So, instead of a statement like $A=$A ◔ $B,
you can use the $A ◔= $B instruction. For example, instead of the
$A=$A+$B statement, you can use the $A+=$B command, and the $A.=$B
command is an analog to the $A=$A.$B instruction.

The Ternary Operator

Operators are usually unary (they have one operand) or binary (they have
two operands). But there is one operator that has three operands. That
operator is called the *ternary* one. In general, if you do not focus on the
terminology, you may consider it as a specific syntactic construction that
allows you to assign a value to a variable depending on a condition that
can be true or false. The syntax for the ternary operator is as follows.

```
condition?value_1:value_2
```

First, place the condition (as usual, an expression that returns a
boolean value). Then enter a question mark (?), the value returned if
the condition is true, a colon (:), and the value returned if the condition
is false. The described construction can be assigned to a variable. For
example, after executing the $number=($x<0)?-10:10 statement, $number
is set to -10 if the value of $x is less than zero (if the condition $x<0 is true),
and 10 otherwise (if the condition $x<0 is false). A simple example that
uses the ternary operator is shown in Listing 2-4.

Listing 2-4. The Ternary Operator

```php
<?php
    print("Enter a number: ");
    # Reads a value and converts it
    # to the integer format:
    $number=(int)trim(fgets(STDIN));
```

```
# The ternary operator is used:
$word=($number%2==0)?"even":"odd";
# The result of the test for even/odd:
print("This is an $word number");
?>
```

The program is simple, but it contains some notable instructions. First, the $number=(int)trim(fgets(STDIN)) statement reads the integer value entered by the user from the keyboard and writes it to the $number variable. Then, using the ternary operator, the $number variable is tested for even/odd, and depending on the test result, the $word variable is assigned the value "even" or "odd". The test result is displayed on the screen.

When you run the program, you are prompted to enter a number. The program is waiting for the user input. The user enters a number and presses the Enter key. After that, another message appears, which contains information about whether the number is even or odd. Depending on the value entered by the user (highlighted in bold), the result of the program execution can be as follows (an odd number is entered).

The output of the program (from Listing 2-4)
Enter a number: **123**
This is an odd number

Or the result can be as follows (an even number is entered).

The output of the program (from Listing 2-4)
Enter a number: **124**
This is an even number

Now, let's analyze the main statements. First, consider the $number=(int)trim(fgets(STDIN)) instruction. It is based on a call of the fgets() function, which reads a string from the input stream.

The function argument is the STDIN constant identifier for the standard input stream (which, in this case, is associated with the console). But the fgets() function reads any entered value as text, and, in addition, the text can contain special escape sequences (like a break-line instruction). To remove all "redundant" characters, use the trim() function. It removes all leading and trailing spaces and special characters from the string passed as an argument. Thus, if the user enters an integer, then the trim(fgets(STDIN)) expression contains the textual representation of that number. For example, if the user enters the number 123, then the value read (taking into account the call to the trim() function) is "123". Frankly speaking, accounting for automatic type conversion, calculations could be performed even with that value.

Nevertheless, for reliability, you convert the read text into a number. To do that, place the (int) instruction before the entire expression. In addition to the settype() function mentioned, that is another way to cast a type explicitly.

Details

Instead of the $number=(int)trim(fgets(STDIN)) statement, which reads the value for the $number variable from the console, you could use the $number=123 or $number=124 statement, which explicitly assigns the value to the $number variable.

The $word=($number%2==0)?"even":"odd" command assigns the ($number%2==0)?"even":"odd" expression (based on the ternary operator) to the $word variable. If the $number%2==0 condition is true (which means that the remainder of dividing the $number variable by 2 is zero), then the $word variable gets the text "even". If the $number%2==0 condition is false, then the $word variable gets the text "odd". The value of the $word variable is used when displaying the test result.

Summary

- A variable is a named block of memory that allows you to refer to that block of memory by name. If you want to create a variable in PHP, it is enough to assign a value to the variable. The variable name begins with the $ character.

- A variable does not have a type, but the value that the variable refers to has a type. The main types include integer (integer numbers), double (real numbers), string (text), boolean (boolean values), array (an array), and object (an object). You can obtain the type of value a variable refers to using the gettype() function.

- For explicit type conversion, you can use the settype() function or specify the final type in parentheses before the converted value. PHP also has an automatic type conversion system.

- Basic operations use arithmetic, logical, bitwise, and comparison operators. The *dot* operator is used to concatenate strings.

- The assignment operator returns a value that is the same as the variable's value (to which the value is being assigned). There exist simplified forms of assignment operators.

- The ternary operator returns a value that depends on a specific condition that can be true or false.

- The fgets() function can read data from the console.

CHAPTER 3

The Control Statements

I was sitting quietly, peacefully. Then I got hungry. Further, as if in a fog.

—*ALF* (TV series)

This chapter discusses control statements, which are instructions designed to create branch points in a program and instructions to repeat statement blocks. In other words, it covers the conditional, loop, and selection statements.

The if Conditional Statement

The conditional if statement allows you to execute different blocks of commands depending on some condition. The conditional statement has two alternative syntaxes. Usually, you use the following option.

```
if(condition){
    # commands
}
else{
    # commands
}
```

The if keyword is followed by a condition in parentheses. Then, in curly braces, commands follow. After the block of commands, the else keyword is placed with other commands in curly braces.

© Alex Vasilev 2024
A. Vasilev, *PHP by Example*, https://doi.org/10.1007/979-8-8688-0258-4_3

Let's discuss how the conditional statement is executed. First, the condition after the if keyword is checked. If the condition is true, the commands after the condition are executed. If the condition is false, the commands in the block after the else keyword are executed.

The else block is optional. It is allowed not to use it. The syntax of the conditional statement, in that case, is as follows.

```
if(condition){
    # commands
}
```

If the else block is not used, the conditional statement is executed. First, the condition is checked; if it is true, the commands after the condition are executed. If the condition is false, then nothing happens, and the instruction after the conditional statement starts to execute.

---

i **Note**   Curly braces can be omitted if the if block or else block consists of a single command. However, the absence of curly braces reduces the readability of the code and leads to errors. Therefore, it is reasonable to use curly braces always.

Another way to describe the conditional statement is to use no curly braces but a colon after the condition, the else keyword, and the endif statement (followed by a semicolon) at the end of the whole construction. The general syntax of the conditional statement, in that case, looks as follows.

```
if(condition):
    # commands
else:
    # commands
endif;
```

As in the previous case, the else block can be omitted. If so, the conditional statement is declared according to the following pattern.

```
if(condition):
    # commands
endif;
```

A small example that uses the conditional statement is shown in Listing 3-1.

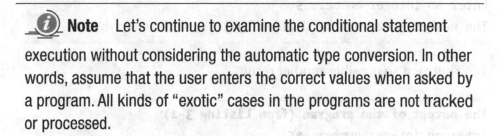 **Note**   Let's continue to examine the conditional statement execution without considering the automatic type conversion. In other words, assume that the user enters the correct values when asked by a program. All kinds of "exotic" cases in the programs are not tracked or processed.

The program is simple. The user enters a number there, and the program checks whether the number can be divided by another known number.

Listing 3-1. The Conditional Statement

```php
<?php
    print("Enter an integer number: ");
    # Reads a number:
    $number=(integer)trim(fgets(STDIN));
    # The divider:
    $A=3;
    # Checks whether the numbers can be divided:
    if($number%$A==0){
        print("The number $number can be divided by $A");
    }
```

55

```
    else{
        print("The number $number can not be divided by $A");
    }
?>
```

The result of the program execution is shown next (the number entered by the user is marked in bold).

The output of the program (from Listing 3-1)

Enter an integer number: **5**
The number 5 can not be divided by 3

There is also possibly another result.

The output of the program (from Listing 3-1)

Enter an integer number: **15**
The number 15 can be divided by 3

In the conditional statement, the $number%$A==0 condition is checked, which is true if the value of the $number variable (entered by the user) is divisible without a remainder by the value of the $A variable (explicitly specified in the program).

Details

The $number=(integer)trim(fgets(STDIN)) command is used to read the value of the $number variable. The value of the variable is determined by the (integer)trim(fgets(STDIN)) expression. The fgets() function reads a line from the standard input (the STDIN identifier). This means that the value entered by the user is read as a string. The trim() function removes leading and trailing spaces and escape sequences from that string. The (integer) instruction converts the textual representation of the number to the integer.

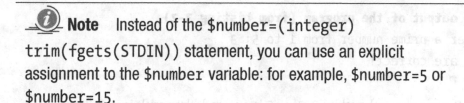 **Note**   Instead of the $number=(integer) trim(fgets(STDIN)) statement, you can use an explicit assignment to the $number variable: for example, $number=5 or $number=15.

Another example of using the conditional statement is shown in Listing 3-2. It uses a complex condition (it contains logical operators) and an alternative form of the conditional statement syntax.

Listing 3-2. The Alternative Form of the Conditional Statement Syntax

```php
<?php
    print("Enter a prime number from 1 to 5: ");
    // Reads a number:
    $number=(int)trim(fgets(STDIN));
    // Checks the value:
    if($number==2 || $number==3 || $number==5):
        print("You are correct!");
    else:
        print("You are wrong!");
    endif;
?>
```

When the program is run, the user is prompted to enter a prime number between 1 and 5. If the user enters the number 2, 3, or 5, the message You are correct! appears. If any other number is entered, the message You are wrong! appears. The following shows what the program's output looks like if the user enters a prime number from the specified range (the entered value is marked in bold).

The output of the program (from Listing 3-2)
Enter a prime number from 1 to 5: **3**
You are correct!

If a number other than 2, 3, or 5 is entered, the result is as follows.

The output of the program (from Listing 3-2)
Enter a prime number from 1 to 5: **4**
You are wrong!

You can use nested conditional statements to check several conditions sequentially. But it is better to use a modification of the conditional statement with the elseif blocks. The following shows the syntax for calling such a conditional statement.

```
if(condition){
    # commands
}
elseif(condition){
    # commands
}
elseif(condition){
    # commands
}
else{
    # commands
}
```

Two elseif blocks are used here, but in principle, you can use as many elseif blocks as you like. Let's discuss how the conditional statement is executed. First, the condition after the if keyword is checked, and if the condition is true, the corresponding block of commands is executed.

If the condition is false, the condition in the elseif block is checked. If that condition is true, the commands from the corresponding elseif block are executed. If the condition is false, the condition in the next elseif block is checked, and so on. The commands in the else block are executed if all the checked conditions are false. The else block is optional.

The following is an alternative syntax for calling the conditional statement with the elseif blocks.

```
if(condition):
    # commands
elseif(condition):
    # commands
elseif(condition):
    # commands
else:
    # commands
endif;
```

Namely, curly braces are not used, a colon is placed at the beginning of the blocks, and the entire structure ends with the endif keyword (followed by a semicolon).

Let's look at an example program that solves an equation of the form $Ax = B$. Depending on the values of the parameters A and B, there three options are possible. The first case is if $A \neq 0$, so the equation has a single solution $x = B/A$. The second case is if both parameters are zero, that is, $A = 0$ and $B = 0$. If so, then the solution of the equation is any number. Finally, and this is the third case, if $A = 0$ and $B \neq 0$, then the equation has no solutions. All these cases are tracked using the conditional statement in the program shown in Listing 3-3.

Listing 3-3. Solving the Equation

```php
<?php
  print("Solving the equation Ax=B\n");
  // Reads the parameters:
  print("A = ");
  $A=(double)trim(fgets(STDIN));
  print("B = ");
  $B=(double)trim(fgets(STDIN));
  // Calculates the solution:
  if($A!=0){
      $x=$B/$A;
      print("x = ".$x);
  }
  elseif($B==0){
      print("The solution is any number");
  }
  else{
      print("There are no solutions");
  }
?>
```

The user is prompted to enter the parameters of the equation, and after that, the result is calculated. Much depends on what values are entered. The following is the result of the program execution if the equation has a single solution (the values entered by the user are marked in bold).

The output of the program (from Listing 3-3)
Solving the equation Ax=B
A = **5.0**
B = **12.6**
x = 2.52

60

The following is the result of the program execution when both parameters are set to zero.

The output of the program (from Listing 3-3)
```
Solving the equation Ax=B
A = 0
B = 0
The solution is any number
```

There may be no solutions at all.

The output of the program (from Listing 3-3)
```
Solving the equation Ax=B
A = 0
B = 1
There are no solutions
```

In the program, the user enters the values for the $A and $B variables. You use the instruction (double) to cast to the double type. The search for a solution is performed using the conditional statement. First, the $A!=0 condition is checked (the value of the $A variable is not 0). If so, the $x=$B/$A command calculates the value for the root of the equation, which is displayed in the console.

If the $A!=0 condition is false (that is, the value of the $A variable is 0), the $B==0 condition in the elseif block is checked. The truth of this condition (considering the falsity of the $A!=0 condition) means that any number can be a solution.

Finally, the equation has no solutions if the $B==0 condition is also false. The else block of the conditional statement handles this situation.

The while Loop Statement

The loop statements make it possible to execute instructions or commands repeatedly. There are several loop statements in PHP. Their action is the same (in the sense that they allow solving the same tasks and are equivalent in their functionality).

The while loop statement has perhaps the simplest syntax of all loop statements. It begins with the while keyword, after which some condition is placed in parentheses, and then a block of commands in curly braces follows. In general, it looks as follows.

```
while(condition){
    # commands
}
```

Let's discuss how the while loop statement is executed. First, the condition is checked. If it is true, then the commands in the body of the loop statement are executed. Then, the condition is rechecked. If the condition is true, the commands are executed, and the condition is checked again? and so on. That continues until the next test of the condition is false. If so, then the loop statement terminates.

(i) **Note**   If the body of the loop statement contains a single command, then curly braces can be omitted. But that is not a good practice.

There is another form of the while loop statement, in which curly braces are not used, a colon is placed after the condition, and the operator ends with the endwhile instruction (and a semicolon).

```
while(condition):
    # commands
endwhile;
```

Listing 3-4 uses the while loop statement to calculate the sum of numbers.

Listing 3-4. The Sum of Numbers

```php
<?php
    // The upper limit of the sum:
    $n=100;
    // The initial value of the sum:
    $s=0;
    // A term for the sum:
    $k=1;
    // Calculates the sum:
    while($k<=$n){
        $s+=$k; // Adds the term
        $k++;    // The new term
    }
    // The result of the calculation:
    print("1+2+...+$n=$s");
?>
```

The result of the program execution is as follows.

The output of the program (from Listing 3-4)

1+2+...+100=5050

The program uses three variables: the upper limit of the sum (the count of terms) is saved to the $n variable, the value of the sum is saved to the $s variable (the initial value of the variable is 0), and the value for the next term is saved to the $k variable (the initial value is 1).

The loop statement checks the $k<=$n condition, which is true if the value of the $k variable does not exceed the value of the $n variable. In the body of the loop statement, the $s+=$k command adds a term to the sum. The $k++ command increments the value of $k by one. On the next iteration, that is the new term for the sum.

After the loop statement is terminated, the $s variable contains the sum of numbers from 1 to the value stored in the $n variable. This result is displayed in the console.

> ⓘ **Note**   The sum of numbers from 1 to n can be calculated using the formula $\dfrac{n(n+1)}{2}$. You do not use this formula but calculate the sum directly by adding the terms.

Another example that calculates the divisors of a certain number is shown in Listing 3-5. In this case, you use an alternate form of the while statement.

Listing 3-5. The Divisors of a Number

```php
<?php
    # The number for which we calculate the dividers:
    $number=315;
    # The variable to store a divider:
    $A=1;
    print("The number $number can be divided by:\n$A");
    while(2*$A<$number):
        $A++;
        if($number%$A==0){
            print(" ".$A);
        }
    endwhile;
    print(" ".$number)
?>
```

The following is the result of the program execution.

The output of the program (from Listing 3-5)
The number 315 can be divided by:
1 3 5 7 9 15 21 35 45 63 105 315

The number for which the program calculates divisors is stored in the $number variable (use the value 315). It also uses the $A variable, whose initial value is 1. You need that variable to store the value of the next divisor for the number saved to the $number variable. Finding divisors is simple: iterate over the numbers in a particular range and check if it is a divisor. To do that, you use the loop statement.

The loop statement checks the 2*$A<$number condition. Here, a divisor of a number (except for the number itself) cannot be more than half of the number. In the body of the loop statement, the $A++ command increments the $A variable, and in the conditional statement (in the simplified form without the else block), the $number%$A==0 condition is checked (the remainder of dividing $number by $A is zero). The print(" ".$A) command is executed if the condition is true. That is, the corresponding number is identified as a divisor. If the condition is false, then nothing happens.

(i) **Note**   The value of the " ".$A expression is the text resulting from the concatenation of the space " " and the value of the $A variable. The latter is automatically converted to the text format.

The last print(" ".$number) instruction adds the number to the list of its divisors. That is done without checks since any number can be divided by itself.

The do-while Loop Statement

The other loop statement is the do-while statement. The following is the syntax for the statement.

```
do{
    # commands
}while(condition);
```

It begins with the do keyword followed by a block of commands in curly braces that form the loop statement's body. Then the while keyword follows, and, in parentheses, some condition. Let's discuss how the do-while loop statement is executed. First, the commands in the body of the loop statement are executed. After that, the condition after the while keyword is checked. If the condition is true, the commands in the body of the loop statement are executed again, and the condition is checked. If it is true, the commands are executed, and so on. The execution of the loop statement terminates if the next time the condition is checked, it gives false.

ⓘ Note   The fundamental difference between the do-while statement and the while statement is that in the while statement, the condition is checked first, and then the commands are executed. At the same time, in the do-while statement, the commands are executed first, and then the condition is checked. When using the while statement, it may turn out that the commands in the statement's body are not executed at all. That happens if the condition is false the first time it is tested. If the do-while statement is used, then the commands in the loop statement are executed at least once.

As an example of using the do-while loop statement, Listing 3-6 is a program that tests a user-entered number for being prime.

 Note   A number is called prime if it has no divisors but one and the number itself.

Listing 3-6. A Prime Number

```php
<?php
    print("A number to check: ");
    // Reads a number:
    $number=(int)trim(fgets(STDIN));
    // The divisor for the number:
    $A=2;
    // Text with the check result:
    $result="It is a prime number";
    do{
        // Checks whether the numbers are divisible:
        if($number%$A==0){
            // Changes the message:
            $result="The number can be divided by $A";
            // The termination of the loop statement:
            break;
        }
        // The next divisor:
        $A++;
    }while($A<=sqrt($number));
    // The result:
    print($result);
?>
```

If the user enters a prime number (marked in bold), the program's output is as follows.

The output of the program (from Listing 3-6)

```
A number to check: 37
It is a prime number
```

If the number is not prime, the result is somewhat different.

The output of the program (from Listing 3-6)

```
A number to check: 91
The number can be divided by 7
```

The program runs as follows. First, the user enters a number to check. That number is stored in the $number variable. The text "It is a prime number" is saved to the $result variable, which is displayed in the console if it turns out that the number entered by the user is prime.

The do-while loop statement uses the conditional statement that tests the $number%$A==0 condition. The truth of the condition means that $number is divisible without remainder by $A (whose initial value is 2). If so, the $result="The number can be divided by $A" command assigns a new value to the $result variable, after which the break statement is executed. It terminates the execution of the loop statement.

If, when checking the $number%$A==0 condition in the conditional statement, it gives false, then the break statement is not executed, and the loop statement goes on. In such a case, the $A++ command increments the value of $A by one, and at the next iteration, the test for divisibility is performed for that new value.

The loop statement is executed while the $A<=sqrt($number) condition is true. Here, the sqrt() function is used; it calculates the square root of the number passed as an argument to the function.

Details

If when searching the smallest (after 1) divisor for a certain number X, some value A is found, that means the initial number can be presented as the product $X = A \cdot B$ and here $A \leq B$. That is why $A^2 \leq X$. This relation gives you the upper limit for the range where you search for divisors.

If the loop statement is terminated not due to the break instruction but because the $A<=sqrt($number) condition becomes false, then the $result variable remains with its original value. If so, the print($result) command prints a message stating that the number is prime. If the break statement "works," then the $result variable gets a new value, and the message in the console states that the number being checked has a divisor. That means that the number is not prime.

Details

The break instruction terminates the execution of the loop statement in which it is called. Here, the do-while statement and the while and for statements (discussed later in the chapter). In addition to this instruction, the continue instruction may be helpful, which terminates the current iteration (while the entire loop statement goes on).

The for Loop Statement

The for loop statement has the following syntax.

```
for(first block;second block (condition);third block){
    # commands
}
```

The for keyword is followed by three blocks of commands placed in parentheses. Semicolons separate the blocks. If a block contains multiple commands, they are separated by commas. After the closing parenthesis, another block of commands follows in curly braces. Those commands form the body of the for loop statement.

(i) **Note**   Curly braces can be omitted if a command block in the statement body consists of a single command. However, it is better to have them.

Let's discuss how the for loop statement operates. At the very beginning, the commands from the first block are executed. They are executed once and only once. Then, the condition in the second block is checked. If the condition is true, then the commands from the body of the loop statement and the commands in the third block are executed. After that, the condition is checked. If it is true, the commands in the body of the loop statement and the commands in the third block are executed, and after that, the condition is checked again. And so on. The execution of the loop statement is terminated when the condition turns out to be false during the next test.

There is also an alternative way to call the for loop statement. It does not use curly braces. Instead of them, you place a colon after the for-instruction (before the command block in the statement body). And all that ends with the endif instruction (and a semicolon).

```
for(first block;second block (condition);third block):
    # commands
endif;
```

The statement in this form is executed the same as described earlier.

As an example of using the for loop statement, let's consider a program that calculates the sum of odd natural numbers, as shown in Listing 3-7.

Listing 3-7. The Sum of Odd Numbers

```php
<?php
    // The count of terms:
    $n=100;
    // Calculates the sum of odd numbers:
    for($s=0,$k=1;$k<=$n;$k++){
        $s+=2*$k-1;
    }
    // Prints the result:
    print("1+3+...+".(2*$n-1)."=$s");
?>
```

The program's output is as follows.

The output of the program (from Listing 3-7)

```
1+3+...+199=10000
```

The program is simple. It uses the $n variable that determines the count of terms in the sum. The sum itself is calculated using the for loop statement. In the first block, the commands $s=0 (the initial value for the sum) and $k=1 (the first term) are executed. The $k<=$n condition is checked in the loop statement. It is true as long as the value of the $k variable (the count of terms already added to the sum) does not exceed the value of the $n variable (the expected count of terms in the sum). The loop statement is executed while the $k<=$n condition is true. The commands $s+=2*$k-1 (the next term is added to the sum) and $k++ (the term for the next iteration) are performed for each iteration.

Note   Here, odd numbers can be calculated using the formula
$2k - 1$, where the k variable takes the values 1, 2, 3, and so on.

After the loop statement is terminated, the result of the calculations
is displayed in the console with the print("1+3+...+".(2*$n-1)."=$s")
command. This command uses the string obtained by concatenating
several text fragments (including the 2*$n-1 expression, which determines
the last term in the sum, and the $s variable, which determines the sum).

 Note   The sum of the first n odd natural numbers is
equal to n^2.

Listing 3-8 is an alternative form of the for loop statement using a
program in which the Fibonacci numbers are calculated.

 Note   In the Fibonacci sequence, the first two numbers are
equal to one, and each subsequent number is equal to the sum of the
previous two.

Listing 3-8. The Fibonacci Numbers

```php
<?php
    // How many numbers to calculate:
    $n=15;
    // The first and second numbers:
    $a=$b=1;
    // Prints numbers:
    print("$a $b");
```

```
// Calculates other numbers:
for($k=3;$k<=$n;$k++):
    // The new pair of numbers:
    $b=$a+$b;
    $a=$b-$a;
    // Prints the new number:
    print(" ".$b);
endfor;
?>
```

The following is the result of the program execution.

The output of the program (from Listing 3-8)
1 1 2 3 5 8 13 21 34 55 89 144 233 377 610

The count of calculated numbers is stored in the $n variable. The $a
and $b variables get the initial value 1 (the $a=$b=1 command, in which
the assignment operator returns a result). The print("$a $b") command
displays the values of these variables in the console. Assume that the $a
variable contains the last but one number in the sequence, and the $b
variable contains the last calculated value in the sequence. The calculation
process is implemented using the loop statement. There, the $k variable
runs from 3 (because the first two numbers are already known) to the value
of the $n variable (the count of numbers to be calculated in the sequence).
In the body of the loop statement, the $b=$a+$b and $a=$b-$a commands
calculate a new number in the sequence.

Details

Let's discuss how to calculate the numbers. Suppose that $a and $b contain respectively the last but one and the last number in the Fibonacci sequence. Let's formally denote the value of the $a variable as $\triangle$ and the value of the $b variable as $\square$. You need to do the "next step": the $b variable should contain the value $\triangle+\square$, and the $a variable should contain the value $\square$.

After executing the $b=$a+$b command, $b contains the value $\triangle+\square$, and $a contains the original value $\triangle$. To write the value $\square$ to the $a variable, you need to execute the $a=$b-$a command.

After the next number in the sequence is calculated and saved to the $b variable, the print(" ".$b) command displays it in the console.

 Note   It is worth mentioning that the distribution of commands in the blocks of the for loop statement is somewhat arbitrary. For example, commands from the body of the loop statement can be moved to the third block, and commands from the third block can be moved to the main body of the loop statement as long as the commands are executed in the same order.

The switch Selection Statement

Depending on the value of some expression, the switch statement allows you to execute one or another block of commands. In some sense, this statement resembles nested conditional statements. But while in a conditional statement, a condition is checked (an expression with a value of the boolean type or a value that can be cast to the boolean type), in a selection statement, the value of an expression is checked, whose type may differ from the boolean.

The syntax for calling the selection statement is as follows.

```
switch(expression){
    case value:
        # commands
        break;
    case value:
        # commands
        break;
    default:
        # commands
}
```

The switch keyword is followed by an expression in parentheses whose value is being checked. Then, case blocks follow. There are two of them in the preceding template, but generally, the count of such blocks is practically unlimited. The last one can be the default block (it is optional). The whole structure is enclosed in curly braces.

Each case block contains, after the case keyword, a control value. It is followed by a colon and a block of commands, which usually ends with the break instruction. In the default block, if it exists, the break instruction is not used (it simply does not make any sense to use it there).

How is the selection statement executed? The expression in parentheses after the switch keyword is evaluated first. The value of that expression is sequentially compared with the control values in the case blocks until the first match.

Details

That is an ordinary comparison, not a check for identical equality.

75

The commands in the corresponding case block are executed if a match is found. That is the situation when the command block ends with the break instruction. If there is no break instruction at the end of the case block, the commands in the next block are executed, the block after it, and so on. The process continues until a break instruction is encountered or until the closing curly brace of the selection statement is reached.

The selection statement has an alternative syntax.

```
switch(expression):
    case value:
        # commands
        break;
    case value:
        # commands
        break;
    default:
        # commands
endswitch;
```

Here, the curly braces are not used: a colon is used instead of the opening curly brace, and the endswitch statement (followed by a semicolon) is used instead of the closing curly brace.

Listing 3-9 shows a program illustrating how the selection statement can be used.

Listing 3-9. The Selection Statement

```php
<?php
    // The names of the Musketeers:
    $athos="Athos";
    $porthos="Porthos";
    $aramis="Aramis";
    print("A name from \"The Three Musketeers\": ");
```

```
// Reads the name:
$name=trim(fgets(STDIN));
// Checks the name:
switch($name){
    case $athos:
        print("Yes, Athos is a Musketeer");
        break;
    case $porthos:
        print("Yes, Porthos is a Musketeer");
        break;
    case $aramis:
        print("Yes, Aramis is a Musketeer");
        break;
    default:
        print("Strange. Is this a fourth Musketeer?");
}
?>
```

The program prompts the user to enter the name of one of the Three Musketeers: Athos, Porthos, or Aramis.

The program "knows" the names "Athos", "Porthos", and "Aramis". If the user enters one of these names, the program displays the name of the Musketeer. If the name entered by the user is "not known" to the program, then the message "Strange. Is this a fourth Musketeer?" is printed. The following shows the program's output if the user enters the name "Athos".

The output of the program (from Listing 3-9)
A name from "The Three Musketeers": **Athos**
Yes, Athos is a Musketeer

If the user enters "Porthos", the result is as follows.

The output of the program (from Listing 3-9)

```
A name from "The Three Musketeers": Porthos
Yes, Porthos is a Musketeer
```

The following is the result for the case when the user enters the name "Aramis".

The output of the program (from Listing 3-9)

```
A name from "The Three Musketeers": Aramis
Yes, Aramis is a Musketeer
```

Finally, if the program "doesn't recognize" the name, the result is as follows.

The output of the program (from Listing 3-9)

```
A name from "The Three Musketeers": D'Artanian
Strange. Is this a fourth Musketeer?
```

The program uses the $athos, $porthos, and $aramis variables to store the names of the Three Musketeers in them. The $name variable is assigned the name entered by the user. The switch statement is used to find matches. The expression to be tested is the value of the $name variable. The $athos, $porthos, and $aramis variables are used as control values in the case blocks.

Let's discuss how the selection statement is executed. The value of the $name variable is sequentially compared with the values of the $athos, $porthos, and $aramis variables. As soon as a match is found, the commands of the corresponding case block are executed. If there are no matches, then the commands in the default block are executed.

Listing 3-10 illustrates how to use the selection statement in the alternative form. In this program, the number the user enters is checked for divisibility by 2 and 4.

Listing 3-10. The Divisibility of a Number

```php
<?php
    print("Enter a number: ");
    # Reads the number:
    $number=(int)trim(fgets(STDIN));
    # Checks the numbers for divisibility:
    switch($number%4):
        case 0:
            print("The number can be divided by 4");
            break;
        case 2:
            print("The number can be divided by 2");
            break;
        default:
            print("The number can not be divided by 2");
    endswitch;
?>
```

If the user enters a number that can be divided by 4, the result is as follows.

The output of the program (from Listing 3-10)

Enter a number: **140**
The number can be divided by 4

If the number can be divided by 2 but not by 4, the result is as follows.

The output of the program (from Listing 3-10)
```
Enter a number: 70
The number can be divided by 2
```

Finally, if the number the user enters is not divisible by 2, the program produces the following result.

The output of the program (from Listing 3-10)
```
Enter a number: 123
The number can not be divided by 2
```

In this case, the integer entered by the user is stored in the $number variable. The switch statement checks the value of the $number%4 expression (the remainder of dividing $number by 4). If the remainder is 0, the print("The number can be divided by 4") command is executed. If the remainder is 2, the print("The number can be divided by 2") command displays the message. Here, the number is divisible by 2 but not by 4. Finally, all other situations are handled in the default block. If so, the print("The number cannot be divided by 2") command is executed.

The case blocks ended with the break instructions in the considered examples. However, that is not required. There exist situations when the same set of commands must be executed for several control values. The program in Listing 3-11 shows how that could be done.

Listing 3-11. A Day of the Week

```php
<?php
    print("A day of the week: ");
    // Reads a day of the week:
    $day=trim(fgets(STDIN));
```

```
// Checks the day of the week:
switch($day){
    case "Monday":
    case "Tuesday":
    case "Wednesday":
    case "Thursday":
    case "Friday":
        print("It is a working day");
        break;
    case "Saturday":
    case "Sunday":
        print("It is a holiday");
        break;
    default:
        print("There is no such day");
}
?>
```

The result of the program execution can be as follows (the value entered by the user is marked in bold).

The output of the program (from Listing 3-11)

A day of the week: **Wednesday**

It is a working day

It could also look as follows.

The output of the program (from Listing 3-11)

A day of the week: **Saturday**

It is a holiday

Or it could look as follows.

The output of the program (from Listing 3-11)
A day of the week: **Midday**
There is no such day

In the program, the user enters the name of a day of the week, and the program determines whether it is a working day or a holiday. The critical point is that for the values "Monday", "Tuesday", "Wednesday", "Thursday", and "Friday", the same print("It is a working day") command must be executed. To not duplicate the code five times, create four empty case blocks (they do not contain commands), and only the last (out of five) case block contains the necessary command and the break instruction. If, for example, the user enters "Wednesday", the code from the case block with the control value "Wednesday" is executed until the first break instruction. It turns out that the same commands are executed for each of the five control values.

A similar tactic handles the "Saturday" and "Sunday" values. The commands in the default block are executed if the user enters a value other than one of the controls.

The goto Instruction

PHP has the goto instruction that can be used to jump to a particular position in a program marked with a label. Frankly speaking, using the goto instruction is usually considered not a very good programming style. Nevertheless, such a possibility exists, and it is better to know about it.

So, you can place a label in a program. It is an identifier that determines the transition point in the program. Declaring a label is simple. You specify the name of the label followed by a colon. To jump to that place in the program, you must call the goto statement followed by the label (that determines the place in the program to jump to). Listing 3-12 shows a program that emulates a loop statement using a conditional statement, a label, and the goto instruction. As a result, a sequence of numbers is displayed in the console.

Listing 3-12. The goto Instruction

```php
<?php
    // Variables:
    $number=10;
    $k=1;
    // A label:
    start:
    print($k." ");
    // The new value:
    $k++;
    if($k<=$number){
        // Jumps to the label:
        goto start;
    }
?>
```

The result of the program execution is as follows.

The output of the program (from Listing 3-12)

1 2 3 4 5 6 7 8 9 10

The program uses two variables: $number (how many numbers to display) and $k (the current number). The place in the program marked with the start label begins with the print($k." ") command (prints the value of the $k variable and a space). After that, the $k++ command increments $k by one. Then, the program checks the $k<=$number condition in the conditional statement. If it is true, goto start is executed. As a result, the program's execution continues from the place

marked with the label start. Namely, the commands print($k." ")
and $k++ are executed, after which the condition in the conditional
statement is checked again, and so on. It looks like a loop statement. When
$k<=$number evaluates to false, the goto start instruction is ignored,
and the program is over (since there are no other commands).

The match Selection Statement

PHP 8 introduces yet another selection statement. That is the match
statement. In a certain sense, the match statement is like a combination of
the switch statement and the ternary operator. Like the switch statement,
the match statement allows you to check expressions. But unlike the
switch statement, the match statement returns a result (similar to the
ternary operator). The following shows the general syntax for using the
match statement.

```
$variable=match(expression){
    value=>resulr,
    value=>result,
    value=>result,
    ...
    $value=>result,
    default=>result
};
```

At the very beginning of the statement, you place the match keyword
followed by the expression (in parentheses) whose value has to be
checked. The next block is enclosed in curly braces. As mentioned, the
match statement returns a result, so the whole expression is assigned to
some variable. At the end of the statement, you put a semicolon.

In the main body of the match statement, place blocks of the form
value=>result in curly braces. These elements are separated by commas.

The last one can be a block like default=>result with the default keyword, but it is optional.

Let's discuss how the match statement is executed. First, the value of the expression in parentheses after the match keyword is evaluated. Then, that value is sequentially compared (up to the first match) with the values specified in the body of the match statement. If a match is found, the result after the corresponding => arrow is returned. If no matches are found, the result for the block with the default keyword is returned.

Details

The match selection statement must return a result. When executing the statement, an error occurs if it turns out that none of the blocks work (no matches are found, and there is no default block).

The comparisons are performed until the first match. If a match is found, the remaining values are not checked.

If the result should be the same for several values of the tested expression, then such values can be collected (separated by commas) within one block. Let's look at such a situation in more detail.

🔔 **The PHP 8 Standard**   The following code runs in PHP 8 only.

The program that uses the match selection statement is shown in Listing 3-13.

Listing 3-13. Getting Familiar with the match Statement

```php
<?php
    // The loop statement for iterating values:
    for($num=1;$num<=10;$num++){
        // The selection statement:
        $res=match($num){
```

```
        1=>"one",
        2,3,5,7=>"a prime number",
        4,6,8=>"an even number",
        9=>"nine",
        default=>"a great number"
    };
    // Prints the result:
    echo "[$num] ",$res,"\n";
  }
?>
```

The result of the program execution is as follows.

The output of the program (from Listing 3-13)

```
[1] one
[2] a prime number
[3] a prime number
[4] an even number
[5] a prime number
[6] an even number
[7] a prime number
[8] an even number
[9] nine
[10] a great number
```

The program's core is the for loop statement, in which the $num variable runs through the range from 1 to 10 inclusively. For each iteration, the $res variable is assigned a value, after which that value (along with the value of the $num variable) is displayed by the echo "[$num] ",$res,"\n" command.

Use the match selection statement to assign a value to the $res variable. It checks the value of the $num variable. If the variable's value is 1, the string "one" is returned as a result (the 1=>"one" block). For the values 2, 3, 5, and 7 of the $num variable, the statement returns the result "a prime number" (the 2,3,5,7=>"a prime number" block). If $num is 4, 6, or 8, the result is the text "an even number" (the 4,6,8=>"an even number" block). For the value 9, the result "nine" is returned (the 9=>"nine" block). In all other cases, the result is the string "a great number". The default=>"a great number" block is responsible for that result.

Another example of using the match selection statement is shown in Listing 3-14.

Listing 3-14. Using the match Selection Statement

```php
<?php
    // The loop statement for iterating numbers:
    for($num=1;$num<=10;$num++){
        // The selection statement:
        $res=match(true){
            ($num<=3)=>"a small number",
            ($num<8)=>"just a number",
            ($num>=5)=>"a great number"
        };
        // Prints the result:
        echo "[$num] ",$res,"\n";
    }
?>
```

The following is the program output.

The output of the program (from Listing 3-14)
[1] a small number
[2] a small number
[3] a small number
[4] just a number
[5] just a number
[6] just a number
[7] just a number
[8] a great number
[9] a great number
[10] a great number

This example is similar to the previous one, but significant changes
were made. The keyword true is specified as the expression to be checked.
The results of the $num<=3, $num<8, and $num>=5 expressions are compared
against that value. They are checked one by one until the first match. In
particular, it first checks if the value of the $num<=3 expression is true. If
so, then the result of the match statement is "a small number". If there is
no match, then the value of the $num<8 expression is checked if it is true.
If there is a match, the statement returns the string "just a number"
as a result. If there is no match, the $num>=5 expression is checked. If
that expression is true, the result of the statement is the string "a great
number".

Details

The conditions $num<=3, $num<8, and $num>=5 are such that at least one of them is true. Therefore, the selection statement returns a result for any value of the $num variable.

It is also worth mentioning that for the values 5, 6, and 7 of the $num variable, the $num<8 and $num>=5 conditions are true at the same time. But the $num<8 condition is checked before the $num>=5 condition. Therefore, if it turns out that the $num<8 condition is true, the $num>=5 condition is not checked.

Summary

- The if statement allows you to execute different blocks of commands depending on the truth or falsity of some condition. The condition is specified in parentheses after the if keyword, followed by the commands to be executed when the condition is true. Commands executed when the condition is false are placed in the else block.

- The while loop statement allows you to execute a block of commands repeatedly. Commands are executed while the condition specified after the while keyword is true.

- The do-while statement differs from the while statement as follows. In the do-while statement, the block of commands is executed first, and then the condition is checked, while execution of the while statement begins with checking the condition.

- The for loop statement has a more complex syntax than the while and do-while statements, but it is pretty convenient to use, and its capabilities are not inferior to those of other loop statements.

- The break instruction allows you to terminate the execution of a loop statement. The continue instruction is used to terminate the current iteration (without terminating the loop statement execution).

- The switch statement allows you to execute different blocks of commands depending on the value of some expression. It contains case blocks with control values. If the value of the checked expression matches the control value, the commands in the corresponding case block are executed. The commands in the optional default block are executed if no matches are found.

- The goto statement allows you to jump to a particular place marked with a label in the program. The label is specified after the goto keyword. To mark a place in a program with a label, put the label name followed by a colon.

- PHP 8 introduces the match selection statement. The statement allows you to check the value of some expression and returns a result depending on that value. In a certain sense, the match selection statement can be interpreted as a symbiosis of the switch selection statement and the ternary operator.

CHAPTER 4

Arrays

> —*This is such a toy—puzzles.*
> —*She's broken!*
> —*That's the point, Alf. You have to collect it.*
> —*What's that? I didn't break it!*
>
> —*ALF* (TV series)

An array is generally a set or group of values united by a common name. Arrays are usually used when there are many values, and creating a separate variable for each is impossible. If so, a common name is used for the entire set of values, and specific values (array elements) are identified using an index or indexes. In the "classic" version, the indexes are integers. In PHP, integers and strings can be used as indexes. In that case, the term *key* may be used instead of *index*. An array with string keys is usually called an *associative array*.

ⓘ Note   About the terminology, there are a lot of possible terms. For example, the term list is sometimes used along with the term array. Instead of the *associative array*, the term *dictionary* or *table* is used. Let's name all arrays (integer indexes and string keys) as arrays. A *list* is an array with integer indexes. The index is interpreted as a particular case of an integer key.

© Alex Vasilev 2024
A. Vasilev, *PHP by Example*, https://doi.org/10.1007/979-8-8688-0258-4_4

Next, let's consider some cases of creating and using arrays.

Getting Familiar with Arrays

An array in PHP can be created differently, and all methods are acceptable.
Let's examine the main and simplest possibilities and other tricks for
creating and using arrays. You do that step by step as you solve problems.

So, you can create an array using the array() function. If that
function is called without arguments, an empty array is created. If you
pass arguments to the array() function, they determine the values of the
array elements. If so, element indexes are integers, and indexing begins
from zero. Also, there are other ways to create arrays. A small example that
creates arrays is shown in Listing 4-1.

Listing 4-1. Creating an Array

```php
<?php
    // An empty array:
    $A=array();
    print("Array \$A:\n");
    // The contents of the array:
    print_r($A);
    // Elements are added to the array:
    $A[0]="Red";
    $A[1]="Yellow";
    $A[2]="Green";
    print("Array \$A:\n");
    // The contents of the array:
    print_r($A);
    // An array with three integer elements:
    $B=array(100,200,300);
    print("Array \$B:\n");
```

```
// The contents of the array:
print_r($B);
print("\$B = [ ");
// Prints the elements one by one:
for($k=0;$k<count($B);$k++){
    print($B[$k]." ");
}
print("]\n");
// An array with elements of different types:
$C=["First",2,3.3];
print("Array \$C:\n");
// The contents of the array:
print_r($C);
?>
```

The result of the program's execution is as follows.

The output of the program (from Listing 4-1)
```
Array $A:
Array
(
)
Array $A:
Array
(
    [0] => Red
    [1] => Yellow
    [2] => Green
)
Array $B:
Array
(
```

```
    [0] => 100
    [1] => 200
    [2] => 300
)
$B = [ 100 200 300 ]
Array $C:
Array
(
    [0] => First
    [1] => 2
    [2] => 3.3
)
```

The program creates and performs simple operations on three arrays. The first array is created with the $A=array() statement. The array is empty, and a reference to it is written to the $A variable. To check the contents of an array, you use the print_r() function, whose argument is a variable that refers to the array.

Details

To display the dollar symbol $ in text, use the combination \$.

If you try to display the contents of an array using the print() function or the echo statement, the text Array appears. Therefore, it is better to use the print_r() function to display the array. The contents of the array in the output area are represented as follows: the word Array appears followed (in parentheses) by the keys/indexes and values of the array elements in the [index] => value format.

After checking the array, you see that the array is indeed empty. However, you can add elements to the array: the $A[0]="Red", $A[1]="Yellow", and $A[2]="Green" commands. The commands mean that you add the "Red" element with the 0 index, the "Yellow" element with the 1 index, and the "Green" element with the 2 index to the $A array. Here, to refer to an element of an array, you specify the name of the array followed by the index in square brackets. Having displayed the array's contents using the print_r() function, you ensure that the elements were added to the array.

Details

If a value is assigned to the array element that does not exist, then the element is added to the array. If you assign a value to an already existing element, then that element changes its value. In this case, the array is empty. By assigning values to the elements of the array, you add elements to the array. Moreover, there was no need to create the array first. It was enough to assign a value to an element of the array. The array is created automatically in that case.

The $B=array(100,200,300) command creates an array with three integer elements whose values are 100, 200, and 300. The values of the elements of the created array are passed as arguments to the array() function. The indexes of the elements are defined automatically. They are 0, 1, and 2, respectively. The contents of the $B array are displayed using the print_r() function and then using the for loop statement, where you explicitly iterate over the elements of the array. The elements are iterated using the index stored in the $k variable. The count() function determines the count of elements in the array. You also saw that indexing begins from zero, and the index of the last element is one less than the count of elements in the array.

ⓘ **Note**   In addition to the count() function, you can use the sizeof() function to determine the size of an array.

Another way to create an array is to list the values of the array elements in square brackets. That is how the $C array is created. The $C=["First",2,3.3] statement is used to create it. It is worth mentioning that the elements of that array have values of different types. In PHP, that is an acceptable situation. Indexes for the array elements are determined automatically (0, 1, and 2).

It may happen that you are not satisfied with the situation when the indexes of the array elements are determined automatically, or you want to use non-numeric values as indexes. If so, when creating an array, you pass constructions of the form key=>value as arguments to the array() function or list them in square brackets. Namely, you specify the key of the element and, after the "arrow" =>, its value. In addition, as before, you can assign values to the elements of an array. In that case, the array is automatically created, and elements with the corresponding keys are added to it.

ⓘ **Note**   Once again, let's go over the terminology. Arrays contain elements. Elements have a *value* and a *key* (or keys for multidimensional arrays). For integer keys, the term *indexes* is also used.

An example of creating an array with elements whose keys are explicitly specified is shown in Listing 4-2.

Listing 4-2. Explicitly Specifying Keys When Creating an Array

```php
<?php
    // Adds elements to the array:
    $A["Red"]=100;
    $A["Yellow"]=200;
    $A["Green"]=300;
```

```
print("Array \$A:\n");
// The contents of the array:
print_r($A);
// An array with three elements:
$B=array(100=>"One hundred",200=>"Two hundred", 300=>"Three
hundred");
print("Array \$B:\n");
// The contents of the array:
print_r($B);
// An array with elements and keys of different types:
$C=[5=>"First","X"=>0,"Last"];
print("Array \$C:\n");
// The contents of the array:
print_r($C);
?>
```

The following is the program's output.

The output of the program (from Listing 4-2)
```
Array $A:
Array
(
    [Red] => 100
    [Yellow] => 200
    [Green] => 300
)
Array $B:
Array
(
    [100] => One hundred
    [200] => Two hundred
    [300] => Three hundred
```

```
)
Array $C:
Array
(
    [5] => First
    [X] => 0
    [6] => Last
)
```

The program starts with the $A["Red"]=100, $A["Yellow"]=200, and $A["Green"]=300 commands. As a result, the $A array with three elements is created: the elements have the keys "Red", "Yellow", and "Green", and the values are 100, 200, and 300, respectively.

The $B=array(100=>"One hundred",200=>"Two hundred",300=>"Three hundred") command creates the $B array with three elements. Elements have the integer indexes 100, 200, and 300. Their values are "One hundred", "Two hundred", and "Three hundred".

Finally, the $C=[5=>"First","X"=>0,"Last"] command creates the $C array, whose elements have keys of different types. Namely, the element with the value "First" has the integer key 5. The element with the value 0 has the "X" string key. The element with the value "Last" has no specified key. In that case, the index is calculated automatically: one greater than the highest integer index of the elements already included in the array. Therefore, the element with the value "Last" gets the integer key 6.

Details

You can add a new element to an array with a command like `array[]=value`. Here, you refer to an element, specifying empty parentheses without specifying a key. In that case, the key (index) is calculated automatically (the highest index among the array elements, plus one).

To remove an element from an array, you can use the `unset()` function, passing the element to be removed as an argument to the function.

Suppose multiple elements with matching indexes are specified in the array description. In that case, the array has a single element with the corresponding index, and its value is determined by the last of the values specified for the element with that index.

A Loop over an Array

You have examined a case where the index is used the for loop statement to iterate array elements. The inconvenience of that approach is that the indexes must form an ordered sequence. But that may not be the case. Therefore, another loop statement is usually used. It is called `foreach`. Its syntax is as follows.

```
foreach(array as key=>value){
    # commands
}
```

The `foreach` keyword is followed by a special "construct" in parentheses. First comes the array name, the `as` keyword, and then the `key=>value` expression. The keys and values are realized by employing variables. The body of the loop statement contains statements enclosed in curly braces.

The `foreach` loop statement is executed as follows. The elements are iterated sequentially in the array specified in the `foreach` statement. The commands in the body of the loop statement are executed for each element of the array. The variable specified as a key in the key=>value statement gets the value of the element's key, and the variable specified as a value gets the element's value.

An alternative syntax uses a colon instead of the opening curly brace and the endforeach keyword (and a semicolon) instead of the closing curly brace.

```
foreach(array as key=>value):
    # commands
endforeach;
```

Listing 4-3 illustrates the foreach loop statement in practice.

Listing 4-3. Iterating over Elements in an Array

```php
<?php
    // An array:
    $A=["X"=>100,"Y"=>200,"Z"=>300];
    // Iterating over the array elements:
    foreach($A as $k=>$v){
        echo "Key ",$k," -> value ",$v,"\n";
    }
?>
```

The following shows the result of the program's execution.

The output of the program (from Listing 4-3)

```
Key X -> value 100
Key Y -> value 200
Key Z -> value 300
```

In this case, everything is quite simple. First, with the $A=["X"=>100, "Y"=>200,"Z"=>300] instruction, you create an array. Then, use the loop statement. After the foreach keyword, the parentheses contain the $A

as $k=>$v construction. It means that the elements of the $A array are
iterated, and the $k variable gets the keys of the elements; meanwhile, the
$v variable gets the values of the elements. There is only one command,
echo "Key ",$k," -> value ",$v,"\n", in the body of the loop
statement, which displays the "Key" string, the value of the $k key of the
element, the " -> value " string, the value $v of the element, and the
break-line escape sequence (the "\n" instruction).

Details

For the first loop, $k is set to "X", and $v is set to 100. For the second loop, $k is set
to "Y", and $v is set to 200. For the third loop, $k is set to "Z", and $v is set to 300.

Another example of using the foreach statement (in its alternative
form) is shown in Listing 4-4.

Listing 4-4. Deleting Elements from an Array

```php
<?php
    // An array:
    $A=[5=>100,"Two hundred",300];
    print("Array \$A:\n");
    print_r($A);
    // Iterates over the elements in the array:
    foreach($A as $k=>$v):
        print("\$A[$k] = $v");
        // Checks the element type:
        if(gettype($v)=="string"){
            print(" - delete\n");
            // Deletes the element from the array:
            unset($A[$k]);
        }else{
            print(" - remain\n");
```

101

```
    }
  endforeach;
  print("Array \$A:\n");
  print_r($A);
?>
```

The following is the result of the program's execution.

The output of the program (from Listing 4-4)
```
Array $A:
Array
(
    [5] => 100
    [6] => Two hundred
    [7] => 300
)
$A[5] = 100 - remain
$A[6] = Two hundred - delete
$A[7] = 300 - remain
Array $A:
Array
(
    [5] => 100
    [7] => 300
)
```

The program creates an array and then removes the elements with text values from the array. The array is created by the $A=[5=>100,"Two hundred",300] command. It has three elements. The value of the element with the 5 index is 100. The indexes of the other two elements are calculated automatically. Thus, the index of the element with the value "Two hundred" is 6, and the index of the element with the value 300 is 7.

The `foreach` loop statement is used to iterate over the elements of the $A array. The key is stored in the $k variable, and the element's value is stored in the $v variable. For each cycle, the `print("\$A[$k] = $v")` command displays the value of the array element. Then, the conditional statement comes into play, in which the `gettype($v)=="string"` condition is checked (the element's value is of the `string` type). If so, the `print(" - remove\n")` command displays a message about removing the element, and then the element is removed from the array using the `unset($A[$k])` command.

If the `gettype($v)=="string"` condition is false, then the `print(" - remain\n")` command displays a message that the element remains in the array.

After the loop statement is terminated, check the array's contents. The check shows that the element with the text value is removed from the array.

Sometimes, you do not need to know and use the keys of the array elements. That means that you are interested only in the values of the elements. If so, a simplified syntax can be used in the `foreach` loop statement.

```
foreach(array as variable){
    # commands
}
```

Here, a variable to store the keys is not specified, and the name of the variable follows the `as` keyword that sequentially, cycle by cycle, takes the values of the elements from the array placed before the `as` keyword. An example of using the `foreach` loop statement in a simplified form is shown in Listing 4-5.

Listing 4-5. Iterating over the Array's Elements

```php
<?php
    # An array:
    $A=["X"=>100,"Y"=>200,"Z"=>300];
    echo "\$A = [ ";
    # Iterates over the values of the elements:
    foreach($A as $v){
        echo $v," ";
    }
    echo "]";
?>
```

The following shows the program's output.

The output of the program (from Listing 4-5)

$A = [100 200 300]

Here, in the loop statement, the $v variable sequentially takes the values of the $A array elements. The keys are not used.

It is worth mentioning that within the framework described, you can access the value of an element in a read-only mode. You cannot assign a new value to the element since the standard scheme for iterating over array elements assumes that a copy of the element's value is written to the corresponding variable. By changing the value of the copy, you do not affect the element's value. Nevertheless, there exists an easy way to change the situation. To do that, in the description of the foreach loop statement, before the name of the variable proposed for storing the values of the array elements, you should place the & symbol. If you do so, the specified variable refers to an array element. In other words, you get access to the element's value and the element itself (and you can, if necessary, change its value).

Details

You can also refer to ordinary variables. A variable reference is an alternative way to get access to that variable. To create a reference to a variable, you must create a new variable (reference) in the program and assign the original variable as a value, prefixing it with the & symbol. For example, the $x=100 command creates the $x variable with the value 100. Then, the $y=&$x command creates the $y reference to the $x variable. That means changing the $x variable automatically changes the $y variable, and vice versa. The reason is simple: the $x and $y variables refer to the same memory area.

Listing 4-6 explains how array elements are accessed.

Listing 4-6. Accessing Elements by a Reference

```php
<?php
    # An array:
    $A=[100,200,300];
    print("The initial array:\n");
    print_r($A);
    # Accessing the values by a variable:
    foreach($A as $v):
        $v++;
    endforeach;
    print("The first try:\n");
    # Checks the result:
    print_r($A);
    # Accessing the values by a reference:
    foreach($A as &$v):
        $v++;
    endforeach;
    print("The second try:\n");
    # Checks the result:
    print_r($A);
?>
```

The following shows the program's output.

The output of the program (from Listing 4-6)
```
The initial array:
Array
(
    [0] => 100
    [1] => 200
    [2] => 300
)
The first try:
Array
(
    [0] => 100
    [1] => 200
    [2] => 300
)
The second try:
Array
(
    [0] => 101
    [1] => 201
    [2] => 301
)
```

The program creates an array and then, using the foreach loop statement, iterates over the elements of the array and attempts to increase the value of the array elements by one (the $v++ command in the body of the loop statement). In the first case, you use an ordinary variable to access the array's elements; in the second case, you use a reference. As you can see, in the first case, the values of the elements do not change; in the second case, the value is increased by one for each array element.

Multidimensional Arrays

The elements of an array can be, among other things, arrays. And the elements of these internal arrays can also be arrays, and so on. In that case, multiple indexes or keys must be used to access an element of the internal array: the first key allows access to the internal array, the second key allows access to an element of that internal array, and the chain can continue. If so, you usually speak of multidimensional arrays. But, in the respect that in PHP, array elements can be of different types, this concept is rather vague. You proceed from the fact that a multidimensional array is an array among the elements of which there are arrays.

From a technical point of view, creating a multidimensional array is not tricky. It is enough to describe one or more elements as an array when creating the initial (external) array. A small example is shown in Listing 4-7.

Listing 4-7. A Multidimensional Array

```php
<?php
    // A multidimensional array:
    $A=[[1,2,3,4,5],["A","B","C"],[6,7,8,9]];
    echo "Array \$A:\n";
    // The contents of the array:
    print_r($A);
    echo "Array \$A:\n";
    // Iterates the elements (with the help of indexes):
    for($i=0;$i<count($A);$i++){
        for($j=0;$j<count($A[$i]);$j++){
            // Displays the value of the elements:
            echo $A[$i][$j]," ";
        }
```

```php
    // Breaks the line:
    echo "\n";
}
// A multidimensional array:
$B=array(7=>array("X"=>2,"Y"=>3),9=>array("D","E","F"));
echo "Array \$B:\n";
// The contents of the array:
print_r($B);
echo "Array \$B:\n";
// Iterates the elements:
foreach($B as $k1=>$v1){
    foreach($v1 as $k2=>$v2){
        // Displays the value of the element:
        echo "\$B[$k1][$k2] = $v2\n";
    }
}
?>
```

The following shows the result of the program's execution.

The output of the program (from Listing 4-7)
```
Array $A:
Array
(
    [0] => Array
        (
            [0] => 1
            [1] => 2
            [2] => 3
            [3] => 4
            [4] => 5
        )
```

```
    [1] => Array
        (
            [0] => A
            [1] => B
            [2] => C
        )

    [2] => Array
        (
            [0] => 6
            [1] => 7
            [2] => 8
            [3] => 9
        )

)
Array $A:
1 2 3 4 5
A B C
6 7 8 9
Array $B:
Array
(
    [7] => Array
        (
            [X] => 2
            [Y] => 3
        )

    [9] => Array
        (
            [0] => D
            [1] => E
```

```
            [2] => F
        )

)
Array $B:
$B[7][X] = 2
$B[7][Y] = 3
$B[9][0] = D
$B[9][1] = E
$B[9][2] = F
```

The program creates two multidimensional arrays and displays their contents in different modes. The first array is created with the $A=[[1,2,3, 4,5],["A","B","C"],[6,7,8,9]] command. That is an array consisting of three elements: the element $A[0] is the [1,2,3,4,5] array, the element $A[1] is the "A","B","C"] array, and the element $A[2] is the [6,7,8,9] array. If you specify the second index, you get access to an element of the internal array. For example, the $A[0][1] expression refers to the element with the 1 index in the array, which is the element with the 0 index in the $A array (the element value is 2). The $A[1][2] instruction refers to the element with the 2 index in the array, which is the element with index 1 in the $A array (the value of the element is "C").

You did not specify indexes for array elements, so they are determined automatically. You can use that fact and enumerate the array elements employing indexes. You do that in the nested for loop statements. In the outer statement, the loop variable $i runs from 0 to count($A) (the count of elements in the $A) array minus one. In the inner loop statement, the loop variable $j runs from 0 to count($A[$i]) (the number of elements in the inner array $A[$i]) minus one. With the given values of the $i and $j variables, the echo $A[$i][$j]," " command is executed, which displays the value of the element $A[$i][$j] (the element with the $j index in the array, which is the element with the $i index in the $A) array and a space.

After the inner loop statement is terminated, the echo "\n" command breaks the line (moves the caret to the new line in the output area).

Another multidimensional array is created by the $B=array(7=> array("X"=>2,"Y"=>3),9=>array("D","E","F")) command. Here, you use the array() function, and for some arrays (including the outer one), you explicitly specify the key values. Nested foreach statements are used to iterate over elements. The outer statement iterates over the contents of the $B array. The key of an $B array element is written to the $k1 variable, and the value of the element of the $B array is written to the $v1 variable. But the $B array consists of arrays, so $v1 is an array. That array is reviewed in the inner foreach loop statement. There, the key of the element in the internal array is written to the $k2 variable, and the value of that element is written to the $v2 variable. The echo "\$B[$k1][$k2] = $v2\n" command displays the keys and the value of the element in the internal array.

Array Assignments

The basic operations performed on array elements are reading the element's value and assigning a value to the element. If you need to know an array element's value, specify the array name and element index/key in square brackets after the array name.

---

i **Note**   You can use curly braces instead of square brackets when referring to array elements, but in PHP 8, such syntax raises an error.

If you want to change the value of an array element, you just assign a new value to the element. As noted earlier, if the element to which a value is assigned does not exist in the array, such an element is created. You also know how to iterate over the elements of an array using the foreach loop statement. All these have been discussed. However, that is not a complete list of operations that can be performed with arrays. Next, let's examine some of the most relevant issues. Let's start with array assignments.

The program in Listing 4-8 assigns an array as a value to a variable.

Listing 4-8. Array Assignments

```php
<?php
    // The initial array:
    $A=[1,[2,[3,4]]];
    print("Array \$A:\n");
    // Checks the contents of the array:
    print_r($A);
    // Assigns an array:
    $B=$A;
    print("Array \$B:\n");
    // Checks the contents of the array:
    print_r($B);
    // Changes the initial array:
    $A[0]="A";
    $A[1][0]="B";
    $A[1][1][0]="C";
    print("Array \$A:\n");
    // Checks the contents of the array:
    print_r($A);
    print("Array \$B:\n");
    // Checks the contents of the array:
    print_r($B);
?>
```

The program creates an array with the $A=[1,[2,[3,4]]] command. Next, with the $B=$A command, the $A array is assigned as a value to the $B variable. Then, you change the values of some array elements $A and check how the $A and $B arrays have changed.

Details

After the $A array is created, the following commands are executed: $A[0]="A" changes the value of the $A array element with the 0; $A[1][0]="B" index changes the value of the element with the 0 index in the array, which is the element with the 1 index in the $A; $A[1][1][0]="C" array changes the element with the 0 index in the array, which is the element with the 1 index in the array, which is the element with the 1 index in the $A array.

The following shows the result of the program's execution.

The output of the program (from Listing 4-8)
```
Array $A:
Array
(
    [0] => 1
    [1] => Array
        (
            [0] => 2
            [1] => Array
                (
                    [0] => 3
                    [1] => 4
                )

        )

)
```

Array $B:
Array
(
    [0] => 1
    [1] => Array
        (
            [0] => 2
            [1] => Array
                (
                    [0] => 3
                    [1] => 4
)

)

)
Array $A:
Array
(
    [0] => A
    [1] => Array
        (
            [0] => B
            [1] => Array
                (
                    [0] => C
                    [1] => 4
)

)

)

```
Array $B:
Array
(
    [0] => 1
    [1] => Array
        (
            [0] => 2
            [1] => Array
                (
                    [0] => 3
                    [1] => 4
                )

        )

)
```

The most important conclusion is that changing the $A array (after executing the $B=$A command) does not affect the $B array. In other words, the $B=$A command creates a copy of the $A array.

ⓘ Note   Such an obvious conclusion might seem strange and naive. However, this situation may surprise those familiar with Java, C#, or Python.

Concatenating Arrays

Another practical operation is the concatenation (addition) of arrays. To do that, you use the + operator. The rule is as follows. If you add an array to an array, you get an array consisting of elements from both arrays. If the merged arrays have elements with the same keys, the resulting array keeps the value presented in the first operand (the value from the first array). The situation is illustrated in Listing 4-9.

Listing 4-9. The Sum of Arrays

```php
<?php
    // The initial arrays:
    $A=["First"=>1,2,"Last"=>3];
    $B=[100,200,"Last"=>300];
    // The sum of the arrays:
    $C=$A+$B;
    // The contents of the resulting array:
    print_r($C);
?>
```

The output of the program is as follows.

The output of the program (from Listing 4-9)
```
Array
(
    [First] => 1
    [0] => 2
    [Last] => 3
    [1] => 200
)
```

Create two arrays using the $A=["First"=>1,2,"Last"=>3] and $B=[100,200,"Last"=>300] commands. Next, calculate the sum of these arrays (the $C=$A+$B instruction). What is the result? The result is an array that contains elements from the two original arrays. There is just some intrigue regarding the elements that have matching indexes. There are two such elements (two pairs). This means the element with the "Last" key, and the element with the 0 index (in the $A array, that is, the element with

the value 2, and in the $B array, that is, the element with the value 100).
As noted, the first array (the $A array) takes precedence in such situations.
Thus, in the $C array, the element with the 0 index has the value 2, and the
element with the "Last" key has the value 3.

Comparing Arrays

Another important procedure is comparing arrays for equality or inequality.
Two arrays are considered equal if they have the same set of elements,
including the keys of those elements and their values. But here, you should
consider the automatic type casting involved when comparing arrays. Namely,
if the == and != operators are used to compare arrays, then the comparison is
performed considering the automatic type conversion. If you want to compare
arrays without involving the automatic type casting, you should use the ===
and !== operators. Here, only the values of the elements are considered. The
keys are compared for a match involving the automatic type casting in any
case. An example of how arrays are compared is shown in Listing 4-10.

Listing 4-10. Comparing Arrays

```php
<?php
    // The arrays to compare:
    $A=["0"=>123,1=>true,2=>""];
    $B=["123",10,0];
    $C=[0=>123,"1"=>true,"2"=>""];
    $D=[0=>123,1=>true,3=>""];
    // Compares the arrays:
    if($A==$B){
        echo '$A==$B',"\n";
    }
    if($A!==$B){
        echo '$A!==$B',"\n";
    }
```

```
   if($A===$C){
      echo '$A===$C',"\n";
   }
   if($A!=$D){
      echo '$A!=$D',"\n";
   }
?>
```

The result of the program's execution is as follows.

The output of the program (from Listing 4-10)

```
$A==$B
$A!==$B
$A===$C
$A!=$D
```

There is the $A=["0"=>123,1=>true,2=>""] array, which is compared to the $B=["123",10,0], $C=[0=>123,"1"=>true,"2"=>""] arrays and $D=[0=>123,1=>true,3=>""]. It appears that the $A==$B condition is true. The reason is like that. The elements of the $A array have the "0", 1, and 2 keys, and the values 123, true, and "" respectively. The elements of the $B array have the 0, 1, and 2 keys (auto-calculated), and the values of the corresponding elements are "123", 10, and 0. The keys match because "0" is automatically converted to 0. The value "123" is converted to 123, the non-zero number 10 is equivalent to true, and the empty string "" is converted to the zero value 0.

△ **The PHP 8 Standard**   In PHP 8, the empty string "" is not equal to the number 0. Therefore, in PHP 8, $A==$B is not true.

If the automatic type conversion is not involved, then the values of the elements of the arrays $A and $B are different, so the $A!==$B expression is true.

118

In the $C array, the values of the elements are the same as in the $A array. Although the elements' keys in the $C array are different from those in the $A array, the keys are interpreted as the same due to the automatic type casting. Therefore, the $A===$C condition is true. Finally, the $D array is compared to the $A array, and only one of the keys differs. That is enough for the $A!=$D condition to be true.

Functions for Handling Arrays

Many interesting operations with arrays can be performed using special functions. One is the list() function (frankly, it is not a function but a special syntax construction). The format for using the function is as follows.

```
list(variables)=array
```

You pass variables as arguments to the function (and these variables may have no values at all) and assign an array to that expression. The consequences are as follows: the variable specified as the first argument of the list() function is assigned the first element of the array, the second variable in the argument list of the list() function is assigned the second element of the array, and so on. Some arguments can be skipped, and the count may not match the count of array elements. Examples of using the list() function are shown in Listing 4-11.

Listing 4-11. Extracting Values from an Array

```php
<?php
    // An array:
    $A=[1,2,3,4,5];
    list($x,,$y,$z)=$A;
    // The result:
    print("\$x = $x\n");
```

119

```
    print("\$y = $y\n");
    print("\$z = $z\n");
?>
```

The following is the program's output.

The output of the program (from Listing 4-11)

```
$x = 1
$y = 3
$z = 4
```

The $A=[1,2,3,4,5] array is assigned as the value in the
list($x,,$y,$z)=$A statement. The command is executed as follows. The
value 1 of the first element of the $A array is stored in the $x variable. The
next argument of list() is omitted, so the element with the value 2 is not
written anywhere. The value 3 is written to the $y variable, the value 4 is
written to the $z variable, and the value 5 is not written anywhere because
the corresponding variable is not specified in the list() argument list.

There are also some other functions and utilities that can be useful
when handling arrays. For example, the array_keys() function returns
an array with the keys of the array passed as an argument to the function.
The array_combine() function allows you to create an array based on
two arrays: one defines the keys, and the second defines the values of the
elements. Another useful function is range(), which creates an array with
the values of the elements in the specified range (function arguments).
The array_pop() function removes the last element from the array, and
the array_push() function adds an element (or elements) to the end
of the array. The array_slice() function allows you to get a slice of an
array (that is, extract a subarray from the array). The first argument of the
function is the array to be sliced. The second argument is the index of
the element from which the slice is to be performed. If that argument is
negative, then the index is counted from the last element of the array

(-1 means the last element, -2 means the last but one element, and so on). The third argument specifies the number of elements in the slice.

 Note   In general, there are a lot of functions for manipulating arrays. A separate book could be devoted to their description.

Listing 4-12 is a program in which the functions described are used.

Listing 4-12. Functions for Handling Arrays

```php
<?php
    // The first array:
    $K=range(3,5);
    print("Array \$K:\n");
    print_r($K);
    // The second array:
    $A=["X"=>100,"Y"=>200,"Z"=>300];
    print("Array \$A:\n");
    print_r($A);
    // The third array:
    $B=array_keys($A);
    print("Array \$B:\n");
    print_r($B);
    // The fourth array:
    $C=array_combine($K,$B);
    print("Array \$C:\n");
    print_r($C);
    array_pop($C);
    print("Array \$C:\n");
    print_r($C);
    array_push($C,"A","B");
```

```
    print("Array \$C:\n");
    print_r($C);
    // The fifth array:
    $D=array_slice($C,0,3);
    print("Array \$D:\n");
    print_r($D);
    // The sixth array:
    $E=array_slice($C,-3,2);
    print("Array \$E:\n");
    print_r($E);
?>
```

The following is the program's output.

The output of the program (from Listing 4-12)

```
Array $K:
Array
(
    [0] => 3
    [1] => 4
    [2] => 5
)
Array $A:
Array
(
    [X] => 100
    [Y] => 200
    [Z] => 300
)
Array $B:
Array
(
```

```
    [0] => X
    [1] => Y
    [2] => Z
)
Array $C:
Array
(
    [3] => X
    [4] => Y
    [5] => Z
)
Array $C:
Array
(
    [3] => X
    [4] => Y
)
Array $C:
Array
(
    [3] => X
    [4] => Y
    [5] => A
    [6] => B
)
Array $D:
Array
(
    [0] => X
    [1] => Y
    [2] => A
)
```

123

```
Array $E:
Array
(
    [0] => Y
    [1] => A
)
```

The $K=range(3,5) command creates an array of numbers from 3 to 5 inclusively (that is, the [3,4,5] array). Another array is created by the $A=["X"=>100,"Y"=>200,"Z"=>300] command. The $B=array_keys($A) command creates the third array. It is an array consisting of the keys of the $A array (that is, the ["X","Y","Z"] array). The $C=array_combine($K,$B) command creates an array whose keys are determined by the values of the elements of the $K array, and the values of the elements of the $C array are determined by the values of the elements of the $B array.

The array_pop($C) command removes the last element from the $C array. And due to the array_push($C,"A","B") command, the elements with the values "A" and "B" are added to the end of the $C array.

The $D=array_slice($C,0,3) command creates an array obtained by extracting three elements (due to argument 3) from the $C array, beginning from the element with the 0 index (due to argument 0).

The $E=array_slice($C,-3,2) command creates an array obtained by extracting two elements (since the third argument is 2) from the $C array, beginning from the third from the end (due to the second argument -3) element.

Summary

- An array is a collection of values joined by a common name. The values, in general, can be of different types.

- An array element is accessed by the key or index (indicated in square brackets after the array name). Keys/indexes can be integers or strings.

- There are several ways to create an array. Namely, you can assign values to array elements, use the `array()` function (syntax construction), or list the values of the array elements in square brackets. If the keys/indexes are not specified explicitly, they are calculated automatically.

- You can use the `foreach` loop statement to iterate over the contents of an array. It allows you to access the keys and values of the array elements.

- The array elements can be arrays. In that case, the elements of the internal arrays are accessed using multiple keys.

- You can perform various operations on arrays, including assignment and comparison for equality/ inequality. You can also concatenate arrays.

- There exist special functions designed to handle arrays.

CHAPTER 5

Functions

—I notice you spend a lot of time fixing stuff, Willie.

—That's because you spend a lot of time breaking stuff, Alf.

—Well, it's nice that our hobbies are so compatible.

—ALF (TV series)

This chapter introduces functions, which play an essential role in any programming language. The PHP language is not an exception. You learn how to create functions, how they can be used, and what is unique about functions in the PHP language.

Creating Functions

Very often in programs, you must execute many times the same sequence of commands. It is convenient to write such commands as a separate block of code and then, if necessary, simply put the instruction that means the execution of the corresponding block of commands. In general terms, that idea underlies the use of functions.

A function is a named block of code that can be called by that name. In other words, you form a block of commands, specify a name for that block of commands, and every time you need the block of commands executed, you just specify its name. As usual, you use commands to process some values or data. If you are intended to process such values

© Alex Vasilev 2024
A. Vasilev, *PHP by Example*, https://doi.org/10.1007/979-8-8688-0258-4_5

during the function call, the function should be called with an argument (or arguments). Traditionally, function arguments are specified in parentheses after the function name. If there are multiple arguments, they are separated by commas.

Before calling a function, it must be declared (or created). The description of a function implies that you must define what commands are executed when the function is called and what operations are performed on the arguments (if any). So, how is a function defined in PHP?

A function declaration begins with the `function` keyword followed by the function name and a list of arguments in parentheses. Arguments are similar to variables and are identified with the values passed to the function when called. If the function has no arguments, empty parentheses are placed after the function name in the function's description. The commands executed when the function is called are placed in a block enclosed in curly braces. The following is the general function declaration template.

```
function name(arguments){
    // commands
}
```

Commands in the body of a function may refer to the function arguments, and the function arguments are described as variable names (the argument names begin with the $ symbol). When a function is called and arguments are passed to it, the commands described in its body are executed. In that case, in those places where the arguments are put in the code, the actual values passed to the function are used.

Details

Function names are not case-sensitive. In other words, whether the function name is in uppercase or lowercase letters doesn't matter. For example, if you have the show() function, then that is the same as the SHOW() or Show() function.

It is also worth mentioning that traditionally, function names are specified with empty parentheses after the function name. That is usually done to distinguish function names from variable names. As you know, in PHP, the distinguishing feature of variable names is the $ symbol with which the name begins. Nevertheless, the tradition is held.

To call a function, it is enough to specify its name and parentheses: empty if the function has no arguments and with a list of values if there are arguments. A small example in which you declare and then call a function is shown in Listing 5-1.

Listing 5-1. Getting Familiar with Functions

```php
<?php
    // The function declaration:
    function show($argument){
        echo "Calling the function show()\n";
        echo "The argument type: ",gettype($argument),"\n";
        echo "The argument value: $argument\n\n";
    }
    // Calls the function:
    show(123);
    SHOW("We learn PHP");
    Show(2.5);
?>
```

129

The following is the result of the program execution.

The output of the program (from Listing 5-1)
```
Calling the function show()
The argument type: integer
The argument value: 123

Calling the function show()
The argument type: string
The argument value: We learn PHP

Calling the function show()
The argument type: double
The argument value: 2.5
```

The straightforward show() function has been described. It has only one argument, which is named $argument. That means that when you call the function, you should put some value (the function argument) in parentheses after the function name.

(i) **Note**   It is essential to understand that the description of a function does not imply the execution of its code. For the function code to be executed, the function must be called.

You should refer to the code in the function's body to understand what happens when a function is called. In this case, there are only three commands, each using the echo statement. So, three messages appear in the output window whenever you call the function. The first message states that the show() function has been called. The second message contains information about the type of argument passed to the function. To determine the type of the argument, the gettype($argument) instruction is used to explicitly refer to the $argument argument.

Note When the function is described, the type of the argument and its value are not known. Those circumstances "reveal" when the function is called. Now, you can simply describe what needs to be done with the function argument.

Another message contains information about the value of the $argument argument.

Note After the last message, a line break is performed twice using two \n instructions. That is purely for aesthetic purposes so that message blocks displayed due to different function calls are separated by a blank line.

After the function is declared, you call it with three different arguments (an integer, a string, and a real number). To illustrate the case-insensitivity of the function name, you specify each time the function name using a different combination of uppercase and lowercase letters. In particular, you write the name of the function in small letters (the show(123) command), in capital letters (the SHOW("We learn PHP") command), and also indicate the first capital letter in the function name (the Show(2.5) command). In all three cases, the same show() function is called.

Note Let's hold a simple principle: call a function according to how it is described (i.e., the name of the function).

The Function Result

A function can return a result. The result of a function is the value that remains "for memory" after the function has completed its execution. If a function returns a result, the instruction by which the function is called has a value, which is the result of the function. Therefore, you can, for example, assign a function call instruction to a variable or use it as an operand in a complex statement. To understand the result of an expression containing function call instructions, you should replace those instructions with the values returned by the corresponding functions in the expression.

To show in the function description that the function returns a result, you use the `return` instruction followed by the value the function returns.

Details

Executing a command with the `return` statement terminates the execution of the function. The function code can contain several `return` instructions (for example, in a conditional statement), but as soon as one of them is executed, the function execution is terminated.

If a function does not return a result, then the `return` statement can be used to terminate the execution of such a function without specifying a return value. Generally, a function that does not return a result is interpreted as returning a `null` reference. Therefore, in principle, for such functions, instead of the `return` instruction (without a value), you can use the `return null` statement.

Listing 5-2 shows a program in which you use several functions that return a result.

Listing 5-2. A Function That Returns a Result

```php
<?php
    // The function calculates the factorial:
    function factorial($n){
        $s=1;
        for($k=2;$k<=$n;$k++){
            $s*=$k;
        }
        return $s;
    }
    // The function calculates a number in a power:
    function power($x,$n){
        $s=1;
        for($k=1;$k<=$n;$k++){
            $s*=$x;
        }
        return $s;
    }
    // The function checks whether a number is even/odd:
    function test($number){
        if($number%2==0){
            return "even";
        }else{
            return "odd";
        }
    }
    // Variables:
    $z=2;
    $num=10;
    // Calls the function:
```

```
    $res=power($z,$num);
    echo "Calculate $z in the power $num: $res\n";
    // Calls the function:
    echo "$num! = ",factorial($num),"\n";
    // Calls the function:
    echo "The number $num is ".test($num)."\n";
    $num--; # Decreases the variable by one
    echo "The number $num is ".test($num)."\n";
?>
```

The following is the result of the program execution.

The output of the program (from Listing 5-2)
```
Calculate 2 in the power 10: 1024
10! = 3628800
The number 10 is even
The number 9 is odd
```

Three functions are described in the program. The factorial() function is designed to calculate the factorial of a number. Its argument is named $n. It is assumed that that is the number for which the factorial is calculated.

ⓘ **Note**   The factorial of an integer number n (denoted as $n!$) is the product of all numbers from 1 to n inclusively. That is, by definition, $n! = 1 \cdot 2 \cdot 3 \cdot \ldots \cdot (n - 1) \cdot n$.

You use the local variable $s with the initial value 1 in the function's body. Then, a loop statement is executed. There, the $k variable gets values from 2 to $n inclusively. For each loop, the $s*=$k command is executed. According to the command, the current value of the $s variable is multiplied by the current value of the $k variable. As a result, after executing the loop statement, the product of numbers from 1 to $n is stored in the $s variable. Finally, with the return $s command, the computed value is returned as the result of the factorial() function.

Details

The variables in the body of a function are called *local variables*. They are the first assigned values in the function's body. Local variables exist while the function code is executed and are available only in the function's body. Two important conclusions follow from that. First, it makes sense to refer to a local variable only in the function body. Second, you can use local variables with the same names in different functions; these are different variables since they have different scopes.

The arguments specified in the function declaration have the "power" of local variables. They are available only in the function's body. If you specify the same names for the arguments in the description of different functions, they are different variables independent of each other.

The power() function is designed to raise a number to a power. The function has two arguments, separated by a comma in the function description. The first argument $x, is the number to be raised to a power, and the power is determined by the second argument $n.

Note   Even though the name of the second argument $n of the power() function is the same as the name of the argument of the factorial() function, there is nothing in common between these arguments. The same remark applies to the local variable $s used in the body of the power() function.

In the power() function, the local variable $s is initialized with the initial value 1. After that, the $s*=$x command is executed in the loop statement, which multiplies the current value of the $s variable by the first argument $x of the power() function. The number of cycles is determined by the second argument $n. As a result, the $s variable contains the value of $x in the power $n. The return $s statement returns the result of the function.

Another function used in the program is named test(). It is designed to check the number passed as an argument (denoted as $number) to see if it is even or odd. If the number is even, the function returns the "even" string as a result, and if the number is odd, the "odd" string is the result of the function.

The core of the function code is a conditional statement, which checks the $number%2==0 condition (the remainder of dividing the $number argument by 2 is 0). If the condition is true, then the result is returned by the return "even" command. Otherwise, the result is returned by return "odd".

You use two variables to test how the functions operate: $z with the value 2 and $num with the value 10. Using the $res=power($z,$num) command, you call the power() function with arguments $z and $num, and you store the result, returned by the function, to the $res variable. That is the value of the $z variable in the power determined by the $num variable.

The factorial of the number saved in the $num variable is calculated by the factorial($num) instruction.

Finally, the program uses expressions like "The number $num is ".test($num)."\n". That is the string obtained by concatenating the "The number $num is ", test($num), and "\n" strings. The dot is used as a concatenation operator, and the second of the strings to be concatenated (the test($num) instruction) is the result returned by the test() function.

Details

The PHP interpreter generates a special intermediate bytecode based on the source code. This process is called translation. After the code is translated, the code execution begins. In PHP, the translation and the code execution are separated. Because of that, functions do not have to be declared before they are called. In other words, you can first place a function call instruction in a program and only after that describe the function. However, such a style should not be overused, especially in the practical use of PHP codes, since that can increase the probability of error raising.

The Type of Arguments and Result

When describing functions in the examples, it is assumed that the values passed to the functions belonged to a specific type. It was essential and accounted for when processing the arguments. However, there is no guarantee that when a function is called, a value of the correct type is passed to it as an argument. A similar situation is with the result type returned by a function.

Note   The fact that the type of the arguments or the type of the result is not explicitly specified is not always a disadvantage; rather, it is on the contrary. There are often situations when you need to create a function whose argument could be values of different types. But there are also opposite situations when you must pass a value of a strictly defined type to a function. It all depends on the specifics of the problem being solved.

Of course, you can add some code to the function to check the passed arguments' type. But that is not always convenient. Fortunately, there is an easier way to "restrict" the range of allowed types for arguments. Namely, you can explicitly specify the type of the arguments and the result of the function in the function description. That could be done quite simply. For arguments, the type is specified before the argument name in the function description, and the function result type is specified, separated by a colon, after the closing parenthesis. The function description template, in that case, is as follows.

```
function name(type argument, type argument,...): type{
    // commands
}
```

An error arises with such a function description if you call it and pass an argument of a different type than the one specified in the function description.

Details

PHP has a system for catching and handling exceptions (errors) of various types. That system allows you to create programs that operate efficiently even if errors arise. Catching exceptions is discussed later.

Listing 5-3 uses functions with explicit type specifications for their arguments and results.

Listing 5-3. Type of Arguments and Results

```
<?php
    // To switch to the hard typing mode, we need
    // to uncomment the next statement:
    # declare(strict_types=1);
```

```
// The type of arguments and result
// is specified explicitly:
function power(float $x,int $n): string{
    for($s=1,$k=1;$k<=$n;$s*=$x,$k++);
    return "The number $x in the power $n: ".$s."\n";
}
// Calls the function:
echo power(3,4);
echo power(1.5,2.7);
echo power("2","10.1");
?>
```

The result of the program execution is as follows.

The output of the program (from Listing 5-3)
The number 3 in the power 4: 81
The number 1.5 in the power 2: 2.25
The number 2 in the power 10: 1024

This program modifies the power() function designed to calculate a number in a power. In the new version, the first function argument $x is declared to be of the float type (a real number), the second argument $n is of the int type (an integer), and the result of the function is a value of the string type (text).

There are only two commands in the body of the function. The first one is a call of the for loop statement. In the first block of that statement, the $s=1 and $k=1 commands are executed, which set the $s and $k variables to the initial value 1. The loop statement is executed while the $k<=$n condition is true. Two commands, $s*=$x and $k++, are executed for each loop. Both commands are placed in the third block of the loop statement, so the body of the loop statement is empty (there are no commands at all). You end the instruction that calls the loop statement with a semicolon since the command following the loop statement does not belong to it.

The result of the function is returned by the "The number $x in the power $n: ".$s."\n" statement. Thus, the result is a string formed by combining string fragments and contains information about the results of calculations.

You test the created function using the echo power(3,4), echo power(1.5,2.7), and echo power("2","10.1") commands. It may seem strange, but all three commands run without errors, although the type of the arguments passed to the power() function does not match the declared one. The reason is that the automatic type casting comes into play by default. For example, the second argument must be of the integer type. If a real number is passed as the second argument, then the fractional part is automatically discarded in that real number. If you pass a string with a number "hidden" in it as an argument, then such a string is converted to the number format, and so on.

⌂ The PHP 8 Standard

In versions higher than PHP 8, on the echo power(1.5,2.7) and echo power("2","10.1") commands, you get a warning that the implicit conversion from float (float-string) to integer is deprecated since it leads to losing precision.

If unsatisfied with such code execution, you can switch to the hard typing mode. To do that, the declare(strict_types=1) statement should be added to the program.

Note   In the preceding program, the instruction is a comment (the line begins with the # symbol). If you want to switch to the hard typing mode, remove the # symbol at the beginning of the corresponding line.

If so, only the first of the three instructions to test the power() function operates correctly. Attempting to execute the other two cause an error.

Details

In the power(3,4) statement, the first argument is an integer despite the corresponding argument being declared a real number. In such a case, the integer value is automatically extended to the real type. Notably, from the mathematical point of view, the set of integers is a subset of the set of real numbers.

🔔 **The PHP 8 Standard**

In PHP 8, the ability to define type unions is introduced. In that case, the types are listed with the vertical bar | as a separator. For example, the int|string|double expression means that the corresponding variable (function argument or result) can be int, string, or double.

Also, PHP 8 introduces the mixed type, the broadest possible union of types.

The Argument Passing Mechanism

Take a look at the program in Listing 5-4.

Listing 5-4. Passing Arguments by Value

```php
<?php
    // A function with two arguments:
    function swap($a,$b){
```

```
    echo "Input: the arguments $a and $b\n";
    $x=$a;
    $a=$b;
    $b=$x;
    echo "Output: the arguments $a and $b\n";
}
// Variables:
$A=100;
$B=200;
// The values of the variables:
echo "\$A = $A and \$B = $B\n";
// Calls the function:
swap($A,$B);
// Checks the values of the variables:
echo "\$A = $A and \$B = $B\n";
?>
```

The following is the result of the program execution.

The output of the program (from Listing 5-4)

```
$A = 100 and $B = 200
Input: the arguments 100 and 200
Output: the arguments 200 and 100
$A = 100 and $B = 200
```

You create the swap() function in the program with two arguments. When the function is called, it displays the arguments passed to the function. Then, you try to change the values of the arguments (the first argument is assigned the value of the second argument, and the second argument is assigned the value of the first argument) and check their values again.

142

Two variables are used, $A and $B, with the values 100 and 200 respectively. First, check the values of these variables. Then, you pass the variables to the swap() function as arguments (the swap($A,$B) command). Next, check the values of the variables again.

What is the program's output? As you can see, the $A and $B variables do not change their values. Nevertheless, the second check of the arguments in the body of the swap() function shows that the values of the arguments are switched. What does all that mean, and how do you understand the situation? Indeed, everything is quite simple. You should consider that when passing arguments to a function, the function gets copies of the variable passed to the function as the arguments. In other words, when executing the swap($A,$B) command, it is not the $A and $B variables that are passed to the swap() function but their copies. So, the copies of the variables swap values when executing the code of the swap() function. When the function execution is over, the copies of the arguments are removed from memory, and the $A and $B variables remain with their previous values. Such a mechanism of passing arguments to functions is the default one called passing arguments *by value*. Besides passing arguments by value, arguments can be passed *by reference*. In that case, not copies of the arguments but "originals" are passed to the function. If you want to pass arguments by reference, you should put the & instruction before the argument name in the function declaration. A modification of the previous program, but this time with passing the arguments to the swap() function by reference, is shown in Listing 5-5.

Listing 5-5. Passing Arguments by Reference

```php
<?php
  // Passing arguments by reference:
  function swap(&$a,&$b){
    echo "Input: the arguments $a and $b\n";
    $x=$a;
    $a=$b;
```

```
    $b=$x;
    echo "Output: the arguments $a and $b\n";
}
$A=100;
$B=200;
echo "\$A = $A and \$B = $B\n";
swap($A,$B);
echo "\$A = $A and \$B = $B\n";
?>
```

Now, the result of the program execution is as follows.

The output of the program (from Listing 5-5)

```
$A = 100 and $B = 200
Input: the arguments 100 and 200
Output: the arguments 200 and 100
$A = 200 and $B = 100
```

You see that the values of the $A and $B variables have changed after these variables were passed to the swap() function.

Note   The mechanism of the argument's passing is essential if you change the values of the function arguments during the function's execution. If the argument values are not going to be changed, then the default mechanism of passing the arguments by value is perfectly acceptable.

The Argument Value by Default

You can set default values for the arguments of a function. The default value is used when calling the function if you do not specify a value for such an argument.

To set a default value for an argument, you put the assignment operator and that default value after the argument name in the function declaration. The arguments with default values must be placed at the end of the arguments list in the function declaration.

(i) **Note**   In other words, arguments without default values are described first, followed by those with default values.

Listing 5-6 is a program with functions whose arguments (some or all) have values by default.

Listing 5-6. The Argument Values by Default

```php
<?php
    // All arguments of the function
    // have values by default:
    function show($first="Alpha",$second="Bravo"){
        echo "The first argument: ",$first,"\n";
        echo "The second argument: ",$second,"\n\n";
    }
    // Not all arguments of the function
    // have values by default:
    function display($x,$y=200,$z=300){
        echo "The first number: ",$x,"\n";
        echo "The second number: ",$y,"\n";
        echo "The third number: ",$z,"\n\n";
    }
```

145

```
   // Calls the functions:
   show();          # No arguments
   show("A");       # One argument
   show("A","B");   # Two arguments
   display(100);    # One argument
   display(1,2);    # Two arguments
   display(1,2,3);  # Three arguments
?>
```

The following is the program's output.

The output of the program (from Listing 5-6)
```
The first argument: Alpha
The second argument: Bravo

The first argument: A
The second argument: Bravo

The first argument: A
The second argument: B

The first number: 100
The second number: 200
The third number: 300

The first number: 1
The second number: 2
The third number: 300

The first number: 1
The second number: 2
The third number: 3
```

The program uses two functions: show() with two arguments and display() with three arguments. Both arguments of the show() function have values by default. The last two arguments have default values in the display() function. You call these functions and pass them a different count of arguments each time.

When the show() command is executed, the default values are used for both arguments to the show() function. In other words, the command is executed as if the first argument were "Alpha" and if the second argument were "Bravo".

The show("A") command means that the value "A" is used for the first argument, and the default value "Bravo" is used for the second argument. Finally, the show("A", "B") statement means that the value "A" is passed as the first argument, and the value "B" is passed as the second argument to the function.

A similar situation takes place for the display() function. The only difference is that since there is no default value for the first argument, the first argument must always be specified. So, when you run the display(100) command, the values of the arguments are 100, 200, and 300, respectively. The display(1,2) command means that the first argument's value is 1, the second argument is 2, and the third is the default value 300. When executing the display(1,2,3) command, all function arguments are explicitly specified and have the values 1, 2, and 3.

An Arbitrary Number of Arguments

The peculiarity of PHP is that you can pass more arguments than specified in the function declaration without any tragic consequences when calling a function. For example, if a function is described with two arguments, and when you call the function, you pass five arguments, then the last three arguments are ignored.

That peculiarity of functions can be used to create ones with an arbitrary number of arguments. This means the situation when a function can be called with any number of arguments, and all those arguments are processed in the function.

ⓘ **Note**   You are dealing with default values for function arguments. That makes it possible to specify a different number of arguments when calling a function (less than indicated in the function description). But in that case, the number of processed arguments is limited to those specified in the function description. Contrary to that, you want all arguments to be processed, no matter how many you pass to the function when called.

It is also worth mentioning that there are several modes of declaring a function with an arbitrary number of arguments. You would name one as "old" and the other as "new" (it's available since PHP 5.6). Let's explore both.

To process the arguments passed to a function, they need to be accessed somehow. Moreover, you want to process arguments not mentioned in the list of arguments in its declaration. You can get a list of the arguments passed to the function using the func_get_args() function. The func_get_args() function has no arguments, and it returns a list (array) of arguments passed to the function in whose body the func_get_args() function is called.

Details

The functions func_num_args() and func_get_arg() can also be useful.
The first of these functions returns the count of passed arguments (meaning the
arguments of the function in whose body func_num_args() is called). The second
one returns the value of the argument (of the function in which the func_get_
arg() function is called) with a specific index (the argument of the func_get_
arg() function).

Listing 5-7 is a program that uses functions that accept an arbitrary
number of arguments.

Listing 5-7. An Arbitrary Number of Arguments

```php
<?php
    // The function calculates the sum of the arguments:
    function sum(){
        // The initial value of the sum:
        $s=0;
        // Iterates over the arguments and calculates the sum:
        foreach(func_get_args() as $a){
            $s+=$a;
        }
        // The result of the function:
        return $s;
    }
    // The function counts the arguments of a certain type:
    function count_type($type){
        // The number of passed arguments:
        $num=func_num_args();
        // The number of arguments of a certain type:
        $count=0;
```

```php
    echo "Arguments at all: $num\n";
    // If there is one argument:
    if($num==1){
        echo "The search is over\n";
        // The function is terminated:
        return;
    }
    // Iterates over the arguments:
    for($k=1;$k<$num;$k++){
        // Checks the type of the argument:
        if(gettype(func_get_arg($k))==$type){
            $count++;
        }
    }
    // The result of calculations:
    echo "Arguments of the type $type: $count\n";
}
// Calls the function for calculating the sum:
echo "[1] The sum: ",sum(5,9,6),"\n";
echo "[2] The sum: ",sum(),"\n";
echo "[3] The sum: ",sum(1,3,5,7,9),"\n";
// Calls the function for calculating the number
// of arguments of a certain type:
count_type("integer",2,8,"12",3.5,2,"hello");
count_type("integer");
count_type("string",2,8,"12",3.5,2,"hello");
?>
```

The result of the program execution is as follows.

The output of the program (from Listing 5-7)
```
[1] The sum: 20
[2] The sum: 0
[3] The sum: 25
Arguments at all: 7
Arguments of the type integer: 3
Arguments at all: 1
The search is over
Arguments at all: 7
Arguments of the type string: 2
```

Two functions are declared in the program. The sum() function is declared without arguments, while the count_type() function has one argument. But in fact, the code of the functions provides the processing of all arguments passed to the functions.

Note   The sum() function can be called with an arbitrary number of arguments, including none. At least one argument must be passed when calling the count_type() function.

The sum() function calculates the sum of the arguments passed to the function when called. To store the sum's value in the function's body, you use the $s variable with the initial zero value. The iteration of arguments is performed in the foreach loop statement. The func_get_args() expression is specified as the array to iterate over it. Since the func_get_args() function returns a list with the arguments passed to the function (in this case, sum()), it is these values that are iterated over. The $a variable is used to store the arguments. For each loop, the $s+=$a command

151

increments the current value of the $s variable by the value of $a, so after terminating the loop statement, the sum of the arguments of the sum() function is written to the $s variable. The return $s command returns that number as the result of the function.

Details

If you call the sum() function with no arguments, the result is zero. That is the initial value of the $s variable, which does not change during the execution of the function code.

The count_type() function does not return a result but only displays messages. They contain information about how many arguments were passed to the function in total and the count of arguments of a specific type. The type is determined as a string by the first argument $type of the function (for example, "integer" or "string").

In the function's body, the $num=func_num_args() command assigns the number of arguments passed to the function to the $num variable. That value is returned as the result of func_num_args(). To count the number of arguments of the type given by the $type argument, you use the $count variable with the initial zero value.

Before starting the count, you use the conditional statement to check the $num==1 condition. The true condition means that only one argument is passed to the function, which, following the assumptions, determines the type of the arguments, and there are no other arguments. If so, then echo "The search is over\n" displays a message, and then the function is terminated due to the return instruction.

If there are more arguments than one, the return statement is not executed, and the for loop statement comes into play. There, the $k variable takes the values from 1 and strictly less than $num. Here, you iterate over all but the first argument: ignore the first one because it is unique.

Note Argument indexing begins from zero.

To check the type of an argument, use the conditional statement with the gettype(func_get_arg($k))==$type condition to be checked. The gettype() function returns a string with the type name for the value passed as an argument to the gettype() function. In this case, the func_get_arg($k) expression is passed as an argument. It gives the value of the count_type() function argument with the $k index. If the type of that argument matches the type specified in $type, then the $count++ command increments the $count variable by one. After the loop statement is terminated, the $count variable contains the count of arguments of the given type passed to the count_type() function.

 Note The func_num_args() and func_get_arg() functions are used to implement the count_type() function code (although the func_get_args() function could be as well) to illustrate different ways of handling arguments passed to a function.

After creating the functions, you check how they operate. Thus, the sum(5,9,6) expression gives the sum of the numbers 5, 9, and 6. When the function sum() is called without arguments, the result is 0. The value of the sum(1,3,5,7,9) expression is the sum of the numbers 1, 3, 5, 7, and 9.

In the count_type("integer",2,8,"12",3.5,2,"hello") command, the count_type() function is called with seven arguments, and the count of integer arguments is three. In the count_type("string",2,8,"12",3.5, 2,"hello") command, the count_type() function gets the same number of arguments, but now the string arguments have to be counted, and there are two (not counting the first one) such arguments. Finally, when the count_type() function is called with the count_type("integer") command, only one argument is passed to it, so it does not come to counting the integer type arguments.

As noted, a more convenient way to create functions with an arbitrary number of arguments exists. It assumes declaring a function with one argument with the ellipsis before the argument. Such an argument identifies the entire list of arguments passed to the function and is treated as an array. Let's re-examine the previous program but adjust it for the new way of declaring functions with an arbitrary number of arguments. The code is shown in Listing 5-8 (the comments are removed to keep the code short).

Listing 5-8. One More Way to Declare a Function with an Arbitrary Number of Arguments

```php
<?php
    function sum(...$nums){
        $s=0;
        foreach($nums as $a){
            $s+=$a;
        }
        return $s;
    }
    function count_type($type,...$args){
        $num=sizeof($args)+1;
        $count=0;
        echo "Arguments at all: $num\n";
        if($num==1){
            echo "The search is over\n";
            return;
        }
```

```
    for($k=0;$k<sizeof($args);$k++){
      if(gettype($args[$k])==$type){
        $count++;
      }
    }
    echo "Arguments of the type $type: $count\n";
  }
  echo "[1] The sum: ",sum(5,9,6),"\n";
  echo "[2] The sum: ",sum(),"\n";
  echo "[3] The sum: ",sum(1,3,5,7,9),"\n";
  count_type("integer",2,8,"12",3.5,2,"hello");
  count_type("integer");
  count_type("string",2,8,"12",3.5,2,"hello");
?>
```

The program's result is the same as in the previous case. The main part of the code has not changed either. But there are still some innovations, and they are important ones. Let's analyze them.

The sum() function has an argument described by the ...$nums instruction. The ellipsis before $nums means that it "hides" a set of values, which can be identified with an array of the function arguments. That "array" is what you use in the foreach loop statement when iterating over the arguments.

The count_type() function is declared with two arguments. The first $type argument has the same meaning as in the previous example. The second argument $args, described by the ...$args instruction, is identified with a set (or "array") of other arguments (except the first one) passed to the function.

The value of the $num variable is now determined by the $num=sizeof($args)+1 command, which uses the sizeof() function to get the size of the "array" $args. Since there is also the first argument that is not included in the $args argument, one is added to the result of the sizeof() function.

155

The initial value of the $k variable in the for loop statement is now 0 instead of 1 as it used to be. It is taken into account here that the first argument $type is not included in the "array" $args, and the indexes of all elements from $args must be handled.

Finally, the gettype($args[$k])==$type condition is checked in the conditional statement, in which the $args[$k] instruction is used to access the argument.

Recursion

There is a method of defining functions that deserves special attention. It is about *recursion*. In that case, the function is declared to call itself. That can be achieved by placing a command that calls the same function (usually with a different argument) in the function's body. Listing 5-9 is a program in which several functions are defined using recursion.

Listing 5-9. Recursion

```php
<?php
    // The factorial of a number:
    function factorial($n){
        if($n==0) return 1;
        else return $n*factorial($n-1);
    }
    // The sum of numbers:
    function sum($n){
        if($n==0) return 0;
        else return $n+sum($n-1);
    }
```

```
// A number in a power:
function power($x,$n){
    if($n==0) return 1;
    else return $x*power($x,$n-1);
}
// Variables:
$x=2;
$n=5;
// Calls the functions:
echo "$n! = ",factorial($n),"\n";
echo "1+2+...+$n = ",sum($n),"\n";
echo "The number $x in the power $n: ",power($x,$n),"\n";
?>
```

The following is the program's output.

The output of the program (from Listing 5-9)

```
5! = 120
1+2+...+5 = 15
The number 2 in the power 5: 32
```

The program uses recursion to define functions for calculating the factorial of a number, the sum of natural numbers, and for raising a number to a power.

The factorial is calculated by the factorial() function, which takes one argument (denoted as $n). The function's body consists of only one conditional statement, in which the $n==0 condition is checked. If it is true, then the function returns 1 as a result (by definition, the factorial of 0 is equal to 1). Otherwise, the value of the function is calculated by the $n*factorial($n-1) expression, in which the function calls itself, but with an argument one less than the value of the original argument.

157

Details

In this case, consider that the factorial of some number n is the product of the number n and the factorial of the number $(n - 1)$, that is, $n! = n \cdot (n - 1)!$.

What happens when the function is called? If the function is called with a zero argument, the result is 1. Let's say the argument is non-zero; for example, 5. Then the result is calculated as the product of the number 5, and the result of the function call with argument 4. When the function is called with argument 4, the product of the number 4 and the result of the function call with argument 3 is calculated. When the function is called with argument 3, the product of the number 3 and the result of calling the function with argument 2 is calculated, and so on. The chain of calls ends when the function is called with argument 0. After that, everything is "rolled up": the values of expressions are sequentially evaluated until the result of calling the function with argument 5 is received.

> **Note**   For the sake of clarity and compactness of the code, curly braces were not used in the conditional statement, although that is not very good practice.

The function for calculating the sum of numbers sum( ) also has one argument $n, and when calculating the result, the $n==0 condition in the conditional statement is checked. If the condition is true, the result is zero (the sum of zero terms is assumed to be zero). If the condition is false, the result is calculated by the $n+sum($n-1) expression.

Details

The sum of the numbers from 1 to n can be thought of as the sum of the number n and the sum of the numbers from 1 to $(n - 1)$.

The power() function for raising a number to a power has two arguments: $x (the number to be raised to the power) and $n (the power). If the power is zero (the $n==0 is true condition), then the result is 1 (the number in the power 0 is 1). Otherwise, the result is calculated by multiplying the value of the $x argument by the result of calling the power() function with arguments $x and $n-1 (the $x*power($x,$n-1) expression).

Details

When determining the function, the obvious relation $x^n = x \cdot x^{n-1}$ is taken into account.

In addition to describing functions, the program contains commands that check the correctness of calling the functions with recursion. It is hopeful to believe that they do not require comments.

The eval() Function

In PHP, there are many features worthy to be noted. However, let's focus on the eval() function (more precisely, a syntax construction). It allows you to evaluate the expression passed to it as a string argument. For example, if you pass the '$number=2*3+4;' string as an argument to the eval() function, 10 is written to the $number variable. That result is obtained by evaluating the 2*3+4 expression.

Details

First, the commands with the eval() syntax construction are very dangerous—so much so that the corresponding codes can be blocked by antivirus programs (in that case, you need to "ask" the antivirus to make an exception). The reason for the potential danger is that eval() allows you to execute previously unknown code, which can affect the vulnerability of the entire system. Therefore, the eval() construction should not be overused.

Second, it matters in which quotes (single or double) you pass the string to eval(). The string must contain a valid PHP instruction (including the semicolon at the end of the command). You should also remember that their values are substituted in double quotes instead of variable names. Therefore, for example, an alternative to the eval('$number=2*3+4;') command is the eval("\$number=2*3+4;") command. In the latter case, the \$ instruction is used to include the $ character in the string. The result is the same in both cases.

Listing 5-10 is an example of using the eval() function.

Listing 5-10. Using eval()

```php
<?php
  // The string variables:
  $first='$A=2*3+4;';
  $second="\$B=2*\$A-5;";
  // Calls eval():
  eval($first);
  eval($second);
  echo 'The statement for $x: ';
  // Calls eval():
  eval(trim(fgets(STDIN)));
  // Checks the result:
  echo "\$x = $x\n";
?>
```

The result of the program's execution could look as follows (the user input is marked in bold).

The output of the program (from Listing 5-10)
The statement for $x: **$x=$A+$B;**
$x = 25

The program is small. It uses two string variables $first='$A=2*3+4;' and $second="\$B=2*\$A-5;". These variables contain text with commands executed when the eval($first) and eval($second) instructions are executed.

Details

That is, the $A=2*3+4 and $B=2*$A-5 commands are indeed executed, as a result of which $A is set to 10 and $B is set to 15.

Then, the expression entered by the user is read and passed as an argument to eval() (the eval(trim(fgets(STDIN))) command). The user must enter a command assigning a value to the $x variable. That command is executed because the corresponding text is passed as an argument to eval(). After that, the value of the $x variable is checked using the echo "\$x = $x\n" command.

Details

The preceding is the program's output when the user enters the $x=$A+$B; expression. The expression is read (subject to the transformations due to the trim() function) as the text '$x=$A+$B;' and is passed as an argument to eval(). As a result, the $x=$A+$B command is executed, and the $x variable is set to 25.

Anonymous Functions

In PHP, it is possible to describe functions that do not have a name. Such functions are usually called *anonymous*. The elegance and practical value of anonymous functions come from the fact that they can be assigned as a value to variables.

Details

An anonymous function can be represented as an object (which is not far from the truth) that can be called; that is, used as a function. If such an object (an anonymous function) is assigned to a variable, that variable can be treated as if it were the name of a function.

An anonymous function is described as simply as a regular one but with two important features. First, the function name is not specified (a list of arguments in parentheses follows the `function` keyword). Second, such a function is usually immediately assigned to a variable. The general template for creating an anonymous function looks like the following.

```
$variable=function(arguments){
    # commands
};
```

How this looks in practice is illustrated in Listing 5-11.

Listing 5-11. Anonymous Functions

```php
<?php
    // The function is assigned to a variable:
    $A=function($n){
        for($s=0,$k=1;$k<=$n;$k++){
            $s+=$k*$k;
        }
```

```
    return $s;
};
// Variables:
$n=4;
$x=5;
$y=10;
// Calls the functions by a variable:
echo "\$A($n) -> ",$A($n),"\n";
// Assigning functions:
$B=$A;
// The variable gets a function as a value:
$A=function($x,$y){
    return $x+$y;
};
// Calls the functions by variables:
echo "\$B($n) -> ",$B($n),"\n";
echo "\$A($x,$y) -> ",$A($x,$y),"\n";
?>
```

The result of the program execution is as follows.

The output of the program (from Listing 5-11)

```
$A(4) -> 30
$B(4) -> 30
$A(5,10) -> 15
```

First, the $A variable is assigned the following construction as a value.

```
function($n){
    for($s=0,$k=1;$k<=$n;$k++){
        $s+=$k*$k;
    }
    return $s;
}
```

It defines an anonymous function that, based on the argument $n, calculates (and returns as a result) the sum of the squares of natural numbers from 1 to $n. Once that anonymous function has been assigned to $A (note the semicolon at the end of the assignment statement), $A can be treated like a function—in particular, it can be called. For example, the value of the $A($n) expression (with the value 4 for the $n variable) is the sum of the squared numbers from 1 to 4 (that is, 30). Further, after executing the $B=$A command, which assigns $A to the $B variable, the $B variable also "becomes a function" and is the same as $A. The $A variable is then assigned a new anonymous function, defined as follows.

```
function($x,$y){
    return $x+$y;
}
```

This time, it is a function with two arguments and returns the sum of the arguments. Therefore, the value of the $A($x,$y) expression (with the values 5 and 10 for the $x and $y variables, respectively) is 15.

Named Arguments

When calling a function, you pass the arguments in the same order in which they were specified in the function declaration. That way of passing arguments is called positional one, or passing arguments *by position*.

However, PHP 8 introduced the ability to pass arguments *by name*. In that case, when the function is called, the arguments (all or some) are defined by a name and a value. The function itself is described as usual.

Details

If an argument is specified in the function declaration, then the name of that argument is specified without the $ symbol when the function is called. A colon follows the argument name and then the argument value. For example, if you used the `$arg` argument in the `func()` function declaration, then to pass the argument by name when calling the function, you use the `func(arg: value)` instruction.

Listing 5-12 is a small example illustrating how to pass arguments by name to a function.

⌂ The PHP 8 Standard

The following code only runs in PHP 8.

Listing 5-12. Using the Named Arguments

```php
<?php
    // A function with three arguments:
    function show($first,$second,$third){
        echo "The first argument: $first\n";
        echo "The second argument: $second\n";
        echo "The third argument: $third\n";
        echo "--------------------\n";
    }
```

```
// Passing arguments by position:
show(100,200,300);
// Passing arguments by name:
show(second:200,third:300,first:100);
// The mixed scheme of passing arguments:
show(100,third:300,second:200);
?>
```

The result of the program execution is as follows.

The output of the program (from Listing 5-12)

```
The first argument: 100
The second argument: 200
The third argument: 300
--------------------
The first argument: 100
The second argument: 200
The third argument: 300
--------------------
The first argument: 100
The second argument: 200
The third argument: 300
--------------------
```

In this case, an ordinary function show() with three arguments named $first, $second, and $third is described. When you call the function, it displays the values of the arguments passed to it.

You can call the function in the usual way, using positional argument passing. For example, the show(100,200,300) command means that the value 100 is passed as the $first argument, the value 200 is passed as the $second argument, and the value 300 is passed as the $third argument.

The show(second:200,third:300,first:100) command gives an example of passing all three arguments by name. As in the previous case, the value 100 is passed as the $first argument, the value 200 is passed as the $second argument, and the value 300 is passed as the $third argument.

You can use the mixed argument passing scheme when some arguments are passed positionally and some are passed by name.

ⓘ **Note**   When calling a function, if arguments are passed by position and by name, those arguments that are passed by position are listed first.

Another example is given by the show(100,third:300,second:200) command. The first argument is passed positionally, and the other two are passed by name.

Passing arguments by name can be especially efficient if the function's arguments have default values.

Details

Note that a default argument value is used if that argument is not explicitly specified when the function is called. In a function declaration, the default value is specified after the argument name through the assignment operator.

An example where function arguments have default values and are passed by name is shown in Listing 5-13.

Listing 5-13. Named Arguments and Default Values

```php
<?php
    // The function arguments have default values:
    function show($first=1,$second=2,$third=3){
        echo "The first argument: $first\n";
        echo "The second argument: $second\n";
        echo "The third argument: $third\n";
        echo "--------------------\n";
    }
    // Calls the function:
    show(100,third:300);
    show(second:200);
?>
```

The following is the result of the program execution.

The output of the program (from Listing 5-13)

```
The first argument: 100
The second argument: 2
The third argument: 300
--------------------
The first argument: 1
The second argument: 200
The third argument: 3
--------------------
```

Now, for the show() function, the $first, $second, and $third arguments have the default values 1, 2, and 3 respectively. Therefore, when you call the function with the show(100,third:300) command, the $first argument is set to 100, the $second argument uses the default value 2, and the $third argument is set to 300.

If the show(second:200) command is used, the $second argument is set to 200, and the default values 1 and 3 are used for the $first and $third arguments, respectively.

Summary

- A function is a named block of code that can be called by the name. The function declaration begins with the function keyword, followed by the function's arguments (in parentheses). Then, the commands are enclosed in curly braces. The commands are executed when the function is called.

- A function can return a result. The return value of a function is specified after the return instruction, which terminates the execution of the function.

- For a function, you can explicitly specify the type of arguments and the type of result.

- By default, the arguments of functions are passed by value (copies of the variables specified as the function arguments are created). To pass the arguments by reference, in the function declaration, the name of the corresponding argument is preceded by the & reference symbol.

- Arguments can have default values (specified through the assignment operator after the argument name in the function declaration). The default value is used if no value is specified for the argument when the function is called.

- You can create functions with an arbitrary number of arguments. In that case, the entire set of arguments is identified with one argument, preceded by an ellipsis in the function declaration. The argument is treated as an array.

- Functions can be defined using recursion when the function calls itself (but usually with a different argument).

- The function (syntax construction) eval() allows you to execute the commands in the string passed as an argument to the function.

- It is possible to create anonymous functions that do not have a name. An anonymous function is assigned to a variable; after that, the variable can be called as if it were a function.

- Starting with PHP 8, arguments can be passed by name when calling functions. In that case, you specify the argument's name (without the $ symbol) and, separated by a colon, the argument's value when calling the function.

CHAPTER 6

Useful Tricks and Operations

Imitation is the sincerest form of plagiarism.

—*ALF* (TV series)

This chapter discusses topics that are essential and useful in everyday practice.

References

If the value of a variable is assigned to another variable, then you get a copy of the assigned variable. For example, if $B=$A$ is executed, the value of $A becomes the value of $B. The important thing here is that if the value of $A is subsequently changed, then the value of $B does not change. But another situation is also possible when two variables refer to the same value. In that case, you deal with a *reference*. A reference is, in fact, an alias for a variable, an alternative way to refer to the corresponding value.

 Note   It turns out that there is one value and two variables. Both allow access to that value.

© Alex Vasilev 2024
A. Vasilev, *PHP by Example*, https://doi.org/10.1007/979-8-8688-0258-4_6

To create a reference to a variable, you must place the symbol & after the assignment operator in the assignment statement. Thus, the $R=&$A command creates a reference $R to the $A variable. By changing the value of the $A variable, you change the value of the $R reference, and vice versa—changing the value of the $R reference means changing the value of the $A variable.

Details

When a variable is created, space is allocated in memory to store the value of that variable. The previously allocated memory area is accessed each time you access the variable to read or assign a value. If you create a reference, no memory area is allocated for it. The reference is associated with an existing variable or the memory area allocated for that variable. When accessing a reference, operations are performed on the allocated memory area for the variable with which the reference is associated.

Listing 6-1 uses these references.

Listing 6-1. Creating a Reference

```php
<?php
    // The initial variable:
    $A=100;
    // A copy of the variable:
    $B=$A;
    // A reference to the variable:
    $R=&$A;
    // Checks the values:
    echo "The initial values:\n";
    echo "\$A = $A\n";
    echo "\$B = $B\n";
    echo "\$R = $R\n";
```

```
// Changes the value of the variable:
$A=200;
// Checks the values:
echo "The new values:\n";
echo "\$A = $A\n";
echo "\$B = $B\n";
echo "\$R = $R\n";
// Deletes the variable:
unset($A);
// Checks the values:
echo "After deleting the variable \$A:\n";
echo "\$B = $B\n";
echo "\$R = $R\n";
// Changes the reference:
$R=&$B;
// Checks the values:
echo "Now \$R refers to \$B:\n";
echo "\$B = $B\n";
echo "\$R = $R\n";
// Changes the value through the reference:
$R=300;
// Checks the values:
echo "After changing the value:\n";
echo "\$B = $B\n";
echo "\$R = $R\n";
?>
```

The following are the results of executing the program.

The output of the program (from Listing 6-1)

```
The initial values:
$A = 100
```

```
$B = 100
$R = 100
The new values:
$A = 200
$B = 100
$R = 200
After deleting the variable $A:
$B = 100
$R = 200
Now $R refers to $B:
$B = 100
$R = 100
After changing the value:
$B = 300
$R = 300
```

The program is simple. First, $A=100 sets $A to 100, and $B=$A sets $B to the same value (the value of $A). But the $R=&$A command creates the $R reference to the $A variable. The difference between the $B variable and the $R reference becomes obvious after executing the $A=200 instruction, which assigns a new value to the $A variable. At the same time, the value of the $B variable does not change, and when checking the value of the $R reference, you get the value 200.

In the next step, you use the unset($A) command to remove the $A variable. That does not affect the value of the $R reference, and it still refers to the same value as before the variable was deleted.

After executing the $R=&$B command, you "link" the reference to the $B variable. More precisely, after executing that command, the $R reference is associated with the same memory area as the $B variable. So, after executing the $R=300 command, $B is set to 300.

References like this one are called *hard references*. In addition to hard references, there are also *soft references*. That is a more general mechanism for accessing variables. Let's begin with the brief example shown in Listing 6-2.

Listing 6-2. Soft References

```php
<?php
    // The variable with an integer value:
    $number=123;
    // The value of the variable is a string with a name
    // of another variable:
    $reference="number";
    echo "\$\$reference = ",$$reference,"\n";
    // The new value of the variable $number:
    $$reference=321;
    echo "\$number = ",$number,"\n";
    // The variable with a string value:
    $A="Alpha";
    // Assigns a value to the variable $Alpha:
    $$A=100;
    echo "\$Alpha = ",$Alpha,"\n";
    // The new value of the variable $Alpha:
    $Alpha=200;
    echo "\$\$A = ",$$A,"\n";
    // The new value of the variable $A:
    $A='Bravo';
    // Assigns a value to the variable $Bravo:
    $$A=300;
    echo "\$Alpha = ",$Alpha,"\n";
    echo "\$Bravo = ",$Bravo,"\n";
?>
```

The following are the results of executing the program.

The output of the program (from Listing 6-2)

```
$$reference = 123
$number = 321
$Alpha = 100
$$A = 200
$Alpha = 200
$Bravo = 300
```

Let's analyze the program's code. The $number=123 and $reference="number" commands define two ordinary variables. The string value of the second variable is the same as the name of the first variable (but without the $ symbol). Then, the value of the $$reference expression is checked. Based on the program results, it is easy to guess that that is the value of the $number variable. Thus, adding another $ symbol at the beginning of the $reference variable name leads to the following: the $ symbol is "appended" to the text value of the $reference variable, and the resulting text is interpreted as the name of the variable being accessed. That is confirmed by the $$reference=321 command, which causes the $number variable to get the value 321.

Using the method described, you can get a reference to a variable that does not yet exist. The $A="Alpha" command writes the text "Alpha" to the $A variable. Therefore, when the $$A=100 command is executed, the $Alpha variable is assigned the value 100, and thus such a variable appears in the program.

After executing the $Alpha=200 command, the new value 200 is returned by the $$A expression. If the $A variable is assigned a new value (as is done by the $A='Bravo' command), then the $$Aexpression refers to the $Bravo variable. In particular, after executing the $$A=300 command, the $Bravo variable is set to 300, while the $Alpha variable remains with the old value 200.

Constants

Constants are fundamentally different from variables in that the value of a constant cannot be changed. The `define()` function (more precisely, a syntax construction) is usually used to add a constant to a program. The function's first argument is a string with the constant's name. The second argument specifies the value of the constant. The $ symbol is not used at the beginning of the constant name. Following the generally accepted convention, the names of constants consist of capital letters (that is, this is not necessary, but good manners oblige). For example, the `define("PI",3.141592)` command defines the constant `PI` with the value `3.141592`. After executing that command, the value of the constant `PI` cannot be changed.

A constant cannot be deleted after it has been created. To check the existence of a constant, the `defined()` function is used, the argument of which is a string with the name of the constant; for example, `defined("PI")`. The result is `true` or `false` depending on whether the constant is defined.

There is another way to add a constant to a program. In that case, the keyword `const` is used, after which the name of the constant is specified (without the $ symbol at the beginning of the name), and, through the assignment operator, the value of the constant. For example, the constant TEN with the value 10 can be defined with the `const TEN=10` command.

The fundamental difference between these two ways of creating constants is that constants defined by the `define()` function are created at runtime. In contrast, constants created using the `const` statement are created at the compilation time. That circumstance has consequences. For example, the command to create a constant using the `const` statement cannot be placed in a conditional statement but can be done using the `define()` function. On the other hand, the `define()` function cannot be used in classes and interfaces (discussed in later chapters of the book) to create constant fields; in that case, an expression based on the const statement is used.

A small example in which you use constants is shown in Listing 6-3.

Listing 6-3. Constants

```php
<?php
    // The constant is the number "pi":
    define("PI",3.141592);
    // Using constants:
    echo "The number PI = ",PI,"\n";
    echo "sin(PI/6) = ",sin(PI/6),"\n";
    // Declares constants:
    const ONE=1;
    const TWO=2;
    const THREE=ONE+TWO;
    // Checks the constants:
    echo "ONE = ",ONE,"\n";
    echo "TWO = ",TWO,"\n";
    echo "THREE = ",THREE,"\n";
?>
```

The following are the results of executing the program.

The output of the program (from Listing 6-3)

```
The number PI = 3.141592
sin(PI/6) = 0.49999990566244
ONE = 1
TWO = 2
THREE = 3
```

The program uses the define("PI",3.141592) statement to define the PI constant, and after that, you check its value and calculate the sin(PI/6) expression.

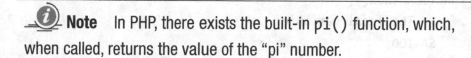 **Note**   In PHP, there exists the built-in pi() function, which, when called, returns the value of the "pi" number.

Three more constants are created using the const ONE=1, const TWO=2, and const THREE=ONE+TWO commands. In the latter case, the value of the THREE constant is calculated as the sum of the ONE and TWO constants.

Details

In PHP, some built-in constants allow us to get important information about the working document and program components. For example, using the __LINE__ constant, you can get the current line number in the file. The __FILE__ constant allows you to get the name of the file, the value of the __DIR__ constant is the name of the directory in which the file is located, and the name of the function (in which the constant is requested) can be obtained using the __FUNCTION__ constant. The names of all these (and some other) constants begin and end with a double underscore.

Global Variables

Earlier, you dealt with functions and used *local* variables in them. Local variables are created in the body of a function (by assigning a value to the variable) and exist while the function is operating. After executing the function, the local variables are removed from memory. The next time the function is called, local variables are created again, and everything repeats. The situation is illustrated in the program in Listing 6-4.

Listing 6-4. Local Variables

```php
<?php
    // The function with a local variable:
    function show(){
        // The local variable:
        $A=100;
        echo "The local variable \$A = ",$A,"\n";
    }
    // The global variable:
    $A=200;
    // Calls the function:
    show();
    // Checks the value of the variable:
    echo "The global variable \$A = ",$A,"\n";
?>
```

The following are the results of executing the program.

The output of the program (from Listing 6-4)
```
The local variable $A = 100
The global variable $A = 200
```

You use the show() function, which creates a local variable $A with the value 100 in its body and displays the variable's value in the output window. Before calling the function, you use the $A=200 command to create the $A global variable with the value 200. When the show() function is called, the value 100 is displayed, while the value of the global variable does not change. The explanation is simple: the variable created when the show() function is called has nothing to do with the $A global variable.

On the other hand, there are situations when, in a function, it is necessary to perform operations on a variable declared outside the function—that is, with a *global* variable. If so, then in the function, you should indicate that the variable is global. To do that, you use the global keyword, after which you put the name of the global variable. An example of using global variables in a function is shown in Listing 6-5.

Listing 6-5. Global Variables

```php
<?php
    // The function:
    function show(){
        // The global variable:
        global $A;
        // Displays the value of the variable:
        echo "[1] In the function: \$A = ",$A,"\n";
        // The new value:
        $A=200;
        echo "[2] In the function: \$A = ",$A,"\n";
    }
    // The global variable:
    $A=100;
    // Calls the function:
    show();
    // Checks the value of the variable:
    echo "The variable \$A = ",$A,"\n";
?>
```

The program's output is as follows.

The output of the program (from Listing 6-5)
```
[1] In the function: $A = 100
[2] In the function: $A = 200
The variable $A = 200
```

181

In the function's body, the global $A command declares that the $A variable is global. Next, the variable's value is displayed, the value 200 is assigned to it, and then the value is checked again.

In the program, the $A variable is assigned the value 100. Then, you call the show() function and, after calling it, check the value of the $A variable. All operations are performed with the same $A global variable.

(i) **Note**   The programming style, which implies using global variables in functions, should not be called very successful. The corresponding global variable is an "external factor" when a function is called. That does not fit well with functional programming principles, according to which the passed to the function arguments must determine its result.

Details

A built-in $GLOBALS array contains all global variables available in the program. The array is accessible anywhere in the program and does not need to be declared in any way.

Static Variables

Quite interesting is the concept of *static variables*. Such a variable is declared with the static keyword. It is not removed from memory after the function is terminated, and the same variable is used for each subsequent function call. The program in Listing 6-6 shows how static variables can be used.

Listing 6-6. Static Variables

```php
<?php
    // The function with a static variable:
    function calc(){
        // The static variable:
        static $value=0;
        $value+=100;
        return $value;
    }
    // Calls the function within the loop statement:
    for($k=1;$k<=5;$k++){
        echo "[$k] calc() -> ",calc(),"\n";
    }
?>
```

The result of the program execution may seem a little unexpected.

The output of the program (from Listing 6-6)
```
[1] calc() -> 100
[2] calc() -> 200
[3] calc() -> 300
[4] calc() -> 400
[5] calc() -> 500
```

Briefly, everything is simple. You have the calc() function that is called with no arguments. The first time the function is called, the result is 100. The second time the function is called, the result is 200. The third time, the function returns 300, and so on. Thus, you use the same instruction but get a new (predicted) result each time. To understand why that happens, let's analyze the code of the calc() function.

In the function's body, the `static $value=0` command creates the static variable $value with the value 0. Then, with the $value+=100 command, that value is incremented by 100 and returned as the result of the function.

Let's see what happens when the function is called for the first time. It's simple: the $value variable is created, it gets the value 100 after all, and the function returns the result. That completes the execution of the function. If the $value variable were normal (not a static one), then it would be removed from memory, and the next time the function is called, everything would start with creating the new variable $value. But the variable is static. Therefore, the variable is not deleted from memory after the function is terminated.

Moreover, the next time the `calc()` function is called, it is the variable that is used, and with the value that the variable had at the last function call. That value is incremented by 100 and returned as the result. It turns out that each time the `calc()` function is called, the value of the $value variable is increased by 100. Therefore, the function returns a new value each time.

Details

The command that initializes the static variable $value with the zero value is executed only once, the first time the function is called. It is also worth mentioning that the $value variable (despite being static) is available only in the function's body.

Multiline Strings

From a practical point of view, strings are very important when using PHP. And often, you must deal with multiline strings. There are several ways to create them.

To create a multiline string, you can use the following construction. The <<< instruction is followed by an identifier, and then a new line is entered. That is followed by text (without quotes) that can span multiple lines. The whole construction ends with the same identifier that begins, and a semicolon is placed at the very end. It must be the last instruction in the line with no additional characters. An example of using such a string is shown in Listing 6-7.

Listing 6-7. Getting Familiar with Multiline Strings

```php
<?php
    // A variable:
    $word="wind";
    // A multiline string:
    $text=<<<MYTEXT
    The mighty Dnieper roars and bellows,
    The $word in anger howls and raves,
    Down to the ground, it bends the willows,
    And mountain-high lifts up the waves.
    MYTEXT;
    echo $text;
?>
```

The output of the program is as follows.

The output of the program (from Listing 6-7)

The mighty Dnieper roars and bellows,
The wind in anger howls and raves,
Down to the ground, it bends the willows,
And mountain-high lifts up the waves.

Here, the $text variable is assigned a rather complex expression, which begins with the <<< instruction followed by the MYTEXT identifier. (You determine the name of the identifier.) Then, the text follows, ending with the MYTEXT instruction and a semicolon.

Details

The text indentation should be made relative to the position of the instruction that terminates the text value (in this case, the MYTEXT identifier). An error arises if the text is placed to the left of that instruction.

Notably, the name of the $word variable in the text fragment is used. As a result, the variable's value is inserted instead of its name. That means the text behaves like a string literal enclosed in double quotes.

There is another way to create a multiline string. It is similar to the previous one, but the initial identifier after the <<< instruction is enclosed in single quotes. An example of such a multiline string is shown in Listing 6-8.

Listing 6-8. Another Way to Create a Multiline String

```php
<?php
    // A multiline string:
    $text=<<<'MYTEXT'
An example of programming code:
$number=123;  // Creates a variable
echo "\$number = ",$number,"\n";
MYTEXT;
    echo $text;
?>
```

186

The following is the result of the program execution.

The output of the program (from Listing 6-8)
```
An example of programming code:
$number=123;  // Creates a variable
echo "\$number = ",$number,"\n";
```

In this case, the MYTEXT identifier after the <<< instruction is enclosed in single quotes, and the text itself contains commands, including variable names. All the text content is displayed "as it is"—that is, it is similar to the situation when a string literal is enclosed in single quotes.

Using Files

Another important aspect of using PHP is related to operating with files. Let's discuss the most common techniques for getting data from files and writing data to files.

First of all, the file needs to be opened. To do that, you use the fopen() function. The function's first argument is a string specifying the path to the file. The second argument is a string with special characters. That argument determines the access mode under which you use the file. Table 6-1 lists and describes combinations for the second argument of the fopen() function.

Table 6-1. *The Access Modes for Using Files*

Instruction	Access Mode
'r'	The file is opened for reading. The pointer for reading is set at the beginning of the file.
'r+'	The file is opened for reading and writing. The pointer for reading/writing is set at the beginning of the file.
'w'	The file is opened for writing. The pointer for writing is set at the beginning of the file. The original contents of the file are deleted. If the file does not exist, it will be created.
'w+'	The file is opened for reading and writing. The pointer for reading/writing is set at the beginning of the file. The original contents of the file are deleted. If the file does not exist, it will be created.
'a'	The file is opened for writing only. The pointer for writing is set at the end of the file. If the file does not exist, it will be created.
'a+'	The file is opened for reading and writing. The pointer for reading/writing is set at the end of the file. If the file does not exist, it will be created.
'x'	The file is created for writing. The pointer for writing is set at the beginning of the file. If the file already exists, an error is raised.
'x+'	The file is created and opened for reading and writing. The pointer for reading/writing is set at the beginning of the file. If the file already exists, an error is raised.
'c'	The file is opened for writing only. If the file does not exist, it will be created. If the file already exists, then the contents of the file are not deleted. The pointer for writing is set at the beginning of the file.
'c+'	The file is opened for reading and writing. The pointer for reading/writing is set at the beginning of the file. If the file does not exist, it will be created. If the file exists, its contents are not deleted.

As a result, the fopen() function returns a numeric identifier that can be used to access the opened file.

Details

Data can be written and read in byte or character stream mode. As it is easy to understand from the name, operating with a byte stream implies that data is written and read byte by byte. If the stream is a character one, then reading and writing are performed character by character. The type of the stream (character or byte) is determined by the characters b (the byte stream) and t (the character stream), which are placed in the string after the instruction that specifies the file access mode.

There is a set of functions designed to work with files. The most important among them are the following. The fgets() function reads a line starting at the pointer in the file. The fread() function is used for byte reading. The fwrite() function allows you to write bytes. The file() function allows you to read a file into an array. You can use the file_exists() function to check if a file exists. The is_readable() function checks if a file is readable. The feof() function lets you know if the end of the file has been reached.

Details

After operations with a file are completed, it is recommended to close the file. The fclose() function is used for that.

In some cases, creating (for reading or writing) a file with a random name may be necessary (so no one gets unauthorized access to it by mistake). The tmpfile() function can be used for doing that.

Listing 6-9 uses some of the functions discussed.

Listing 6-9. Reading a File Line by Line

```php
<?php
    // The full path to the file:
    $path="D:/books/php/myfile.txt";
    // We open the file for reading
    // as the character stream:
    $h=fopen($path,"rt");
    // The variable to count lines:
    $k=1;
    // While the end of the file is not reached:
    while(!feof($h)){
        // Reads a string line:
        $line=fgets($h);
        // Displays the read line:
        echo "[$k] ",$line;
        // The new value for the counter:
        $k++;
    }
    // Closes the file:
    fclose($h);
?>
```

For this program to run successfully, there must be the myfile.txt file with some text in the D:\books\php folder. In this case, the contents of the text file are as follows.

```
The mighty Dnieper roars and bellows,
The wind in anger howls and raves,
Down to the ground, it bends the willows,
And mountain-high lifts up the waves.
Taras Shevchenko
```

The full path to the file is written to the $path variable. Then, the $h=fopen($path,"rt") command attempts to open the file, and if successful, the file identifier is written to the $h variable. Next, using that variable, you get access to the file. In particular, you read the contents of the file line by line and display the read string in the output area. Each line is preceded by its number in square brackets. The $k variable is used to count the lines.

The second argument, "rt" passed to the fopen() function, means that the file is opened for reading only under the character stream mode.

Details

An error arises if the file you are trying to open does not exist. In that case, instead of the $h=fopen($path,"rt") command, you can use a command like $h=fopen($path,"rt") or die("File access error"). Here, the or logical operator is used. It performs the *logical or* operation in a simplified form: the second operand, die("File access error"), is evaluated only if the first operand, $h=fopen($path,"rt"), has a value equal to false. If the file is opened successfully, the first operand is non-zero, which is equivalent to true. In that case, the second operand is not evaluated. If the file cannot be opened, then the second operand die("File access error") is evaluated, and as a result, a message about the error appears in the output area, and the code execution stops.

To read the file's contents, you use the while loop statement. The condition is defined by the !feof($h) expression. The feof() function determines whether the end of the file whose identifier is passed as an argument to the function has been reached. Therefore, the !feof($h) expression is true if the end of the file has not been reached.

Until the end of the file is reached, the $line=fgets($h) command writes the line read to the $line variable using the fgets() function. Then the echo "[$k] ",$line instruction displays the read line in the output area. Finally, the $k++ command increments the counter variable $k value.

That process is terminated as soon as the end of the file is reached. The fclose($h) command closes the file. The result of running the program is as follows.

The output of the program (from Listing 6-9)

[1] The mighty Dnieper roars and bellows,

[2] The wind in anger howls and raves,

[3] Down to the ground, it bends the willows,

[4] And mountain-high lifts up the waves.

[5] Taras Shevchenko

Listing 6-10 shows how to write into a file in the program.

Listing 6-10. Writing into a File

```php
<?php
    // The full path to the file:
    $path="D:/books/php/mytext.txt";
    // We open the file for writing:
    $h=fopen($path,"wt");
    echo "Writing into the file.\n";
    echo "Enter text. To terminate, enter exit:\n";
    // The variable to count lines:
    $k=1;
    // Reads the string entered by the user:
    $line=trim(fgets(STDIN));
    while($line!=="exit"){
        // Writes the line number into the file:
        fwrite($h,"[$k] ");
        // Writes the line into the file:
        fwrite($h,$line."\n");
        // The new value for the counter:
```

```
    $k++;
    // Reads a new string:
    $line=trim(fgets(STDIN));
}
// Closes the file:
fclose($h);
echo "The program is over.";
?>
```

The result of the program execution could be as follows (the text entered by the user is marked in bold).

The output of the program (from Listing 6-10)
Writing into the file.
Enter text. To terminate, enter exit:
The mighty Dnieper roars and bellows,
The wind in anger howls and raves,
Down to the ground, it bends the willows,
And mountain-high lifts up the waves.
Taras Shevchenko
exit
The program is over.

But the most important thing is that in the D:\books\php folder, there appears (if it was not there) the mytext.txt file with the following content.

```
[1] The mighty Dnieper roars and bellows,
[2] The wind in anger howls and raves,
[3] Down to the ground, it bends the willows,
[4] And mountain-high lifts up the waves.
[5] Taras Shevchenko
```

Let's find out why that happens. Namely, let's analyze the program. The $path variable, as in the previous case, stores the full path to the file where you intend to write the text. In particular, that is the mytext. txt file from the D:\books\php folder. You open the file using the $h=fopen($path,"wt") instruction. The second argument, "wt", means the file is opened for writing under the character stream mode. Next, several messages are displayed, and then, with the help of the $line=trim(fgets(STDIN)) command, you read the text entered by the user (in which all leading and trailing spaces and special characters are previously discarded). After that, the while loop statement is launched, in which the $line!=="exit" condition is checked. The condition is true if the user has not entered the text "exit".

 Note   Thus, to terminate the input process, you must enter the word exit.

The fwrite($h,"[$k] ") command writes the line number in square brackets into the file, after which the fwrite($h,$line."\n") command adds the read string into the file, supplemented by the instruction to move to a new line in the file. The $k++ instruction changes the value of the counter variable $k, and then the $line=trim(fgets(STDIN)) command reads the next line the user enters. Finally, you close the file using the fclose($h) instruction.

Including a File in the Program

Often, there is a need to include some code from another file into a program. Next, let's examine a small example that shows (at an elementary level) how that could be done. The main idea is as follows. You describe some function in a file and then call it in another. Namely, you create a file called show.php with the following code.

```php
<?php
    // The function:
    function show($n){
        echo "The argument - $n\n";
    }
?>
```

Let's create a file (see Listing 6-11) in the same folder that contains the show.php file with the show() function code.

Listing 6-11. Including a File in the Program

```php
<?php
    // Includes a file into the program:
    require_once 'show.php';
    // Creates a variable:
    $val=123;
    // Calls the function from the file:
    show($val);
?>
```

The output of the program is as follows.

The output of the program (from Listing 6-11)
The argument - 123

The code begins with the require_once 'show.php' command, which imports the contents of the show.php file into the program. Then, you create the $val variable and pass it to the show() function as an argument. The function is called, and a corresponding message appears in the output area.

Summary

- References provide alternative access to variables. When creating a reference to a variable, the variable name preceded by the & instruction is assigned to the reference. That kind of reference is called the hard one.

- When using a soft reference, some variable is assigned a string with the name of another variable (without the $ symbol). Adding a second $ character to the name of the first variable allows access to the variable, whose name contains the string assigned to the first variable.

- In addition to variables, you can use constants. The value of a constant cannot be changed after the first assignment. Constants can be created using the define() function or the const statement. The $ symbol is not used in the constant names.

- Functions can use global variables. These are variables that are also available outside the scope of the function. In the body of a function, global variables are declared using the global statement.

- Functions can use static variables. (The static keyword to declare such a variable was used.) A static variable is created and gets its initial value the first time the function is called. After the function is terminated, the static variable is not removed from memory, and the next time the function is called, that variable is used again.

- In some cases, a multiline string is used. If so, a variable is assigned an expression that begins with the <<< instruction followed by some label. The text is entered without quotes in multiple lines. The expression ends with the same label and a semicolon. That is the equivalent of a string in double quotes. If the first occurrence of the label is enclosed in single quotes, you get an analog of a string enclosed in single quotes.

- A set of functions is designed for working with files. The fopen() function is used to open a file. The first argument specifies the full path to the file, and the second argument specifies the access mode. When the file has been handled, it is closed using the fclose() function.

- To import the contents of a file, the require_once instruction is added to the program, after which you put the string with the name of the imported file.

CHAPTER 7

Classes and Objects

—As you may have gathered, I'm in big trouble.

—You're always in trouble.

—ALF (TV series)

This chapter discusses how the principles of object-oriented programming (OOP for short) are implemented in PHP. Let's start by introducing the concept of *classes* and *objects*. That is the cornerstone of the OOP paradigm, and how the main conceptual points are learned will largely determine the success of using the broad features of PHP to create OOP projects.

The OOP Principles

The study of the OOP principles often begins with their enumeration: *encapsulation*, *polymorphism*, and *inheritance*. That may sound a little bit scary. However, not everything is as scary as it seems at first glance. To understand the concept of OOP, it makes sense to clarify what it is and why you need it to create programs.

The OOP paradigm must imply a certain way of organizing a program. In other words, OOP is about how to organize a program. And here, an analogy would help us.

© Alex Vasilev 2024
A. Vasilev, *PHP by Example*, https://doi.org/10.1007/979-8-8688-0258-4_7

Let's say there is a small café with a kitchen, and you need to organize the work in the kitchen. The kitchen receives orders from visitors and prepares dishes following those orders. If the cafe is not very large and there are not many visitors, you need a chef to manage the process for the successful operation of the kitchen. You also need to have several assistant chefs. Each assistant chef is responsible for preparing a specific dish or dishes. For example, one chef specializes in meat dishes, another in fish dishes, the next one prepares salads, someone specializes in desserts, and so on. One or more refrigerators can be used to store food, and all chefs store products there and use those products to prepare meals. All chefs have access to all refrigerators. The distribution of tasks to the assistant chefs is the responsibility of the main chef. The main chef also controls the contents of the refrigerators: are there all the products, and are their quantities sufficient?

Note   Even if, in reality, the work of a kitchen is organized differently, it does not matter. The example is illustrative; you just need to explain the difference in approaches, but not to organize the work of a real kitchen.

Let's compare how a kitchen works to how a program works. Assistant chefs are analogous to functions, and food stored in the refrigerator is analogous to data. The overall goal is to "connect" the data and the "functionality" associated with processing that data. In "culinary" language, that means you need to define for each assistant chef the functional responsibilities and the products they can use in their work.

Let's say you make everything right, and the kitchen operates like a clock. What can break the situation? One of the main reasons is the expansion of the "enterprise." In a programming language, an increase in the amount of code. Imagine that there are a lot of visitors, and the kitchen is huge—lots of assistant chefs, lots of refrigerators. Unavoidably, problems will arise due to someone incorrectly taking an order, collecting another chef's products, or dropping out of the process. That is a pure scaling problem. It can be solved by changing the structure of production. Namely, let's divide the kitchen into departments. Each department has its own specialization. Products in each department are stored in separate refrigerators. Each department has its own main chef. That may increase staff and overall costs, but it makes the kitchen more reliable since some problems are automatically removed due to how the production is organized. For example, if the refrigerator is located in the fish department, no one from the meat department can access it.

What is important in this new model? The important thing is that you use a system of departments that interact with each other. Previously, in the original scheme, individual assistant chefs interacted with each other. As part of the new approach, the chefs also interact with each other within the department. At the next level, there is an interaction between departments. You can do the same with the program. Namely, you can organize it as an interaction of some blocks which contain the data and which can process that data. Such blocks are called *objects*. The scheme itself describes the paradigm of object-oriented programming (OOP).

(i) **Note**   OOP principles were developed for creating large programs. A large program usually contains several thousand lines of code or more.

Thus, writing a program within the framework of OOP implies the creation of objects. Objects are created based on patterns called *classes*.

Let's consider another analogy to understand the difference between a class and an object. Let's say you want to build a house (an analogy to an object). But to build a house, you need a plan or scheme according to which you build (an analogy to a class). You take a plan and build a house following the plan. Similarly, you take a class and create an object based on the class. Several houses can be built based on the same plan. They are of the same type but physically different. And if you build houses based on different plans, you get different houses. As well multiple objects can also be created based on a class. They are also of the same type (with the same functionality), but at the same time, physically, they are different. If you create objects based on different classes, the objects are also different. It is also possible that there is a plan but no buildings. Similarly, you can create a class but not create any object based on it.

That is the main idea. Next, you must learn how to declare classes and create objects based on them.

_(i)_ **Note**   Returning to encapsulation, polymorphism, and inheritance, it is worth mentioning the following. These are the three basic mechanisms of OOP. Encapsulation means that the data and the code for processing it are combined into a single unit, which is an object. Polymorphism implies using generic interfaces for interacting with objects, functions, and methods. Finally, inheritance allows you to create new classes based on existing ones by inheriting their properties. All these mechanisms are examined step by step in examples.

Creating Classes and Objects

It is time to go deep into the practical issues. Let's start by creating classes.

A class declaration begins with the class keyword followed by the class name. Then, in a block defined by curly braces, the contents of the class are described. The class declaration template looks as follows.

```
class name{
    # The contents of the class
}
```

But the intrigue remains: what can be described in a class? The short answer is that you can describe methods and fields there. The fields are actually variables. Unlike ordinary variables, the fields are described in the class. There is no need to assign values to them; it is just enough to specify their presence in the class. Methods are the same as functions. But contrary to the functions, the methods are described in the class.

(i) **Note**   The fields are sometimes also called properties or attributes. The fields and methods of a class are called members of the class.

The following is an example of a simple class with only a single field.

```
class MyClass{
    public $number;
}
```

The class contains only one public $number statement, which means that the class describes a field called $number. The public keyword is called an *access level specifier*, meaning the field is public. The "publicity" of the field, in turn, allows you to access the field not only inside the class but also outside of it.

(i) **Note**   In addition to the public access level specifier, the private (a private field) and protected (a protected field) keywords can be used. How the access level specifier affects the field properties is discussed later.

So, there is the MyClass class with a single $number field. What does that mean? That means if you create an object based on the MyClass class, the object has the $number field.

Details

A field is like a variable. If you imagine an object as a container, then the field of the object is a variable put in that container. If you have several objects created based on the same class, they have the same set of fields. However, these are different variables since each object has its own fields. Therefore, it is not enough to specify the field's name when referring to an object field. You must also specify the object to which that field belongs.

To create an object based on a class, use the new instruction followed by the name of the class to be the basis for creating the object. A reference to that object is written to a variable (an object variable) identified with the object. The template of the statement that creates an object is as follows.

```
$variable=new ClassName;
```

For example, if you want to create an object of the MyClass class, the corresponding command could look like the following.

```
$obj=new MyClass;
```

This command creates an object of the MyClass class, and a reference to the created object is written to the $obj variable. If you need to access the object, use the $obj variable.

☺ The PHP 8 Standard

In PHP 8, you can use the $obj::class statement to get the name of that class based on which the $obj object was created. In the previous versions of PHP, the get_class() function is used for that purpose, and the corresponding command looks like get_class($obj).

But an object is primarily its fields and methods. Therefore, access to the object is access to its fields and methods. To do that, put the arrow -> after the object variable and then place the field name without the $ symbol. In this case, you access the $number field of the $obj object using the $obj->number instruction.

Listing 7-1 is a program in which you describe a class, create an object based on the class, and then perform some operations with the object's field.

Listing 7-1. Creating an Object

```php
<?php
   // Description of a class:
   class MyClass{
      public $number;
   }
   // Creates an object:
   $obj=new MyClass;
   // The field is assigned a value:
   $obj->number=123;
   // Displays the field:
   echo "The field \$number: $obj->number\n";
   // The new value of the field:
   $obj->number=321;
```

205

```
// Displays the field:
echo "The field \$number: $obj->number\n";
?>
```

The following is the result of the program execution.

The output of the program (from Listing 7-1)

```
The field $number: 123
The field $number: 321
```

The program begins with a description of the MyClass class. Based on the class, the $obj=new MyClass instruction creates the $obj object. It has the $number field, assigned the value 123 using the $obj->number=123 statement. Then, use the echo "The field \$number: $obj->number\n" statement to display the $number field of the $obj object.

---

i **Note**   Instead of the $obj->number instructions in the string literal in double quotes, the value of that instruction is displayed.

After that, the $obj->number=321 command assigns the new value 321 to the $number field of the $obj object. The check shows that the field value has changed.

Details

The public access level specifier in the description of the $number field in the MyClass class makes it possible to access the field in the $obj->number format outside the MyClass code.

The Methods

As mentioned, in addition to describing fields in a class, you can describe methods there. A method is described in the same way as a function, but only in the body of the class. The main feature of the method is related to how it is called. When you call a function, you have to specify the name of the function and the list of its arguments. When you call a method, you need to specify the object from which the method is called. The method has access to all fields and methods described in the class.

Note   From here, you examine ordinary (non-static) fields and methods. In addition to ordinary class members, there exist static members. Operations with them have their own peculiarities, which are discussed later.

Listing 7-2 is a small modification of the previous example. Now, the MyClass class contains two methods besides the $number field.

Listing 7-2. Using Methods

```php
<?php
    class MyClass{
        public $number;
        // The method to display the field:
        function show(){
            print("The field \$number: $this->number\n");
        }
```

```
        // The method to assign a value to the field:
        function set($n){
            $this->number=$n;
        }
    }
    // Creates objects:
    $A=new MyClass;
    $B=new MyClass;
    // The fields are assigned values:
    $A->set(100);
    $B->set(200);
    // Displays the fields:
    $A->show();
    $B->show();
?>
```

The following is the result of the program execution.

The output of the program (from Listing 7-2)
```
The field $number: 100
The field $number: 200
```

The main changes are related to the MyClass code. In addition to
the $number field, the class contains the methods show() and set(). The
show() method has no arguments and allows you to display the $number
field of the object from which the method is called. The set() method
assigns a value to the $number field of the object from which the method is
called. The method's argument (named $n) determines the value assigned
to the $number field.

You are faced with an essential problem in the description of these methods. Namely, a method is called from an object. That means that to call the method, it is necessary to specify the name of the method and the object from which the method is called. The method, in turn, accesses the field $number of the object. When accessing the field, you must specify the object (which owns the field). But when you describe the method, the object does not yet exist. In other words, you need to denote somehow the object from which the method is called. That is what the $this identifier is used for. The $this instruction, when used within the method code, denotes the object from which the method is called. Therefore, for example, the $this->number command is a reference to the $number field of the object from which the method is called. In particular, in the body of the show() method, use the print("The field \$number: $this->number\n") statement, which displays the $number field of the object from which the method is called. In the body of the set() method, the $this->number=$n statement assigns the $n argument of the method to the $number field.

In the program, create two objects, $A and $B, of the MyClass class. To do that, use the $A=new MyClass and $B=new MyClass commands, respectively. Each object has the $number field, but these are different fields despite the coinciding names: one belongs to the $A object, and the other belongs to the $B object. You use the set() and show() methods to perform operations with fields. The $A->set(100) instruction assigns 100 to the field $number of $A, and the $B->set(200) instruction assigns 200 to the field $number of $B. After that, using the $A->show() command, display the $number field of the $A object, and to display the $number field of the $B object, use the $B->show() command.

Details

It might be interesting that when trying to assign a value to a field that doesn't exist in an object, such a field appears (a so-called dynamic property). For example, if the $obj object has no $name field, then after executing the $obj->name="php" command, the $obj object gets the $name field with the value "php". Nevertheless, since PHP 8.2, that possibility is deprecated. If you still want to use it, you should put the #[\AllowDynamicProperties] annotation before the class description.

You can use the unset() function to remove a field from an object. For example, to delete the $name field from the $obj object, the unset($obj->name) instruction could be helpful.

It is also worth mentioning that methods, like fields, can be described with the public, private, and protected specifiers of access level. If a method is described without a specifier of access level (as in the earlier examples), then the method is a public one by default.

A good practice is to specify the public access level explicitly for public methods. Nevertheless, let's use the default (public) access level (so the public keyword is not used) for some methods to demonstrate PHP's flexibility and power.

Also, you can assign values to fields in the description of a class. In that case, when creating an object based on the class, the corresponding field of the object has the value assigned to the field in the class.

🔔 The PHP 8 Standard

In the PHP 8 version, you can use the ?-> instruction instead of -> when accessing the fields and methods of objects. For example, you can use an expression like $object?->method instead of the expression like $object->method. The former option is safer because if the value of the $object variable is an empty null reference, then there is no fatal error.

The Constructor and the Destructor

In the examples, you created objects based on a class, and then the fields of the objects were assigned values. If there are many objects and they have many fields, then the process can become tedious. So, it is advisable to automate it. In that sense, two special methods may be useful: the *constructor* and the *destructor*.

The constructor is a method called automatically when an object is created. The constructor's name is __construct() (the name starts with a double underscore). The constructor can take arguments. Typically, the constructor contains commands that assign values to fields or perform other operations.

Details

If the constructor has arguments, then those arguments must be specified when an object is created. Arguments of the constructor are specified in parentheses after the class name in the command based on the new instruction that creates the object.

The destructor is a method automatically called when an object is removed from memory. The destructor's name is __destruct(), and it has no arguments. Listing 7-3 illustrates how to use the constructor and the destructor.

Listing 7-3. The Constructor and the Destructor

```php
<?php
    # The class with the constructor and the destructor:
    class MyClass{
        # The field:
        public $code;
        # The constructor:
```

```
    function __construct($code=123){
        $this->code=$code;
        echo "The object is created: ",$this->code,"\n";
    }
    # The destructor:
    function __destruct(){
        echo "The object is deleted: ",$this->code,"\n";
    }
}
# Creates objects:
$A=new MyClass();
$B=new MyClass(321);
?>
```

The result of the program execution is as follows.

The output of the program (from Listing 7-3)

```
The object is created: 123
The object is created: 321
The object is deleted: 321
The object is deleted: 123
```

The program describes the MyClass class. The class has the $code field, the constructor, and the destructor. The constructor has a single argument (denoted as $code) with the default value 123. In the constructor, the $this->code=$code command is executed, which assigns a value (the method argument) to the $code field of the object being created.

(i) **Note**   Thus, if an argument is passed to the constructor, its value becomes the value of the $code field of the created object. If no argument is passed to the constructor, the field gets the default value 123.

The echo "The object is created: ",$this->code,"\n" command displays a message that the object has been created and informs about the value of its field.

(i) **Note**   So, when an object is created, a message about that automatically appears, and it also contains information about the value of the object's field.

The destructor contains only one command echo "The object is deleted: ",$this->code,"\n", which informs you that the object is deleted.

In addition to the class description, the program contains two commands, $A=new MyClass() and $B=new MyClass(321), which create objects of the MyClass class. When the $A object is created, no arguments are passed to the constructor, so the $code field of that object is set to 123.

Details

If no arguments are passed to the constructor, you can put empty parentheses or not put them after the class name in the command that creates the object. In other words, instead of the $A=new MyClass() command, you could use the $A=new MyClass command.

When the $B object is created, the value 321 is passed to the constructor as an argument. That is the value of the $code field of the $B object.

Each time an object is created, a constructor is called. The command displays a message in the constructor that the object was created. You create two objects, so two messages appear. Two more messages automatically appear when objects are deleted from memory. You see that the program ends with the commands creating objects. There are no other commands in the program. Therefore, after the objects are created, the program is terminated. But before the program is terminated, all created objects are automatically deleted from memory.

As you already know, the destructor is called before the object is deleted. The command executed in the destructor displays a message that the object is deleted. Two objects were created, so two objects were also deleted.

(i) **Note**   Objects are deleted in the reverse order as they were created: the last created object is deleted first.

Details

In the previous versions of PHP, there was another way to create the constructor. It differs from the one described in that the constructor's name is not __ construct(), but its name matches the name of the class. In this case, that would be the MyClass() method.

🖒 **The PHP 8 Standard**

In PHP 8, a method whose name is the same as the name of its class is no longer interpreted as the constructor.

Static Fields and Methods

The fields and methods that were described in the classes in the previous examples were ordinary—that is, non-static. But, as noted earlier, a class can also contain static members—*static* fields and static methods.

From a formal point of view, creating a static field or method is easy. You describe it with the `static` keyword. But what is the difference between a static field or method and a non-static field or method? If ordinary (non-static) fields and methods are "attached" to an object, then static class members do not belong to any object. They exist on their own (but in the context of the class in which they are described).

To refer to a static field or class method, specify the class name followed by a double colon (`::`), and then the name of the field or method (with arguments in parentheses) follows. If you call a static method or refer to a static field inside the class code, the `self` keyword is used instead of the class name.

Listing 7-4 describes a class with a static field and two static methods.

Listing 7-4. Static Fields and Methods

```php
<?php
  # A class with static members:
  class MyClass{
    # A static field:
    public static $name;
    # Static methods:
    static function rename($name){
      self::$name=$name;
    }
    static function hello(){
      echo "The name: ",self::$name,"\n";
    }
```

```
}
# The value of the static field:
MyClass::$name="Alpha";
// Calls the static methods:
MyClass::hello();
MyClass::rename("Bravo");
MyClass::hello();
?>
```

The output of the program is as follows.

The output of the program (from Listing 7-4)

```
The name: Alpha
The name: Bravo
```

The MyClass class has the static field $name. The rename() static method is designed to change the value of the $name field (the method argument has the same name). Assigning a value to the field is realized by the self::$name=$name command in the method. There, the $name instruction means the method's argument, and the static field is accessed by the self::$name instruction.

The static hello() method has no arguments. When the method is called, the echo "The name: ",self::$name,"\n" command is executed, which displays the value of the static field.

After the class is declared, the MyClass::$name="Alpha" command assigns the "Alpha" string to the $name static field of the MyClass class. Here, you should pay attention to how the static field $name of the MyClass class is accessed: since you are accessing the field outside the class, use the MyClass::$name instruction, which contains the class name. Also noteworthy is that you have not yet created objects for the MyClass class and do not plan to create them.

The MyClass::hello() and MyClass::rename("Bravo") commands
are used to call the static methods. In the first case, the value of the static
field $name of the MyClass class is displayed, and the second command sets
the field to "Bravo" (after which the hello() method is called again in the
program).

Copying Objects

From a practical point of view, such a task as copying objects is important.
Let's look at the example program shown in Listing 7-5.

Listing 7-5. Assigning Objects

```php
<?php
    # The description of a class:
    class MyClass{
        public $code;
        function __construct($code){
            $this->code=$code;
        }
        function show(){
            echo "The field \$code: ",$this->code,"\n";
        }
    }
    # Creates an object:
    $A=new MyClass(100);
    echo "The object \$A\n";
    $A->show();
    # Assigns objects:
    $B=$A;
    echo "The object \$B\n";
    $B->show();
```

```
   # Changes the value of the field of the initial object:
   $A->code=200;
   echo "The object \$A\n";
   $A->show();
   echo "The object \$B\n";
   $B->show();
?>
```

The following is the result of the program execution.

The output of the program (from Listing 7-5)

```
The object $A
The field $code: 100
The object $B
The field $code: 100
The object $A
The field $code: 200
The object $B
The field $code: 200
```

The program defines the MyClass class with the $code field, the one-argument constructor (defines the value of the $code field), and the show() method that displays the field's value.

Based on the MyClass class, the $A=new MyClass(100) command creates the $A object, whose $code field gets the value 100. Using the show() method, check the value of that field. Then, the $B=$A command is executed. But the copying of objects, in that case, does not happen. The $A variable does not contain the object but only refers to it. The situation can be interpreted so that the $A variable contains the object's address. Therefore, as a result of executing the $B=$A command, the address from the $A variable is copied to the $B variable. So, it turns out that the $B variable refers to the same object as the $A variable. Therefore, if you change the value of the $code field of the $A object (the $A->code=200 command), the check shows that the value of the $code field of the $B object has also changed. But once again, you deal with the same object here.

So, how can you create a copy of an object? One of the easiest ways is to use the clone instruction in the object assignment command. In particular, the $B=clone $A command could be used instead of the $B=$A command. The new version of the program that copies objects is shown in Listing 7-6.

Listing 7-6. Copying Objects

```php
<?php
  class MyClass{
    public $code;
    function __construct($code){
      $this->code=$code;
    }
    function show(){
      echo "The field \$code: ",$this->code,"\n";
    }
  }
  $A=new MyClass(100);
  echo "The object \$A\n";
  $A->show();
  # Copies objects:
  $B=clone $A;
  echo "The object \$B\n";
  $B->show();
  $A->code=200;
  echo "The object \$A\n";
  $A->show();
```

```
    echo "The object \$B\n";
    $B->show();
?>
```

The result of the program execution is as follows.

The output of the program (from Listing 7-6)
```
The object $A
The field $code: 100
The object $B
The field $code: 100
The object $A
The field $code: 200
The object $B
The field $code: 100
```

The result of the program execution proves that a copy of the object was indeed created.

Private Fields and Methods

The previous examples used public fields and methods. Their "publicity" allowed access to them outside the class code. However, making fields or methods private is often reasonable and convenient. Such class members are described with the private keyword and are available only inside the class code. What does it give to us? The point is that private members of a class are more difficult to use in an "unsupposed" manner. In other words, if a field or method is used to solve additional routine tasks and is not proposed for the "end user," it is better to "hide" such a field or method. The situation is illustrated in Listing 7-7.

Listing 7-7. Private Members of a Class

```php
<?php
    // A class:
    class MyClass{
        // The private field:
        private $code;
        // The method for reading the field value:
        function get(){
            return $this->code;
        }
        // The method for assigning a value to the field:
        function set($code){
            $this->code=$code;
        }
        // The private constructor:
        private function __construct($code){
            $this->set($code);
        }
        // The static method for creating objects:
        static function create($code){
            return new self($code);
        }
    }
    // Creates an object:
    $obj=MyClass::create(100);
    // Checks the field:
    echo "The field: ",$obj->get(),"\n";
    // Assigns a value to the field:
    $obj->set(200);
    // Checks the field:
    echo "The field: ",$obj->get(),"\n";
?>
```

The following is the program's output.

The output of the program (from Listing 7-7)
```
The field: 100
The field: 200
```

You describe the MyClass class with a private $code field and two public non-static methods. The get() method returns the value of the $code field of the object from which the method is called (the return $this->code statement in the method body).

The set() method has one argument (denoted as $code) and is designed to assign a value to the $code field of the object from which the method is called. The $this->code=$code instruction in the method's body solves the task.

The class has a constructor with one argument to pass when creating an object, and the argument determines the value of the object's $code field. And you do that by calling the set() method. But the tricky moment is that the constructor is described with the private keyword. That is, it is private. So, you cannot create an object outside the class code using the new instruction. Then how can you create objects? For that purpose, you create the public static create() method. The method has one argument (denoted as $code). The argument defines the value of the object's field of the same name, the reference to which is returned by the method as a result. The object itself is created by the new self($code) statement in the method body. The result of the expression is a reference to the created object. It is the reference that is returned by the method. The self keyword is used to identify the class from which the method is called.

Since you cannot create an object in the usual way, you use the $obj=MyClass::create(100) command to create an object of the MyClass class. The $code field of the created object gets the value 100. However, since the $code field is private, you cannot access it directly. If you want to get the value of the field, use the $obj->get() instruction, which calls the public get() method from the $obj object.

To assign a value to the field of the object, call the set() method, as is done with the $obj->set(200) command.

ⓘ **Note** It turns out that the $code field of the object is private, so you cannot perform operations directly with it outside the class code. But you can access the field using public methods. In particular, use public methods to read the field's value and assign a value to the field.

Special Methods

There is a group of methods that solve "special" tasks. The names of those methods begin with a double underscore. Let's explore them next.

ⓘ **Note** As you might guess, the __construct() and __destruct() methods (the constructor and the destructor) are also special ones.

Let's start with the __toString() method. That method is called automatically every time an object is in the place where a string should be. Examples are when the object is concatenated with a string using the dot operator or when the object is passed as an argument to the print() function or to the echo statement. Let's look at the example in Listing 7-8.

Listing 7-8. The __toString() Method

```php
<?php
    // The description of the class
    // with the __toString() method:
    class MyClass{
        // The fields:
        public $name;
        public $code;
        // The constructor:
        function __construct($name,$code){
            $this->name=$name;
            $this->code=$code;
        }
        // The __toString() method:
        public function __toString(){
            $txt="The fields of the object:\n";
            $txt.="The field \$name = $this->name\n";
            $txt.="The field \$code = $this->code\n";
            return $txt;
        }
    }
    // Creates an object of the class:
    $obj=new MyClass("Object",123);
    // Explicitly calls the method __toString():
    echo "Call the method __toString() explicitly:\n";
    echo $obj->__toString();
    // Implicitly calls the method __toString():
    echo "Call the method __toString() implicitly:\n";
    echo $obj;
    $text=$obj."The program is over";
    print($text);
?>
```

The result of the program execution is as follows.

The output of the program (from Listing 7-8)
```
Call the method __toString() explicitly:
The fields of the object:
The field $name = Object
The field $code = 123
Call the method __toString() implicitly:
The fields of the object:
The field $name = Object
The field $code = 123
The fields of the object:
The field $name = Object
The field $code = 123
The program is over
```

The program describes the MyClass class, which has two fields ($name and $code). The class also has a constructor with two arguments that define the values of the fields. In addition, it describes the __toString() method. The method has no arguments and returns a string as a result. The string is formed in several steps and contains information about the values of the object's fields.

Based on the MyClass class, you create the $obj object. In the $obj->__toString() statement, the __toString() method is called explicitly, like an ordinary method. But when the echo $obj instruction is executed, the __toString() method is called automatically from the $obj object, and the result of the method replaces the reference to that object. The method is also called implicitly when the $text=$obj."The program is over" command is executed. There, you concatenate the object with a string. That operation is performed as follows: the __toString() method is called from the $obj object, and the string result of the method is concatenated with the second string operand.

🔔 The PHP 8 Standard

In PHP 8, if the __toString() method is declared in a class, then that class automatically implements the Stringable interface. Interfaces are discussed later.

Let's explore three more special methods: __set(), __get(), and __call(). They are used when referring to members of a class. Namely, the __call() method is called if a call is made to the non-existing object method.

The arguments of the __call() method are the name of the called method and the list of arguments passed to the called method.

Details

If a method is called from an object and the object does not have such a method, then the __call() method is automatically called from the object. The first argument of the __call() method is the name of the non-existing method. The second argument of the __call() method is an array whose elements are the arguments passed to the non-existing method.

Listing 7-9 is an example of using the __call() method.

Listing 7-9. The special __call() Method

```php
<?php
    // The class with a special method:
    class MyClass{
        // The method:
        public function show($txt){
```

```
        echo $txt."\n";
    }
    // The special method:
    public function __call($name,$args){
        if(strlen($name)>5){
            echo "The arguments: ",sizeof($args),"\n";
            echo "The $name() method does not exist!\n";
        }else{
            for($k=0;$k<sizeof($args);$k++){
                echo "[",$k+1,"] $args[$k]\n";
            }
        }
    }
}
// An object of the class:
$obj=new MyClass();
// Calls an existing method:
$obj->show("The MyClass class");
// Calls the non-existing methods:
$obj->display("Alpha");
$obj->hello("Bravo","Charlie","Delta");
?>
```

The following is the result of the program execution.

The output of the program (from Listing 7-9)
```
The MyClass class
The arguments: 1
The display() method does not exist!
[1] Bravo
[2] Charlie
[3] Delta
```

The program uses the MyClass class, which describes the ordinary show() method with one argument. When the method is called, the value of the argument passed to the method is displayed. You need that method to show that the presence of the __call() method does not affect the operation of ordinary methods in a class.

The special __call() method is declared with two arguments. The first argument $name means the name of the method that is called from the object and which the object does not have. The second argument, $args, is an array with the arguments passed to the non-existing called method.

You use a conditional statement in the method's body that tests the strlen($name)>5 condition. The condition is true if the name of the called (non-existing) method consists of more than five characters. If so, echo "The arguments: ",sizeof($args),"\n" displays a message informing about the count of arguments passed to the method. echo "The $name() method does not exist!\n" displays a message stating that the method does not exist.

If the strlen($name)>5 condition is false and the name of the called method has no more than 5 characters, a loop statement is launched that iterates over the elements of the $args array (the arguments passed to the non-existing method) and displays their values.

Details

The sizeof() function is used to calculate the size of an array. The length of a string is calculated using the strlen() function.

Based on the MyClass class, create the $obj object. If you call the existing show() method from that object, everything happens as it should, without surprises.

The $obj->display("Alpha") command calls the non-existing display() method with the "Alpha" argument from the $obj object. The name of the method consists of more than five characters. So, when

228

the __call() method is automatically called, it displays the message that the method does not exist, and it also contains information about the number of arguments passed to the method (in this case, there is one argument).

The other non-existing method is called by the $obj->hello("Bravo", "Charlie","Delta") instruction. The method name is now five characters long, so the automatically called __call() method displays the list of arguments passed to the method hello().

The __set() and __get() methods are automatically called when accessing the non-existing fields of an object. In particular, the __set() method is called if you try to assign a value to the field that does not exist. The arguments of the method __set() are the name of the field to which the value is assigned and the assigned value itself.

Details

By default, if the non-existing field of an object is assigned a value, then such a field is added to the object. If the __set() method is defined in the class, then when a value is assigned to an inaccessible (non-existing or private) field, the __set() method is automatically called.

The __get() method is called if you try to read the value of the non-existing field. The name of that field is passed as an argument to the method __get().

The program that illustrates how to use the __get() method is shown in Listing 7-10.

Listing 7-10. The special __get() Method

```php
<?php
    // The class:
    class MyClass{
        // The public field:
```

```php
    public $number=321;
    // The private field:
    private $code=100;
    // The method to access the private field:
    public function get(){
        return $this->code;
    }
    // The method handles the access
    // to the non-existing field:
    public function __get($name){
        if(isset($this->$name)) return $this->$name/2;
        return 123;
    }
}
// Creates objects:
$obj=new MyClass();
// The reference to the public field:
echo "\$number: ",$obj->number,"\n";
// The reference to the private field:
echo "\$code: ",$obj->code,"\n";
echo "get(): ",$obj->get(),"\n";
// The reference to the non-existing field:
echo "\$value: ",$obj->value,"\n";
?>
```

The result of the program execution is as follows.

The output of the program (from Listing 7-10)

```
$number: 321
$code: 50
get(): 100
$value: 123
```

The MyClass class has the public field $number with the value 321 and the $code private field with the value 100. The class has the ordinary get() method with no arguments, which returns the value of the private field $code.

In addition, the special __get() method is described in the class, automatically called when an attempt is made to access the inaccessible field. The method's only argument is denoted as $name. It identifies the name of the field being accessed.

In the method's body, a conditional statement is executed in a simplified form. It checks the isset($this->$name) condition. The condition is true if the object has the requested field (but unavailable). If the field is present, then the returned value is half the value of the field (the return $this->$name/2 command). Here, implicitly assume that you deal with a numeric field. If the object does not have the requested field, the __get() method returns the value 123.

Details

A field can be inaccessible because the object does not have it or the field is private. The __get() method is automatically called in both cases. You use the conditional statement to check if the object has a private field with the requested name.

You should also pay attention to the $this->$name instruction. Here, the $name variable contains the name of the field. In other words, this is not about the $name field but the field whose name is the value of the $name variable (argument).

After creating the $obj object of the MyClass class, access the fields of that object. The result of the $obj->number expression is the value 321 of the $number field of $obj.

The $obj->code instruction accesses the private field $code of the $obj object. The field is there, but there is no access to it. The value of the private $code field is 100. That is the value returned by the get() method (the $obj->get() instruction). But the value of the $obj->code expression is twice less (that is, 50). It is the value returned by the __get() method. It is called automatically when the $obj->code expression is processed.

The $obj->value instruction accesses the non-existing $value field. In that case, the __get() method returns the value 123.

The program that uses the special __set() method is shown in Listing 7-11.

Listing 7-11. The special __set() Method

```php
<?php
// The class description:
class MyClass{
    // The public field:
    public $number;
    // The private field:
    private $code;
    // The method to access the private field:
    public function get(){
        return $this->code;
    }
    // The method to assign a value
    // to the private field:
    public function set($code){
        $this->code=$code;
    }
    // The special method is called when
    // assigning a value to the inaccessible field:
    public function __set($name,$arg){
        if(isset($this->$name)) $this->$name=$arg/2;
        else $this->$name=2*$arg;
    }
}
```

```
// Creates an object:
$obj=new MyClass();
// Assigns values to the fields:
$obj->number=123;
$obj->set(321);
// Checks the values of the fields:
echo "\$number: ",$obj->number,"\n";
echo "\$code: ",$obj->get(),"\n";
// Assigns a value to the private field:
$obj->code=100;
// Assigns a value to the non-existing field:
$obj->value=100;
// Checks the values of the fields:
echo "\$code: ",$obj->get(),"\n";
echo "\$value: ",$obj->value,"\n";
?>
```

The following is what you get when running the program.

The output of the program (from Listing 7-11)

```
$number: 123
$code: 321
$code: 50
$value: 200
```

🔔 The PHP 8 Standard

In versions higher than PHP 8, the creation of dynamic properties is deprecated. Thus, the $obj->value=100 command causes a warning. To avoid that, you can use the #[\AllowDynamicProperties] annotation for the MyClass class (put the annotation before the class description).

The MyClass class has the public $number field, the private $code field, the public get() method to read the value of the $code field, and the set() method to set the value to that field.

The __set() method is described with two arguments. The first argument $name specifies the field name to which the value is assigned. The second argument $arg is the value to assign to the field.

The core of the method code is a conditional statement. You check the isset($this->$name) condition in the conditional statement. It is true if the object has the corresponding field. If the condition is true, the $this->$name=$arg/2 command is executed. In that case, the field gets half the value passed for assigning. If the condition is false, then $this->$name=2*$arg is executed. As a result, the object gets a corresponding field, and the field's value is twice the value you tried to assign to the field.

ⓘ **Note**   If you assign a value to the unavailable private field, that field gets half the value you assign. If you assign a value to the non-existing field, the field is added to the object and gets twice the value you assign.

Based on the MyClass class, create the $obj object. After that, you use the $obj->number=123 command to assign the value 123 to the public field $number, and the $obj->set(321) command sets the value 321 to the $code private field. Here, everything happens without any intrigue. Therefore, the $obj->number expression gives 123, and the $obj->get() expression gives 321.

In the next step, you try to assign a value to the private $code field with the $obj->code=100 command. In that case, the __set() method is automatically called. Since the $obj object has the $code field, the value of that field is not 100 but 50. Checking it with the $obj->get() instruction confirms the predictions.

The $obj->value=100 command attempts to assign the value 100 to the non-existing $value field. In that case, the __set() method is also called. As a result, the $value field is added to the object and gets the value 200. The field's value can be checked using the $obj->value statement.

Defining Fields in the Constructor

The constructor in a class often assigns values to the fields of the object being created. In that case, the fields are declared in the class, and the constructor contains commands that assign values to the fields (based on the constructor's arguments). In practice, it looks like the following.

```
class MyClass{
    // The field:
    public $code;
    // The constructor:
    function __construct($code){
        // The field is assigned a value:
        $this->code=$code;
    }
}
```

235

Here, you deal with the MyClass class, which has the public $code field and the one-argument constructor. The constructor argument specifies the value of the field. Starting with PHP 8, combining the field declaration and field assignment can significantly reduce the code. Considering the innovations, the code could look like the following.

```
class MyClass{
    function __construct(public $code){}
}
```

What has changed? First, there is no field declaration. Second, in the constructor, no command assigns a value to the field. Third, the $code argument is preceded by the public access level specifier in the constructor declaration. That means the class has the $code field with the public access level. It also means that the argument passed to the constructor is automatically assigned as a value to the field.

Thus, if you specify an access level specifier for the argument in the description of the constructor argument, then that means the following.

- The class has the corresponding field.

- The constructor argument is assigned (automatically, no need to write a command) as a value to that field.

Next, let's analyze a small example.

🔔 The PHP 8 Standard

The code in Listing 7-12 runs only in PHP 8.

Listing 7-12 shows the class declaration with a constructor that defines two fields (one public and one private).

Listing 7-12. Defining Fields in the Constructor

```php
<?php
    // The declaration of a class:
    class MyClass{
        // The fields are declared in the constructor:
        function __construct(public $code,private $name){
            echo "The object is created: $code and $name\n";
        }
        // The method for displaying the fields:
        function show(){
            echo "The field \$code = ",$this->code,"\n";
            echo "The field \$name = ",$this->name,"\n";
        }
    }
    // Creates an object:
    $obj=new MyClass(123,"MyClass");
    // Checks the fields:
    $obj->show();
?>
```

The result of the program execution is as follows.

The output of the program (from Listing 7-12)
The object is created: 123 and MyClass
The field $code = 123
The field $name = MyClass

In the constructor of the MyClass class, the $code argument is declared with the public specifier, and the $name argument is declared with the private specifier. That means the class has the public field $code and the private field $name. The constructor's first argument is assigned as a value to the $code field, and the constructor's second argument specifies the value of the $name field. The constructor contains the echo "The object is created: $code and $name\n" command, which displays a message with information that the object is created and the values of the arguments passed to the constructor.

Details

Constructor arguments are named the same as class fields. In the constructor, the $code and $name instructions refer to the constructor's arguments. You access the fields using the $this->code and $this->name instructions.

The show() method is described in the MyClass class. When the method is called, it displays the $code and $name fields of the object from which the method is called.

After the MyClass class is declared, use the $obj=new MyClass(123,"MyClass") command to create an object based on the class. After that, call the show() method from the object (the $obj->show() statement).

A constructor can have both ordinary arguments and arguments that declare fields. An example similar to the previous one is shown in Listing 7-13.

Listing 7-13. Ordinary Arguments and the Arguments That Declare Fields in the Constructor

```php
<?php
    class MyClass{
        // The private field:
        private $name;
        function __construct(public $code,$name){
            // The field is assigned a value:
            $this->name=$name;
```

```
        echo "The object is created: $code and $name\n";
    }
    function show(){
        echo "The field \$code = ",$this->code,"\n";
        echo "The field \$name = ",$this->name,"\n";
    }
}
$obj=new MyClass(123,"MyClass");
$obj->show();
?>
```

The second argument in the constructor of the MyClass class is a regular argument, and the private field of the same name in the class is traditionally declared. You also added the command that assigns the constructor's second argument to the $name field. In all other aspects, the examples are similar. The result of the program execution is the same as in the previous case.

Summary

- Objects are created from classes and can contain fields and methods.

- The class declaration begins with the class keyword, followed by the class name and, in curly braces, the class description.

- The fields and methods declared in a class are called class members. Methods are described as ordinary functions. When describing fields, field values can be omitted.

- To determine the access level, you can use the keywords (access level specifiers) `private` (the private class member), `protected` (the protected class member), and `public` (the public class member). The absence of an access level specifier means the corresponding class member is public.

- To create an object based on a class, use the `new` instruction followed by the name of the class. The result of the corresponding expression is a reference to the created object. That reference is assigned as a value to an object variable.

- No copy of the object is created when assigning object variables, and the two variables refer to the same object. The assignment statement should contain the `clone` instructions to create a copy of the object.

- The constructor is a method automatically called when an object is created. It is named `__construct()` and can take arguments. If so, the constructor's arguments are specified in the statement that creates an object in parentheses after the class name.

- The destructor is a method called automatically when an object is removed from memory. The destructor is named `__destruct()` and has no arguments.

- A class can contain static fields and methods. Such class members are declared with the `static` keyword. Static class members are not tied to any particular object and exist regardless of whether any objects of the corresponding class were created.

- To access the fields of an object, use the instructions of the $object->field form, and the $ symbol is not indicated in the field name. A method from an object is called by a command like $object->method(arguments). Access to static class members is performed in the class::$field and class::method(arguments) format.

- The $this keyword is used in a class as an identifier for the object from which the method is called. The self keyword is used in a class as the class identifier when accessing static fields and methods.

- There are special methods with a special purpose that are called automatically. The names of those methods begin with a double underscore. Among those methods are __toString() (automatically called to convert an object to a string), __call() (automatically called when trying to call the non-existing method), __get() (automatically called when trying to read the value of the inaccessible field), and __set() (automatically called when trying to assign a value to the unavailable field).

- Starting with PHP 8, you can combine argument descriptions and field declarations in the class constructor. In that case, an access level specifier is supplied for the argument that automatically creates the corresponding field and assigns a value based on the argument passed to the constructor.

CHAPTER 8

Inheritance

It's all very nice, but I didn't get it!

—*ALF* (TV series)

This chapter is devoted to such a critical OOP mechanism as inheritance. Along with encapsulation and polymorphism, inheritance is one of the three pillars on which the knowledge of OOP rests. Next, you learn how inheritance is implemented in PHP.

Creating a Child Class

So, let's say that you have a class that you would like to modify (add some new properties and methods to it). In principle, you can simply modify the code of the corresponding class. But the situation is complicated because the programs already use the class. Therefore, the idea of modifying the code of an already existing class is not the best one. The idea of describing a new class from scratch, duplicating, in addition to new fragments, the contents of the original class is also not productive. First, in that case, you have to repeat the existing code. In programming, such a style is usually a sign of a badly created program. Second, if you later have to make changes to the original class (for example, by changing the code of one

A. Vasilev, *PHP by Example*, https://doi.org/10.1007/979-8-8688-0258-4_8

of the methods), you may need to make changes to the newly created class synchronously. So, what are you going to do? In such a situation, it is reasonable to use the *inheritance mechanism*.

The idea is simple: create a new class based on an existing one. In that case, the newly created class automatically inherits all public and protected methods from the original class. (What happens to the private members of the class is a special case, which is discussed a little later.) The class from which the new class is created is called the *parent* or *base* class. A class created based on the parent class is called a *child* or *derived* class.

Note   PHP allows multilevel inheritance: from a parent class, you can create a child class, from which another child class can be created, and from it, the next child class, and so on. Thus, child and parent classes are relative: a class can be a child for some class and a parent for another class.

However, PHP does not allow multiple inheritance: a child class can have one and only one parent class.

From a technical point of view, creating a child class is very simple: in the class description, after its name, you put the extends keyword and the name of the parent class. The description of the child class specifies only those fields and methods that should be appended to the child class in addition to the members from the parent class. The members of the parent class are automatically available in the child class. The child class declaration template looks as follows.

```
class Bravo extends Alpha{
    # The description of the class
}
```

That pattern means the Bravo class is created based on the Alpha class. In the Bravo class, you need to describe only those members you want to append to the inherited members from the Alpha class.

Details

The situation is as if all public and protected members of the Alpha class were declared in the Bravo class. In the body of the Bravo class, you can directly access those class members.

Listing 8-1 is a program that creates and uses parent and child classes.

Listing 8-1. Creating a Child Class

```php
<?php
    // The parent class:
    class Alpha{
        // The field:
        public $number;
        // The method for assigning a value to the field:
        public function setNumber($number){
            $this->number=$number;
        }
    }
    // The child class:
    class Bravo extends Alpha{
        // The field:
        public $symbol;
        // The method for assigning a value to the field:
        public function setSymbol($symbol){
            $this->symbol=$symbol;
        }
```

```php
    // The method for assigning values
    // to both fields:
    public function setAll($symbol,$number){
        // Calls the method described
        // in the parent class:
        $this->setSymbol($symbol);
        // Calls the inherited method:
        $this->setNumber($number);
    }
    // The method for displaying the fields:
    public function show(){
        // Calls the method described
        // in the parent class:
        echo "The field \$symbol: ",$this->symbol,"\n";
        // Calls the inherited method:
        echo "The field \$number: ",$this->number,"\n";
    }
}
// Creates an object:
$obj=new Bravo;
// Assigns values to the fields:
$obj->setSymbol('A');
$obj->setNumber(100);
// Displays the fields:
$obj->show();
// Assigns values to the fields:
$obj->setAll('B',200);
// Displays the fields:
$obj->show();
?>
```

The result of the program execution is as follows.

The output of the program (from Listing 8-1)
The field $symbol: A
The field $number: 100
The field $symbol: B
The field $number: 200

The program describes two classes: the Alpha parent class and the Bravo child class created based on the Alpha parent class.

The Alpha class has the public $number field and the public one-argument setNumber() method for assigning a value to the field.

Since the Bravo child class is based on the Alpha class, the Bravo class also has the $number field and the $setNumber() method, even though these class members are not defined in the Bravo class. But they are inherited from the Alpha class. In addition to the inherited members, you explicitly declared the public $symbol field and three public methods in the Bravo class. The setSymbol() method with one argument is designed to assign a value to the $symbol field. The setAll() method has two arguments. The method assigns values to the $number and $symbol fields. It contains the commands that call the setSymbol() and setNumber() methods.

The show() method has no arguments. When the method is called, it displays the $symbol and $number fields of the object from which it is called.

(i) **Note**   In the body of the child class, you handle the fields and methods inherited from the parent class as if they were declared directly in the child class.

The $obj=new Bravo command is used to create the $obj object based on the Bravo class.

> ⓘ **Note**   You do not create an object of the Alpha parent class since it is not particularly interesting. It would be an ordinary object of an ordinary class.

First, the $obj->setNumber(100) and $obj->setSymbol('A') commands assign values to the fields of the $obj object. You check the fields using the show() method. The $obj->setAll(200,'B') command is another way to change the fields of the $obj object.

Details

You also could directly access the $number and $symbol fields of $obj. Note that a member must be public to be accessed outside the class.

It is also worth mentioning that there is a way to prevent a particular class from being inherited. In that case, the class should be declared with the final keyword.

Overriding Methods

It is pretty convenient that, due to inheritance, a child class gets the fields and methods of its parent class. However, in some cases, it is necessary for the method inherited in a child class to be performed somewhat differently than it is implemented in the parent class. In other words, there are situations when an inherited method needs to be *overridden*. To override a method in a child class is easy. You just need to declare it explicitly. Listing 8-2 shows how that can be done.

Listing 8-2. Overriding Methods

```php
<?php
    // The parent class:
    class Alpha{
        // The field:
        public $number;
        // The method for assigning a value to the field:
        public function set(...$args){
            $this->number=$args[0];
        }
        // The method for displaying the field:
        public function show(){
            echo "The class Alpha\n";
            echo "The field \$number: ",$this->number,"\n";
        }
    }
    // The child class:
    class Bravo extends Alpha{
        // The field:
        public $symbol;
        // Overrides the method for assigning
        // values to the fields:
        public function set(...$args){
            parent::set($args[0]);
            $this->symbol=$args[1];
        }
        // Overrides the method for displaying
        // the fields:
        public function show(){
            echo "-----------------\n";
            parent::show();
```

```
        echo "The class Bravo\n";
        echo "The field \$symbol: ",$this->symbol,"\n";
    }
}
// An object of the parent class:
$A=new Alpha;
// Assigning a value to the field:
$A->set(100);
// Displays the field:
$A->show();
// An object of the child class:
$B=new Bravo;
// Assigns values to the fields:
$B->set(200,'B');
// Displays the fields:
$B->show();
?>
```

The result of the program execution is as follows.

The output of the program (from Listing 8-2)
```
The class Alpha
The field $number: 100
-----------------
The class Alpha
The field $number: 200
The class Bravo
The field $symbol: B
```

The Alpha parent class has the $number field and two public set()
and show() methods you plan to override in the child class. The show()
method has no arguments. When the method is called, it displays a

message with the name of the Alpha class and the $number field of the object from which the method is called. The set() method, which you need for assigning a value to the $number field, is described as one that can take an arbitrary number of arguments (formally, it is described with the $args argument preceded by an ellipsis). To understand why you did that, it is necessary to consider the following important circumstances. When overriding a method in a child class, the method must be declared with the same arguments as in the parent class. The set() method in the parent class assigns a value to a single field. In the child class, use the method to assign values to two fields. Therefore, use a trick: describe the method with an arbitrary number of arguments and use only those that are needed. In the parent class, that is the first argument accessed using the $args[0] instruction. The value is assigned to the $number field by the $this->number-$args[0] command in the method body.

⌂ The PHP 8 Standard

In PHP 8, a method with an arbitrary number of arguments can override a method with a fixed number of arguments (subject to type compatibility).

The Bravo child class is created by inheriting the Alpha class. The $symbol field also appears, and the set() and show() methods are overridden.

In the description of the set() method, the parent::set($args[0]) command calls the version of the set() method inherited from the parent class. Here, the general rule was used, according to which, if you want to access a parent class method, you should precede it with the parent keyword and a double colon (::). In particular, the parent::set($args[0]) statement means that when the set() method is called from an object of the Bravo class, the version of the method from the parent class (that is, the Alpha class) must be called first. The first argument of that version of the method (from the Alpha class) is defined by the first argument passed to the set() method (from the Bravo class). As a result, the $number field is assigned a value. To assign a value to the $symbol field, the $this->symbol=$args[1] command is used, according to which the second argument determines the value of the field passed to the set() method.

To override the show() method, the following commands were used. First, the echo "------------------\n" statement displays a "decorative" line, purely aesthetic, to separate the results of different calls to the show() method. The parent::show() command calls the version of the show() method from the Alpha parent class, after which the echo "The class Bravo\n" command displays a message, and then the value of the $symbol field is displayed (by the echo "The field \$symbol: ",$this->symbol,"\n" command).

The $A=new Alpha command creates the $A object based on the Alpha class. The set() and show() methods for that object are executed as described in the Alpha class.

The $B object of the Bravo child class is created by the $B=new Bravo command. You check directly that for the object, the show() and set() methods are executed differently (if compared to the $A object), namely, according to how they are overridden in the Bravo class.

ⓘ Note You can disable method overriding by declaring the method with the final keyword.

Constructors and Inheritance

Let's examine the program shown in Listing 8-3.

Listing 8-3. Constructors and Inheritance

```php
<?php
    // The parent class:
    class Alpha{
        // The constructor:
        function __construct(){
            echo "An object of the class Alpha is created\n";
        }
        // The destructor:
        function __destruct(){
            echo "An object of the class Alpha is deleted\n";
        }
    }
    // The child class (with an empty body):
    class Bravo extends Alpha{}
    // Creates an object of the child class:
    $obj=new Bravo;
?>
```

The following is the program's output.

The output of the program (from Listing 8-3)

An object of the class Alpha is created
An object of the class Alpha is deleted

You have created a very simple `Alpha` parent class. The class only has the constructor and the destructor. When you create an object, a message appears that an object of the `Alpha` class is created. When an object is removed from memory, a message appears that an object of the `Alpha` class is deleted.

The `Bravo` child class is based on the `Alpha` class. The body of the `Bravo` class is empty. You don't describe anything in it at all (you may do that, but why to do that is another question). Then, create an object based on the `Bravo` class. As a result, you get messages about creating and deleting an object of the `Alpha` class appearing in the output window. How is that possible? The parent class's constructor and the destructor of the parent class and other public methods are inherited in the child class. In this case, you did not describe either the constructor or the destructor for the `Bravo` child class. If so, the constructor and the destructor inherited from the `Alpha` parent class are used.

Another important point is that the constructor can be overridden in a child class. As you already know, if you override ordinary methods in a child class, you must describe them with the same arguments as in the parent class. But that rule does not apply to the constructors. In the child class, the constructor may have arguments different from the arguments of the constructor in the parent class.

Finally, as with regular methods, you can call the constructor and destructor from the parent class. To do that, use the `parent` keyword. Namely, an instruction of the form `parent::__construct(arguments)` means calling the parent class's constructor with the appropriate arguments. The `parent::__destruct()` statement means calling the destructor of the parent class. The corresponding example is shown in Listing 8-4.

Listing 8-4. The Constructor and the Destructor of a Child Class

```php
<?php
  // The parent class:
  class Alpha{
    // The field:
    public $number;
    // The constructor:
    function __construct($number){
      $this->number=$number;
      echo "The number: ",$this->number,"\n";
    }
    // The destructor:
    function __destruct(){
      echo "Deleted: the number ",$this->number,"\n";
    }
  }
  // The child class:
  class Bravo extends Alpha{
    // The field:
    public $symbol;
    // The constructor:
    function __construct($number,$symbol){
      echo "----------\n";
      parent::__construct($number);
      $this->symbol=$symbol;
      echo "The character: ",$this->symbol,"\n";
    }
    // The destructor:
    function __destruct(){
      echo "~~~~~~~~~~~~~~~~~~~~\n";
```

```
        parent::__destruct();
        echo "Deleted: the character ",$this->symbol,"\n";
    }
  }
  // Creates an object of the child class:
  $obj=new Bravo(200,'B');
?>
```

The result of the program execution is as follows.

The output of the program (from Listing 8-4)

```
The number: 200
The character: B
~~~~~~~~~~~~~~~~~~~~

Deleted: the number 200
Deleted: the character B
```

You have the Alpha parent class with the $number field, the constructor, and the destructor. The constructor is passed one argument that defines the value of the $number field. The constructor and the destructor display messages with the $number field value.

The Bravo child class, derived from the Alpha class, adds another field, $symbol, and overrides the constructor and the destructor. The constructor of the Bravo class has two arguments (named as $number and $symbol). One is passed as an argument to the parent class's constructor (the parent::__construct($number) instruction) and defines the value of the $number field. The other argument specifies the value of the $symbol field (the $this->symbol=$symbol statement).

In the destructor of the Bravo class, among other actions, the destructor from the Alpha class is called. To do that, use the parent::__ destruct() instruction.

The $obj=new Bravo(200,'B') command creates an object of the Bravo class, and due to that, the constructor of the child class is automatically called. Next, the destructor is automatically called before the program terminates.

Inheritance and Private Members

Let's explore what happens to private class members during inheritance starting with the program in Listing 8-5.

Listing 8-5. Private Members and Inheritance

```php
<?php
    // The parent class:
    class Alpha{
        // The private field:
        private $code;
        // The public method for assigning a value
        // to the field:
        public function set($code){
            $this->code=$code;
        }
        // The public method for getting
        // the value of the field:
        public function get(){
            return $this->code;
        }
    }
    // The child class:
    class Bravo extends Alpha{
        // The constructor:
        function __construct($code){
```

```
        // Calls the inherited methods:
        $this->set($code);
        echo "An object is created: ",$this->get(),"\n";
    }
}
// Creates an object of the child class:
$obj=new Bravo(123);
// Calls the inherited methods:
$obj->set(321);
echo "The field \$code: ",$obj->get(),"\n";
?>
```

The following is the result of the program execution.

The output of the program (from Listing 8-5)
```
An object is created: 123
The field $code: 321
```

The Alpha class has the private $code field and two public methods:
the set() method allows you to assign a value to the field, and the get()
method returns the field's value. Based on the Alpha class, the Bravo
class is created by inheritance. It inherits the public set() and get()
methods but does not (according to conventional terminology) inherit
the private $code field. It turns out that the Bravo class has the set() and
get() methods that require the $code field to operate properly, but that
field itself is not inherited. How can that be? To answer the question, it is
necessary to clarify what the phrase "not inherited" means. The matter
of fact is that the private field $code is not inherited in the Bravo class
because you cannot directly access the $code field in the body of the Bravo
class. You can interpret the situation so that the class "does not know"
anything about that field, but technically, such a field exists, and the set()
and get() methods can operate with it.

258

The set() and get() methods are used in the Bravo class constructor. The $this->set($code) command assigns a value to the $code field, and the $this->get() instruction is used to get the field's value.

A child class object is created with the $obj=new Bravo(123) command. The object has public set() and get() methods. The methods, in turn, refer to the "invisible," even for the Bravo class, the $code field. Thus, the $obj->set(321) command writes the value 321 to the field, and the $obj->get() instruction is used to get its value.

Details

You must remember the following important circumstances when working with private class members. If the non-existing field of an object is assigned a value, then the object gets such a field. Therefore, if you assign a value to a non-inherited private field from the parent class in the child class, then the object has such a field, and it is not the field described in the parent class.

Protected Members of a Class

In addition to public and private members, a class can also have protected class members. Protected class members are described with the protected access level specifier. Like private members, protected members of a class are available only within the class's code. But unlike private members, protected members are inherited. An example of using protected class members is shown in Listing 8-6.

Listing 8-6. Protected Class Members

```php
<?php
  // The parent class:
  class Alpha{
```

```
    // The protected field:
    protected $code;
}
// The child class:
class Bravo extends Alpha{
    // The method for assigning a value to the field:
    public function set($code){
        $this->code=$code;
    }
    // The method for displaying the field:
    public function show(){
        echo "The field \$code = ",$this->code,"\n";
    }
}
// Creates an object of the child class:
$obj=new Bravo;
// Assigns a value to the field:
$obj->set(123);
// Displays the field:
$obj->show();
?>
```

The result of the program execution is as follows.

The output of the program (from Listing 8-6)
The field $code = 123

The Alpha parent class has the single protected $code field. The field is only available in the body of the Alpha class. And that field is inherited in the Bravo child class. Therefore, in the body of the Bravo class, in the methods set() (the method for assigning a value to the field) and show() (the method for displaying the field value), you can directly access the inherited $code field (the instruction like $this->code).

The $obj object is created based on the Bravo class. The object has the $code field, but it is not directly accessible. To assign a value to the field, use the set() method (the $obj->set(123) command), and to display the field value, use the show() method (the $obj->show() command).

Virtual Methods

An interesting property of overridden methods is illustrated in Listing 8-7.

Listing 8-7. Virtual Methods

```php
<?php
   # The parent class:
   class Alpha{
      # The public method:
      function hello(){
         print("The class Alpha\n");
      }
      # The method calls another method:
      function show(){
         $this->hello();
      }
      # The constructor:
      function __construct(){
         print("Creates an object:\n");
         # Calls the method:
         $this->hello();
```

261

```
        print("----------------\n");
    }
}
# The child class:
class Bravo extends Alpha{
    # Overrides the method:
    function hello(){
        print("The class Bravo\n");
    }
}
# Creates an object of the child class:
$obj=new Bravo;
# Calls the inherited method:
$obj->show();
?>
```

The following is the result of the program execution.

The output of the program (from Listing 8-7)
Creates an object:
The class Bravo

The class Bravo

The idea behind the program is very simple. There is the Alpha parent class, and it has the public hello() method, which, when called, displays a message with the name of the Alpha class. The Alpha class also has the public show() method, in the body of which the hello() method is called. The class also has the constructor that calls the hello() method.

The Bravo child class, which is derived from the Alpha class, overrides the hello() method. The method now displays a message with the name of the Bravo class. What does happen? It turns out that the Bravo class inherits the show() method and the constructor from the Alpha class. Both the show() method and the constructor call the hello() method. And that method, in turn, is overridden in the Bravo class. The intrigue is which version of the hello() method is called when the show() method is called from an object of the Bravo class. The result of the program execution demonstrates that the constructor and the show() method, despite being described in the Alpha class, call the version of the hello() method described in the Bravo class. Such a feature of methods is called *virtuality*. The version of the called method is determined by the class of the object from which the method is called.

A Function as a Field Value

In the earlier examples, you assigned numeric or string values to fields. That does not mean that the possible values of an object field are limited to only those data types. In fact, the value of an object field can be almost anything. For example, let's investigate a situation when an anonymous function is assigned as a value to a field.

Note   Note that an anonymous function is described similarly to an ordinary function but without specifying a name. That construction can be assigned as a value to a variable or, as in this case, to a field of an object.

Consider the program shown in Listing 8-8.

Listing 8-8. A Function as a Field Value

```php
<?php
    // The class with a field:
    class MyClass{
        public $calc;
    }
    // A variable:
    $number=9;
    // Creates an object:
    $obj=new MyClass;
    // A function is assigned to the field:
    $obj->calc=function($n){
        return $n*$n;
    };
    // Checks the result:
    echo "Argument $number: ",($obj->calc)($number),"\n";
    // A function is assigned to the field:
    $obj->calc=function($n){
        return sqrt($n);
    };
    // Checks the result:
    echo "Argument $number: ",($obj->calc)($number),"\n";
?>
```

The following is the result of the program execution.

The output of the program (from Listing 8-8)

Argument 9: 81
Argument 9: 3

Let's analyze the code using the MyClass class, which has the public $calc field. Based on the MyClass class, create the $obj object. The following command assigns a value to the $calc field of that object.

```
$obj->calc=function($n){
    return $n*$n;
};
```

The anonymous function assigned to the field returns the square of the $n argument. To calculate the result of the function to which the $calc field of the $obj object refers, use the ($obj->calc)($number) instruction. There, you engage parentheses to "calculate" at first the $obj->calc expression (it is a reference to the function). Then specify the $number argument (in parentheses) for that function.

_**i**_ **Note**   If the $number argument is set to 9, the result of the function is 81 (the number 9 squared).

After checking the result of the function, the $calc field is assigned a new value.

```
$obj->calc=function($n){
    return sqrt($n);
};
```

Now, the $calc field refers to the function that returns the square root of its argument.

_**i**_ **Note**   The sqrt() built-in function is used to calculate the square root. If the $number argument is set to 9, the result of the function is 3 (the square root of 9).

Multilevel Inheritance

As noted earlier, PHP allows multilevel inheritance when a child class is created based on a parent class, a new child class is created based on that child class, and so on. In such a case, the child class is a parent one for another child class. At the same time, inheritance allows you to "pass" the contents of the original parent class along the chain, and the overriding of methods makes that process quite flexible. The situation is illustrated in Listing 8-9.

Listing 8-9. Multilevel Inheritance

```php
<?php
    // The first class:
    class Alpha{
        // The protected field:
        protected $number;
        // The constructor:
        function __construct($number){
            $this->number=$number;
            $this->show();
        }
        // The method for displaying the field:
        function show(){
            echo "Alpha: ",$this->number,"\n";
            $this->drawLine();
        }
        // The method for displaying a "line":
        function drawLine(){
            echo "----------------\n";
        }
    }
```

```php
// The second class:
class Bravo extends Alpha{
    // The private field:
    protected $symbol;
    // The constructor:
    function __construct($number,$symbol){
        $this->symbol=$symbol;
        parent::__construct($number);
    }
    // Overrides the method:
    function show(){
        echo "Bravo: ",$this->number,"\n";
        echo "Bravo: ",$this->symbol,"\n";
        $this->drawLine();
    }
}
// The third class:
class Charlie extends Bravo{
    // The private field:
    protected $text;
    // The constructor:
    function __construct($name,$symbol,$text){
        $this->text=$text;
        parent::__construct($name,$symbol);
    }
    // Overrides the method:
    function show(){
        echo "Charlie: ",$this->number,"\n";
        echo "Charlie: ",$this->symbol,"\n";
```

```php
        echo "Charlie: ",$this->text,"\n";
        $this->drawLine();
    }
}
// Creates objects:
$A=new Alpha(100);
$B=new Bravo(200,'B');
$C=new Charlie(300,'C',"Charlie");
?>
```

The result of the program execution is as follows.

The output of the program (from Listing 8-9)

```
Alpha: 100
----------------

Bravo: 200
Bravo: B
----------------

Charlie: 300
Charlie: C
Charlie: Charlie
----------------
```

The scheme is as follows: based on the Alpha class, the Bravo class is created by inheritance, and based on the Bravo class, the Charlie class is created. The Alpha class has the protected $number field, the one-argument constructor, the show() method, and the drawLine() method.

In the constructor, the field is assigned a value, and then the show() method is called, which displays the value of the object's field and the name of the Alpha class.

Note   For convenience, the drawLine() method in the Alpha class is described. When called, it displays a decorative "line." That element separates the results of calling the show() method in all three classes. That is possible since the drawLine() method is inherited in all child classes.

The $number field, the constructor, the show(), and the drawLine() methods are inherited in the Bravo class. But the constructor and the show() method in that class are overridden. The constructor now has two arguments defining the values of the $number and $symbol fields (a protected field described in the Bravo class). The show() method is overridden so that when the method is called, the values of both fields and the name of the Bravo class are displayed.

In the Charlie class, the $number and the $symbol fields, the constructor, the show(), and the drawLine() methods are inherited from the Bravo class. At the same time, the show() method and the constructor are overridden. In the Charlie class, the constructor has three arguments that determine the $number, $symbol, and $text fields (the last one is a protected field described in the Charlie class). The show() method is overridden so that the values of the three fields and the name of the Charlie class are displayed when it is called.

The Alpha, Bravo, and Charlie classes are used to create objects. Executing the $A=new Alpha(100) command causes calling the constructor described in the Alpha class. As a result, the $number field of the $A object is set to 100, and the show() method (the version of the method from the Alpha class) is called from that object. The method displays the name of the Alpha class, the value of the $number field, and a separator line.

269

Executing the $B=new Bravo(200,'B') command leads to calling the constructor described in the Bravo class. Following the code of that constructor, the $symbol field is assigned a value, and then the parent class constructor is called (that is, the code of the constructor described in the Alpha class). So, the $number field gets a value, the show() method is called, and a separator line is displayed. Here, you need to consider an essential circumstance: due to the virtuality of the methods, the version of the show() method is called not from the Alpha class but from the Bravo class (since the object of that class is created). The show() method from the Bravo class displays the name of that class and the values of the created object's $number and $symbol fields.

The $C=new Charlie(300,'C',"Charlie") command results in the call of the constructor described in the Charlie class. That constructor assigns a value to the $text field and then calls the parent class version of the constructor, which for the Charlie class is the Bravo class. The execution of the constructor from the Bravo class starts with assigning a value to the $symbol field, after which the parent class's constructor is called (for the Bravo class, the parent class is the Alpha class). The execution of the constructor from the Alpha class starts with assigning a value to the $number field. Then, the show() method is called. But, due to the same virtuality of the methods, it is the version of the show() method from the Charlie class. As a result, it displays the name of the Charlie class, the values of the three fields of the created object, and a separator line.

Summary

- New classes can be created based on existing ones. Such a mechanism is called inheritance. The class from which the new class is derived is called a *parent class*. The class derived from a parent class is called a *child class*. All non-private fields and methods of a parent class are inherited in the child class.

- In the declaration of a child class, the class name is followed by the keyword extends and the name of the parent class. There can be only one parent class. On the other hand, a child class can be a parent one for another child class.

- The methods (including constructors and destructors) inherited in a child class can be overridden. In that case, a new version of the inherited method (or constructor/destructor) is described in the child class. The arguments in the new version of the method must match the arguments in the original version of the method. The rule does not apply to constructors. To access the version of a method (or constructor/ destructor) from the parent class, use the parent keyword, a double colon (::), and the method's name (or constructor/destructor).

- To prevent a method from being overridden, the final keyword is used in its description. The same keyword is used if you want to disable class inheritance.

- The private class members are not inherited. Such members cannot be directly accessed in a child class. However, they can be accessed by inherited public methods.

- Protected class members are declared using the protected access level specifier. Like the private members of a class, they are available only in the class code, but unlike the private members, the protected ones are inherited.

- Methods and constructors are virtual. That means the version of a method is determined by the class of the object from which the method is called.

CHAPTER 9

Advanced OOP Mechanisms

I don't know whether to laugh or cry.

—*ALF* (TV series)

This chapter explores the crucial mechanisms for implementing the OOP concept in PHP. In particular, you get familiar with interfaces, abstract classes, and traits. You also get some notion about a namespace and anonymous classes. Let's start with abstract classes.

Abstract Classes

When you create a class, you may not describe some methods but only declare them. In other words, you can specify that the class has some method but not specify what that method does. Such methods are called *abstract methods*.

ℹ️ **Note**   Why you would do such a thing is a different question. All that matters now is that it is possible to do so.

Abstract methods are declared with the abstract keyword. If a class has at least one abstract method, that class is also abstract and must be defined with the abstract keyword. But the question remains: why do you need all that?

In its most general form, the answer is that abstract classes are used in inheritance. To understand the depth of the answer, you should look at the inheritance process not in the context that you can pass fields and methods from the parent class to the child but in a slightly different way. The point is that the parent class defines the "structure" of the child class, which is created based on the parent class. To be more specific, let's look at an example (without having to write program code yet).

Suppose you want to create classes to implement objects describing different geometric shapes. More specifically, you want to create objects to implement a square, a circle, and an equilateral triangle. Each of these shapes has a characteristic size (the side of the square, the radius of the circle, and the side of the triangle). For each figure, you can calculate the area. Thus, each object that implements a geometric figure must have a field (the figure's characteristic size) and a method for calculating area.

Note   The area is calculated using the method because this characteristic of a geometric figure is determined by its characteristic size and must change according to how the characteristic size of the figure changes. It is best to use a method that, when called, refers to the field in which the characteristic size of the figure is written.

Note that the area of a square with side R is equal to R^2. The area of a circle of radius R is equal to πR^2. The area of an equilateral triangle with side R is defined by the expression $\dfrac{\sqrt{3}R^2}{4}$.

Thus, in all three cases, the objects have a similar structure. The only difference is how the method that calculates the area is implemented. But those are different objects, and they must be created based on different classes. Then, you can ask yourself: how do you get the different classes to have the same structure (the same set of fields and methods, but the implementation of the methods should be different)? The answer could be as follows: you can describe an abstract class and then create different classes based on it using inheritance. Those classes have the same structure defined by the abstract class.

(i) **Note**   In principle, instead of an abstract class to implement your strategy, you could take a regular class and override the inherited methods. But that is not a good option since if some method is accidentally not overridden, there is no formal error, but the code does not execute correctly. Such situations are pretty challenging to keep track of. Abstract classes are more reliable in that sense.

Let's examine Listing 9-1.

Listing 9-1. An Abstract Class

```php
<?php
    // An abstract class:
    abstract class Figure{
        // Protected fields:
        protected $name;
        protected $R;
        // The constructor:
        function __construct($R,$name){
            $this->R=$R;
            $this->name=$name;
        }
```

```php
    // An explicitly described method:
    function getName(){
        return $this->name;
    }
    // An abstract method:
    abstract function getArea();
}
// The class to realize a square:
class Square extends Figure{
    // The description of the method:
    function getArea(){
        $r=$this->R;
        return $r*$r;
    }
}
// The class to realize a circle:
class Circle extends Figure{
    // The description of the method:
    function getArea(){
        $r=$this->R;
        $k=3.141592;
        return $k*$r*$r;
    }
}
// The class to realize a triangle:
class Triangle extends Figure{
    // The description of the method:
    function getArea(){
        $r=$this->R;
        $k=sqrt(3)/4;
        return $k*$r*$r;
```

```
    }
}
// The function displays information about an object:
function show($F){
    echo $F->getName(),": ",$F->getArea(),"\n";
}
// Creates objects:
$S=new Square(2.5,"Square");
$C=new Circle(3,"Circle");
$T=new Triangle(4,"Triangle");
// Checks the result:
show($S);
show($C);
show($T);
?>
```

The following is the program's output.

The output of the program (from Listing 9-1)

Square: 6.25
Circle: 28.274328
Triangle: 6.9282032302755

In that case, you describe the abstract Figure class and then create the Square, Circle, and Triangle classes based on it.

The Figure class has two protected fields: $name (for the name of the figure) and $R (for the characteristic size of the geometric figure).

Details

On the one hand, you want the fields to be inaccessible outside the class code, but on the other hand, you need the fields to be inheritable. That is why you make the fields protected.

The Figure class has the constructor with two arguments that define the value of the fields $R and $name.

Since the $name field is protected, to read its value, you describe the getName() method, which returns the value of that field. You also declare the abstract getArea() method in the Figure class. Assume that that method should calculate the area of the figure. How exactly the area is calculated is defined in the child classes.

(i) **Note** The abstract class has an abstract method and a method described explicitly. The child class defines the abstract method and inherits the explicitly described method. The constructor and protected fields are also inherited.

The Square, Circle, and Triangle classes differ only in the way they implement the getArea() method; there is nothing else in them besides that method.

You create objects based on each class and then use the show() function to display information about those objects (the name and area). The important thing here is that in the description of the show() function, you refer to the getName() and getArea() methods of the object passed as an argument to the function. The function is called three times, and each time, it takes an object of a different class as an argument. But since all these classes are child classes of the abstract class Figure, each object has the getName() and getArea() methods.

Interfaces

Thus, abstract classes can be used as a template for creating other classes. They have a similar structure, which is very convenient in practice. There is one problem here, however. The point is that a child class can have only one parent class. If you need to "combine" several templates into one child class at the same time, the abstract class is of little help in that case. Fortunately, there is another mechanism that allows you to solve the problem. It is based on using *interfaces*.

An interface is very similar to an abstract class. The only fundamental difference is that an abstract class can have non-abstract methods, while an interface cannot. Also, an interface has no fields (but it can have constants— their description contains the const keyword). An interface can be considered a "very abstract" class. In that sense, the capabilities of an interface are more modest than those of an abstract class. The advantage of interfaces, however, is that a single class can implement several interfaces at once.

To use interfaces in practice, you first need to figure out how to create an interface and, second, how to implement it in a class.

Creating an interface is easy. It starts with the interface keyword, after which the contents of the interface are described in curly brackets. That is a declaration (without a description) of the methods that are part of the interface. There, you can use the access level specifiers public and protected. You can also declare constants.

If a class implements an interface, then all methods from the interface must be described in the class. The fact that the class implements an interface is stated in the class description: the name of the interface implemented in the class is given after the class name, using the keyword implements. If the class implements multiple interfaces, they are listed after the implements keyword, separated by commas. How all that looks like in practice is illustrated in Listing 9-2.

Listing 9-2. Getting Familiar with Interfaces

```php
<?php
    // The first interface:
    interface Alpha{
        function show();
    }
    // The second interface:
    interface Bravo{
        function set($val);
    }
    // The class implements two interfaces:
    class MyClass implements Alpha,Bravo{
        private $num;
        function __construct($val){
            $this->set($val);
        }
        function set($val){
            $this->num=$val;
        }
        function show(){
            echo "\$num = ",$this->num,"\n";
        }
    }
    // Creates an object of the class:
    $obj=new MyClass(100);
    // Checks the result:
    $obj->show();
    $obj->set(200);
    $obj->show();
?>
```

The following shows the result of the program execution.

The output of the program (from Listing 9-2)
```
$num = 100
$num = 200
```

The program describes two interfaces, Alpha and Bravo, and the MyClass class that implements both. The Alpha interface has the show() method (without arguments), and the Bravo interface has the set() method with one argument. Therefore, these methods are described in the MyClass class. In addition, the class has the private field $num and the constructor with one argument. When the constructor is called, it calls the set() method, which assigns a value to the $num field. The show() method is described so that the value of $num is displayed when it is called.

Based on the MyClass class, the $obj=new MyClass(100) command creates the $obj object with the value 100 of the field $num. The $obj->show() command checks the field's value. The $obj->set(200) command assigns a new value to the field.

Interface Inheritance

One interface can inherit another interface. Everything happens the same way as with class inheritance: the interface description is followed by the extends keyword, and then the name of the inherited interface follows. As a result, all the declarations from the inherited interface are "passed" to the interface being created. A small illustration is shown in Listing 9-3.

Listing 9-3. Interface Inheritance

```php
<?php
    // The interface:
    interface Alpha{
        function show();
    }
    // The Bravo interface inherits the Alpha interface:
    interface Bravo extends Alpha{
        function set($val);
    }
    // The class implements the Bravo interface:
    class MyClass implements Bravo{
        public $num;
        function set($val){
            $this->num=$val;
        }
        function show(){
            echo "\$num = ",$this->num,"\n";
        }
    }
    // Creates an object:
    $obj=new MyClass;
    // Checks the result:
    $obj->set(123);
    $obj->show();
?>
```

The following is the result of the program execution.

The output of the program (from Listing 9-3)

```
$num = 123
```

The example is similar to the previous one, but there is a strategic difference. As before, you declare the Alpha interface with the show() method. The Bravo interface declares the set() method. But apart from that, the Bravo interface inherits the Alpha interface. Therefore, the Bravo interface implicitly gets the show() method and the set() method. Accordingly, the MyClass class that implements the Bravo interface should contain (and does contain) descriptions of the set() and show() methods.

Note   A scheme where one interface inherits another interface and then is implemented in a class is not good. Let's explain that using the example. In particular, the Bravo interface only explicitly declares the set() method. You must trace the interface inheritance chain to understand that you must define the show() method when implementing the interface. That is not very good. The first option, when the class implements two different interfaces, is much more convenient since you can immediately identify the contents you need to implement in the class.

Class Inheritance and Interface Implementation

A class can inherit another class and implement an interface or interfaces. In such a case, in the class description after the class name, you put the extends keyword, the name of the inherited class, the implements keyword, and the names of the interfaces to be implemented. An example of that is shown in Listing 9-4.

Listing 9-4. Class Inheritance and Interface Implementation

```php
<?php
  // The parent class:
  class Base{
     public $number;
  }
  // The first interface:
  interface Alpha{
     function show();
  }
  // The second interface:
  interface Bravo{
     function set($number);
  }
  // The child class inherits the parent class
  // and implements two interfaces:
  class MyClass extends Base implements Alpha,Bravo{
     function set($number){
        $this->number=$number;
     }
     function show(){
        echo "\$number = ",$this->number,"\n";
     }
  }
  // Creates an object:
  $obj=new MyClass;
  // Checks the result:
  $obj->set(123);
  $obj->show();
?>
```

The following shows the result of the program execution.

The output of the program (from Listing 9-4)
$number = 123

The program describes the Base class with the $number field. In addition, you describe the Alpha interface with the show() method declared and the Bravo interface with the set() method declared. The MyClass class inherits the Base class and implements the Alpha and Bravo interfaces. The $number field is inherited from the Base class in the MyClass class so that you can refer to it in the description of the set() and show() methods. The $obj object is created based on the MyClass class, so it has the $number field and the show() and set() methods.

Traits

Both class inheritance and interface implementations solve one strategic problem: code reuse. There is another syntax construction designed to solve that problem. You mean *traits*.

A trait is a block of code that can be used when "constructing" a class. Traits do not play an independent role, but you can get a class by putting them together. A trait is described as follows. You use the trait keyword, after which a trait block is placed in curly braces. That is the block of code added to the class if you include the trait. To include traits in a class, you put the use instruction in the class body, then list the traits to be included in the class, separated by commas. Listing 9-5 shows how that looks in practice.

Listing 9-5. Getting Familiar with Traits

```php
<?php
  // The first trait:
  trait First{
    private $number;
    function show(){
      echo "\$number = ",$this->number,"\n";
      echo "\$symbol = ",$this->symbol,"\n";
    }
  }
  // The second trait:
  trait Second{
    function set($number,$symbol){
      $this->number=$number;
      $this->symbol=$symbol;
    }
  }
  // Including the traits in the class:
  class MyClass{
    use First,Second;
    private $symbol;
    function __construct($number,$symbol){
      $this->set($number,$symbol);
      $this->show();
    }
  }
  // Creates an object of the class:
  $obj=new MyClass(100,'A');
?>
```

The following is the program's output.

The output of the program (from Listing 9-5)
```
$number = 100
$symbol = A
```

The program's culmination is creating the MyClass class (with the subsequent creation of the $obj object based on the class). But you "assemble" that class "in parts." In particular, you describe two traits (the First and Second). The First trait contains the private field $number declaration, and the show() method. When the method is called, the values of the $number and $symbol fields are displayed (the $symbol field is not declared in the trait).

The Second trait describes the set() method with two arguments. When called, the method assigns values to the $number and $symbol fields (the fields are not declared in the trait).

The description of the MyClass class begins with the use First, Second instruction, which adds contents of the traits First and Second to the class.

---

i **Note**   The situation is as if the contents of the traits First and Second were described directly in the body of MyClass class.

In addition to the traits, you declare the private field $symbol in the class. You also describe the constructor with two arguments in the class. The set() and show() methods are called in the constructor so that the $number and $symbol fields get values, and then the values of those fields are displayed. So, the $obj=new MyClass(100,'A') command, which creates an object of the MyClass class, automatically displays a message.

Object Type Control

In some cases, ensuring that the object used in a program belongs to a specific class or implements a particular interface is important. Why is that necessary? For example, you describe a function and plan to pass an object as an argument to it, then call a certain method from the object. The object needs to have that method. How can you guarantee that? One way is to specify the argument type in the function description explicitly. But if you just specify the name of the class, then you can pass objects of that class only (or its child classes) as an argument to such a function. There is a more "refined" approach. It consists in creating an interface in which the needed method is declared. Then, you create a function with an argument whose type is the interface's name. If so, an object of any class implementing that interface can be passed as an argument of the function. The fact that the object implements the interface guarantees that the object has the needed method.

Details

You can create an abstract class with a declared method. If you specify the name of that abstract class as a function argument type, you can pass an object of any class that inherits the abstract class as a function argument.

The described approach is implemented in the program shown in Listing 9-6.

Listing 9-6. An Interface as a Type of Function Argument

```php
<?php
    // The interface:
    interface MyInterface{
        function show();
    }
```

```php
// The classes that implement the interface:
class Alpha implements MyInterface{
    function show(){
        echo "The class Alpha\n";
    }
}
class Bravo implements MyInterface{
    function show(){
        echo "The class Bravo\n";
    }
}
// The function with an argument of the interface type:
function display(MyInterface $obj){
    // Calls the method from the object:
    $obj->show();
}
// Creates objects:
$A=new Alpha();
$B=new Bravo();
// Passes the objects to the function as an argument:
display($A);
display($B);
?>
```

The program describes the MyInterface interface, in which the
show() method is declared. It also creates two classes, Alpha and Bravo,
implementing the MyInterface interface. The display() function has one
argument whose type is MyInterface. That means you can pass objects of
the classes that implement the MyInterface interface as an argument to
the function. That ensures the object being the argument has the show()
method. The method is called in the function from the object passed as an
argument.

To check if the display() function operates correctly, you first call it by passing an object of the Alpha class as an argument, and then you call it by passing an object of the Bravo class. The following shows the result of the program execution.

The output of the program (from Listing 9-6)
```
The class Alpha
The class Bravo
```

By specifying an interface type for the function argument, you set a "filter" for the potential function arguments.

ⓘ **Note**   An error arises if you try to pass an object of the class that does not implement the MyInterface interface to the display() function. It happens even if that class contains the show() method.

There is another way to check the type of argument, which is not as tragic in terms of consequences. It is based on the use of the instanceof instruction, which can be exploited to check if an object is of a specific type. Listing 9-7 is a version of the previous program, but this time, the type of the display() function argument is not explicitly specified. Instead, the argument type is checked in the function's body.

Listing 9-7. Checking the Argument Type

```php
<?php
    // The interface:
    interface MyInterface{
        function show();
    }
```

```php
// The class that implements the interface:
class Alpha implements MyInterface{
    function show(){
        echo "The class Alpha\n";
    }
}
// The class does not implement the interface:
class Bravo{
    function show(){
        echo "The class Bravo\n";
    }
}
// The argument type is checked in the function body:
function display($obj){
    if($obj instanceof MyInterface){
        $obj->show();
    }else{
        echo "The argument type error\n";
    }
}
// Creates objects:
$A=new Alpha();
$B=new Bravo();
// The object is passed as an argument to the function:
display($A);
display($B);
?>
```

The result of the program execution is as follows.

The output of the program (from Listing 9-7)
```
The class Alpha
The argument type error
```

Unlike the previous example (from Listing 9-6), the Bravo class contains a description of the show() method, but it does not implement the MyInterface interface. Also, the display() function description does not specify the argument type. But in the body of the function, you use a conditional statement. It checks the $obj instanceof MyInterface condition. It is true if the $obj argument of the function is of the type MyInterface. That is so if the class based on which the $obj object was created implements the MyInterface interface. In that case, the show() method is called from the $obj object. Otherwise, the echo "The argument type error\n" command is executed.

A Namespace

The concept of a namespace is universal and is used in many programming languages. To understand it, let's consider an imaginary situation unrelated to programming. Suppose a student community has two students whose names are identical (the same first, last, and middle names). It would be challenging to distinguish these students in the official documents. But if you separate the whole student community by groups and distribute the namesakes into different groups, then the situation with student identification significantly improves. Something similar happens when using namespaces. A namespace is an analogy to a group of students. Within the namespace, classes, functions, and other utilities should be distinguishable or, in other words, should have unique names. But if, for example, functions belong to different namespaces, they may have the same names.

To include a program into a namespace, you add the namespace instruction into the program and then put the name of the namespace. The instruction must be the first command in the code. Then, if you want to include some utilities in another program, you have to use the require_once instruction to add the file that contains the namespace. When referring to classes, functions, and other utilities from the imported namespace, you put the namespace name and the backslash \ before the class or function name.

Let's analyze a small example in which a namespace is created and used. A description of the MyUtils namespace is shown in Listing 9-8.

Listing 9-8. Creating a Namespace

```php
<?php
    // Creates a namespace:
    namespace MyUtils;
    // The description of a class:
    class MyClass{
        function show(){
            echo "The class MyClass\n";
        }
    }
    // The description of a function:
    function hello(){
        echo "The namespace MyUtils\n";
    }
?>
```

The code begins with the namespace MyUtils instruction, which means that the following MyClass class and the hello() function belong to the MyUtils namespace. It is assumed that the code is written to the listing09_08.php file.

The next step uses the created MyUtils namespace. The code in which that happens is shown in Listing 9-9.

Listing 9-9. Using the Namespace

```php
<?php
    // Includes the file contents into the program:
    require_once "listing09_08.php";
    // The function description:
    function hello(){
        echo "The function hello()\n";
    }
    // Creates an object from the imported namespace:
    $obj=new MyUtils\MyClass();
    // Calls a method from the object:
    $obj->show();
    // Calls the function described in the program:
    hello();
    // Calls the function from the imported namespace:
    MyUtils\hello();
?>
```

The program begins with the require_once "listing09_08.php" instruction, which imports the contents of the listing09_08.php file. The program also describes the hello() function. The name of the function matches the name of the function from the MyUtils namespace.

To create an object based on the MyClass class from the MyUtils namespace, use the $obj=new MyUtils\MyClass() command. Here, the way you refer to the class is remarkable: along with the name of the class, you specify the namespace name (the MyUtils\MyClass expression). Then, you can perform standard operations with the created object. For example, the $obj->show() command calls the show() method from the $obj object.

The hello() command calls the function described directly in the program. To call the function from the MyUtils namespace, use the MyUtils\hello() command. The result of the program execution is as follows.

The output of the program (from Listing 9-9)
The class MyClass
The function hello()
The namespace MyUtils

A single file may describe several namespaces (nevertheless, that is not the best option). If so, the blocks describing the contents of the namespaces (including the namespace instructions) are specified one after another. It is also possible to enclose the code of the same namespace in curly braces. Let's look at a small example. The program in Listing 9-10 describes the Alpha and Bravo namespaces.

Listing 9-10. The Description of Two Namespaces

```php
<?php
    // The first namespace:
    namespace Alpha{
        function show(){
            echo "The namespace Alpha\n";
        }
    }
    // The second namespace:
    namespace Bravo{
        function show(){
            echo "The namespace Bravo\n";
        }
    }
?>
```

Each namespace contains the show() function that displays a message with the namespace name. The namespaces are used in Listing 9-11.

Listing 9-11. Using the Two Namespaces

```php
<?php
    // Includes the contents of the file into the program:
    require_once "listing09_10.php";
    // Calls the function from the namespace Alpha:
    Alpha\show();
    // Calls the function from the namespace Bravo:
    Bravo\show();
?>
```

After importing the contents of the namespace file with the require_ once "listing09_10.php" command, use the Alpha\show() and Bravo\ show() commands to call the functions described in the different namespaces.

(i) **Note**   Assume that the Alpha and Bravo namespaces are described in the listing09_10.php file.

The following shows the result of the program execution.

The output of the program (from Listing 9-11)
The namespace Alpha
The namespace Bravo

When working with namespaces, it is possible to create aliases. In that case, you involve the use instruction followed by the full namespace utility reference. Next, you put the as keyword and the alias for that utility (for functions, the use keyword is also followed by the function keyword). Listing 9-12 is the code for the MyUtils namespace with the show() and display() functions and the MyClass class.

Listing 9-12. One More Namespace

```php
<?php
    // A namespace:
    namespace MyUtils;
    function show(){
        echo "The function show()\n";
    }
    function display(){
        echo "The function display()\n";
    }
    class MyClass{
        function __construct(){
            echo "An object of the class MyClass";
        }
    }
?>
```

The namespace is used in the program in Listing 9-13.

Listing 9-13. Creating Aliases

```php
<?php
    // Imports the file contents:
    require_once "listing09_12.php";
    // Creates aliases:
    use function MyUtils\show;
    use function MyUtils\display as disp;
    use MyUtils\MyClass as MyClass;
```

```
    // Uses aliases:
    show();
    disp();
    $obj=new MyClass();
?>
```

The output of the program is as follows.

The output of the program (from Listing 9-13)
The function show()
The function display()
An object of the class MyClass

After importing the contents of the namespace from the listing09_12.php file, you create aliases by the use function MyUtils\ show, use function MyUtils\display as disp, and use MyUtils\ MyClass as MyClass instructions. For the show() function, you do not specify the as instruction so that the alias is the function's name (without referencing the namespace). For the display() function, the alias is disp(). The alias for the MyClass class is the name of the class itself.

Anonymous Classes

There are situations when you need a class to create only a single object based on it. In such cases, it is convenient to use anonymous classes. It means that you create an object at the same time as you create a class. The corresponding instruction begins with the new keyword, followed by the class keyword and the class description in curly braces. Let's look at a small example that explains the described approach. The program is shown in Listing 9-14.

Listing 9-14. An Anonymous Class

```php
<?php
    // Creates an object based on the anonymous class:
    $obj=new class{
        // The private field:
        private $number;
        // The method for getting the value of the field:
        public function get(){
            return $this->number;
        }
        // The method for assigning a value to the field:
        public function set($number){
            $this->number=$number;
        }
    };
    // Operations with the objects:
    $obj->set(100);
    echo "\$number = ",$obj->get(),"\n";
?>
```

The result of the program execution is as follows.

The output of the program (from Listing 9-14)

```
$number = 100
```

In that case, you create the $obj object with the help of the following instructions (the comments are deleted).

```php
new class{
    private $number;
    public function get(){
        return $this->number;
    }
```

```
public function set($number){
    $this->number=$number;
  }
}
```

That is an expression that could be a description of the class. The difference is that you do not specify the class name, and the new instruction is present. It turns out that the object is created based on the class described by the instruction, but the class just has no name.

(i) **Note**   You put a semicolon at the end of the entire construction, which acts as a command to create an object.

Summary

- An abstract class is described with the abstract keyword and contains abstract methods. An abstract method is not described but only declared. The abstract method declaration also uses the abstract keyword. In addition to abstract methods, abstract classes may contain regular (non-abstract) methods and fields. Abstract classes are used to create (by using inheritance) child classes based on them.

- An interface is like a "totally abstract" class. An interface has no fields (but constants), and methods are only declared in it. An interface is described with the interface keyword. If an interface is implemented in a class, the class must describe each method from the interface. To implement an interface in a class, in the class description, you put the implements keyword and the interface name to be implemented after the class name. If a class implements multiple interfaces, they are listed after the `implements` keyword, separated by commas.

- An interface can inherit another interface. In that case, use the `extends` keyword like in class inheritance.

- A class can inherit another class and implement several interfaces at the same time.

- Traits contain blocks of code that can be included in the class description. Traits are described using the `trait` keyword. To include the trait contents into a class, you place the `use` instruction, then list the traits to be included in the class and separate them by commas.

- If you specify the interface name as a function argument type, you can pass an object of the class that implements the interface as an argument to that function. If you specify a class name (usually abstract) as an argument type, you can pass an object of any child class as the argument. The `instanceof` instruction can be used to check the type of an object or argument.

- To create a namespace, use the `namespace` instruction followed by the name of the namespace. An appropriate file should be imported to include the namespace in a program. Utilities from a namespace are accessed by specifying the namespace name. The `as` instruction is used to create aliases.

- An anonymous class is used when you need only one
  object to be created based on the class. In that case,
  you assign an expression to the object variable, and
  that expression starts with the new and class keywords
  followed by the actual description of the class in curly
  braces, based on which the object is created.

CHAPTER 10

Error Handling

Have I ever broken anything? Well, lately?

—*ALF* (TV series)

Even if the code is reliable and well thought out, it is not always possible to guarantee that no errors will occur during its execution. And the reasons are often objective. For example, the user might enter an invalid value, or the program might not find the file it needs to run. In such cases, error handling is used, which is discussed in this chapter.

Exception Handling Principles

The PHP language is quite democratic in many ways. That is also applicable to the reaction to error raising. While in most programming languages, an error usually means that the program is terminated (unless a special error-handling system is involved), things are not always so tragic in PHP. Even if something unpleasant like an error happens, it does not mean that the program abruptly terminates. Often, it is limited to a warning message or even no warning at all. In other words, there are quite different errors. Errors that cause the program to terminate are usually called fatal errors or *exceptions*. First, let's explore how to handle such errors.

© Alex Vasilev 2024
A. Vasilev, *PHP by Example*, https://doi.org/10.1007/979-8-8688-0258-4_10

The idea behind exception handling is very simple. You must provide some program code to execute when an exception occurs. In PHP, you can implement that idea in many different ways. Let's start with the simplest case and then explore the problem in detail.

(i) **Note**   Once again, it should be noted that errors and exceptions in the context of PHP are not the same. However, from now on, unless it leads to misunderstandings, terms such as *exception* and *error* are synonyms.

So, let's say there is a code block, and you suspect an error may occur during its execution. What do you have to do? There is a simple recipe. It assumes putting the mentioned code (the controlled code) in a special block that begins with the `try` keyword and is enclosed in curly braces. After the `try` block with the controlled code, the `catch` block is placed, containing the code to be executed in an error. The following is the template for the whole `try-catch`.

```
try{
    // The controlled code
}catch(Error_type $object_name){
    // The code to handle the error
}
```

The `catch` keyword is followed by the error class name and a formal notation in parentheses for the error object (the variable identified with the error object).

Details

The point is that when an error occurs, an object that contains information about the error is automatically created. The information can, in principle, be used when processing the error. The `catch` block contains the name of the error class (the error type) and the error object.

You can use different processing methods to handle errors of different types. If so, then in the `try-catch` construction, use several `catch` blocks—each one for an error of a specific type.

🔔 The PHP 8 Standard

In PHP 8, you can (if you need to) specify only the exception class name in the `catch` block description in parentheses after the `catch` keyword without any variable for the exception object.

The code with the `try-catch` construction is performed as follows. First, the controlled code is executed. If there is no error, the `catch` block is ignored. If there is an error in the `try` block while executing the controlled code, the `try` block is stopped, and the `catch` block is executed. Then, the command after the `try-catch` construction is run. How that looks in practice is illustrated in Listing 10-1.

Listing 10-1. The Exception Handling Principles

```php
<?php
    // The controlled code:
    try{
        echo "The value of the variable \$x: ";
        // Reads the value entered by the user
        // and the string with a command:
        $input="\$x=".trim(fgets(STDIN)).";";
```

```
    // Executes the command:
    eval($input);
    // Checks the variable:
    echo "\$x = $x\n";
// If an error occurs:
}catch(ParseError $e){
    echo "There was an error\n";
}
echo "The program is over\n";
?>
```

The program, in this case, is simple. The user is asked to enter an expression specifying the value of the $x variable. You discard leading and trailing spaces in the read string. The $input="\$x=". trim(fgets(STDIN))."; " instruction forms the command that assigns a value to the $x variable. The corresponding string is written into the $input variable. That command is executed when you pass the string from the $input variable as an argument to the eval() function. Next, the value of the $x variable is displayed. All commands are placed inside the try block. The point is that the eval($input) statement may cause an error because the value entered by the user is invalid. That type of error belongs to the ParseError class. To catch errors, use the catch block, in which the echo "There was an error\n" command is executed.

Thus, if no error of the ParseError class occurs during the code execution in the try block, then the catch block is ignored, and the calculated value of the $x variable is displayed. If an error occurs, the value of $x is not displayed, and the code in the catch block is executed instead. But in any case, the echo "The program is over\n" command is executed after the try-catch construction.

The result of the program execution depends on what expression the user enters. If the expression is a correct PHP statement, the result is as follows (the user input is marked in bold).

The output of the program (from Listing 10-1)
The value of the variable $x: **3+4*5**
$x = 23
The program is over

If the expression that should determine the value of the $x variable is incorrect, the result is as follows.

The output of the program (from Listing 10-1)
The value of the variable $x: **3++4**
There was an error
The program is over

You can handle errors of different types in the way described.

Exception Classes

The classes corresponding to errors of different types (exceptions of different classes) form a hierarchy based on the inheritance of classes and the implementation of interfaces. Why is it important? The reason is that if the catch block is designed to handle errors of a specific class, then it also handles errors of all child classes of that class. Next, let's discuss the main classes related to error handling. But let's begin with the Throwable interface. It is important since the classes used for error handling directly or indirectly implement that interface. Therefore, methods declared in the interface are common to many exception classes. Those methods are listed and described in Table 10-1.

Table 10-1. *Throwable Interface Methods*

Method	Description
getMessage()	The method returns a message associated with the exception.
getCode()	The method returns the exception code.
getFile()	The method returns a string with the name of the file in which the exception object was created.
getLine()	The integer result of the method determines the line on the execution of which the exception object was created.
getTrace()	The stack trace is returned (as an array).
getTraceAsString()	The stack trace is returned (as a string).
getPrevious()	Returns a reference to the previous exception object.
__toString()	The method returns a string representation for the exception object.

Note   In the interface, the methods are only declared. The purpose of the methods is given following how they are defined in the classes that implement the interface.

The exception classes are presented in Table 10-2.

Table 10-2. *The Exception Classes*

Class	Description
ArgumentCountError	It inherits the TypeError class. An exception of this class is thrown if fewer arguments than necessary are passed when calling a function or method.
ArithmeticError	It inherits the Error class. Exceptions of this class are generated in errors arising when performing mathematical operations.
AssertionError	It inherits the Error class. An exception of this class is thrown when an assert() statement fails.
CompileError	It inherits the Error class. An exception of this class can be thrown due to a compilation error.
DivisionByZeroError	It inherits the ArithmeticError class. The exception of this class is associated with an attempt to divide by zero.
Error	It implements the Throwable interface. It is the parent class for the built-in (predefined) exceptions.
ErrorException	It is an exception class that is a child of the Exception class.
Exception	It implements the Throwable interface and is the parent class for the custom exception classes (that is, the user-defined classes).
ParseError	It inherits the CompileError class. An exception of this class may occur in an error while interpreting the program (an attempt to execute an incorrect command).

(continued)

Table 10-2. (*continued*)

Class	Description
TypeError	It inherits the `Error` class. An exception of this class can be thrown if the actual type of an argument or result of a function or method does not match the type specified in the description of the function/method and also if the number of arguments passed to the function or method is incorrect.
UnhandledMatchError	It inherits the `Error` class. The exception can be thrown while executing the match expression.
ValueError	It inherits the `Error` class. An exception of this class is thrown if an argument with the incorrect value is passed to a function or method.

In addition to the listed exception classes, you can create your own—usually by inheriting the `Exception` class. The custom class exceptions are used for throwing exceptions artificially.

Throwing Exceptions

It may seem strange at first glance, but exceptions can be generated artificially. Why is that needed? Here, you have to consider that there is a relatively simple and convenient mechanism for catching and handling exceptions of different classes. Therefore, a way to use exception throwing means throwing exceptions of different classes under different circumstances and then handling those exceptions.

> **Note**   In fact, this scheme is similar to the one used in the conditional statement, save that throwing an exception is used instead of the condition.

You use the throw statement followed by the exception object to throw an exception. An exception object is created the same way you create objects of any other class: after the new statement, you put the class name and, if necessary, the arguments passed to the class's constructor.

> **Note**   It is worth mentioning that just creating an exception object does not cause the exception to be thrown.

Listing 10-2 is a program that artificially throws exceptions.

Listing 10-2. Throwing Exceptions

```php
<?php
    echo "Enter a number: ";
    // Reads a number:
    $number=(int)trim(fgets(STDIN));
    // The controlled code:
    try{
        // If the number is positive:
        if($number>0){
            // Throws an exception:
            throw new Exception("A positive number");
        }
```

```
    // If the number is negative:
    if($number<0){
        // Throws an exception:
        throw new Exception("A negative number");
    }
    // The statement is executed
    // if no exception is thrown:
    echo "The zero";
}catch(Exception $e){ // Handling the exception
    // Displays a message:
    echo $e->getMessage();
}
?>
```

During the program execution, the user is prompted to enter a number. The number is saved to the $number variable. The following code is enclosed in the try block and uses two conditional statements in a simplified form. The first one checks the $number>0 condition. If it is true, the throw new Exception("A positive number") command throws an exception of the Exception class. The new Exception("A positive number") statement creates an anonymous object of the Exception class. The string passed to the class constructor describes the thrown exception.

(i) **Note**   An anonymous object is an object the reference to which is not stored in any variable.

The second conditional statement tests the $number<0 condition. If the condition is true, the throw new Exception("A negative number") command throws an exception of the Exception class. Unlike the previous case, use another description for the exception.

The last command in the try block is the echo "The zero" statement.

If an exception is thrown while executing the code, the code in the try block is terminated, and the code in the catch block starts executing. There is a single echo $e->getMessage() command in the block, which displays a message associated with the thrown exception (the text that was passed to the constructor when the exception object was created). The getMessage() method gets the message string from the $e exception object.

If no exception is thrown when executing the code in the try block, the echo "The zero" command is eventually executed, and the catch block is ignored.

Depending on what number the user enters, three outcomes are possible when the program is executed. If the user enters a positive number, the result is like the following (the value entered by the user is marked in bold).

The output of the program (from Listing 10-2)
```
Enter a number: 5
A positive number
```

The following is the result when the user enters a negative number.

The output of the program (from Listing 10-2)
```
Enter a number: -5
A negative number
```

Finally, if the user enters zero, the result of the program execution is as follows.

The output of the program (from Listing 10-2)
```
Enter a number: 0
The zero
```

In this case, you have thrown exceptions of the Exception class. As noted, you can create your own in addition to the built-in exception classes.

The Custom Exceptions

The recipe for creating your own exception class is simple: you just need to create a child class for the Exception class. An example is shown in Listing 10-3.

Listing 10-3. The Custom Exceptions

```php
<?php
    // The exception class is created by inheriting
    // the Exception class:
    class MyException extends Exception{
        // A reference to an object:
        private $error;
        // The constructor:
        function __construct($msg,$error){
            // Calls the constructor of the parent class:
            parent::__construct($msg);
            // Assigns a value to the field:
            $this->error=$error;
        }
        // The method to cast the object to a string:
        function __toString(){
            $txt="The message: ".$this->getMessage()."\n";
            $txt.=$this->error->__toString();
            return $txt;
        }
    }
```

```php
// The class for odd numbers:
class Odd{
    // A private field:
    private $number;
    // The constructor:
    function __construct($number){
        $this->number=$number;
    }
    // The method for casting the object to a string:
    function __toString(){
        return "The number ".$this->number." is odd\n";
    }
}
// The class for even numbers:
class Even{
    // A private field:
    private $number;
    // The constructor:
    function __construct($number){
        $this->number=$number;
    }
    // The method for casting the object to a string:
    function __toString(){
        return "The number ".$this->number." is even\n";
    }
}
// The loop statement:
for($count=1;$count<=3;$count++){
    // The message:
    $msg="attempt ".$count;
```

```
// The prompt to enter a number:
echo "Enter a number: ";
// Reads the number:
$number=(int)trim(fgets(STDIN));
// The controlled code:
try{
    // If the number is entered:
    if($number%2==0){
        // Throws an exception:
        throw new MyException($msg,new Even($number));
    }else{ // If the number is odd
        // Throws an exception:
        throw new MyException($msg,new Odd($number));
    }
// Handles the exception:
}catch(MyException $e){
    echo $e;
    }
}
?>
```

The result of the program execution could be as follows (entered by the user values are marked in bold).

The output of the program (from Listing 10-3)
Enter a number: **123**
The message: attempt 1
The number 123 is odd
Enter a number: **124**
The message: attempt 2
The number 124 is even

```
Enter a number: 5
The message: attempt 3
The number 5 is odd
```

The program creates a custom MyException exception class by inheriting the library class Exception. In that class, you declare the private $error field. It is supposed that the field is assigned a reference to some object.

The class has a constructor with two arguments. The first argument (denoted as $msg) is passed as an argument to the parent class constructor (the parent::__construct($msg) command in the constructor body). The second argument (denoted as $error) is a reference to an object and is used to assign a value to the field of the same name (the $this->error=$error command in the constructor body).

To be able to use objects of the MyException class as strings, you override the __toString() method in the class. The method returns a string, which is obtained by concatenating the text "The message: ", the result of the getMessage() method, the result of the __toString() method called from the object referenced by the $error field (the $this->error->__toString() instruction), as well as the break line instruction "\n".

In addition to the MyException class, you create two classes: Odd and Even. They have a similar structure and differ in some details (namely, by the result that the __toString() method returns). Each class has the private field $number and the constructor with a single argument specifying that field's value. The __toString() method returns a string containing the value of the $number field and information about whether the number is even or odd.

After describing the classes, you run the loop statement for three iterations (the $count variable is used as a counter). For each loop, the $msg="attempt ".$count command generates a string with the current iteration's count, then reads a number and writes it to the $number variable. After that, the controlled code in the try block is executed. In the conditional statement, you check the $number%2==0 condition, and then an exception of the MyException class is thrown. The second argument of the MyException class constructor depends on the condition. It can be an object of the Even class (if the number is even) or an object of the Odd class (if the number is odd).

Details

The throw statement is used to throw an exception. It is followed by an anonymous object of the MyException class. The constructor's first argument is the string written to the $msg variable. The second argument is an anonymous object of the Even or Odd class (depending on the $number%2==0 condition). When creating anonymous objects of the Even or Odd class, the number stored in the $number variable is passed as an argument to the constructor of the corresponding class.

Exceptions are handled in the catch block. The class of exceptions to be checked is MyException. The block contains the single echo $e command. In such a case, the __toString() method is automatically called from the $e exception object, and the result returned by the method is displayed in the output window.

Handling Exceptions of Different Classes

In the previous example, when throwing an exception, you passed different arguments to the exception class's constructor in different situations. You can go even further and throw different types of exceptions. And handle those exceptions differently. It is implemented quite simply. After the try block, several catch blocks are placed. Each catch block is designed to handle an exception of a specific class.

Details

If the catch block is designed to handle exceptions of a certain class, it also handles exceptions of its child classes.

Let's look at an example in which the linear equation of the form $Ax = B$ is solved. If the parameter A is nonzero, the equation has a single solution $x = B/A$. If the parameter A has a zero value, then two situations are possible. When the parameter B is zero, the solution of the equation is any number. And if the parameter B is nonzero, then the equation has no solutions.

Let's examine the program shown in Listing 10-4.

Listing 10-4. Solving the Linear Equation

```php
<?php
    // The exception classes:
    class AnyNumberException extends Exception{}
    class NoRootsException extends Exception{}
    echo "The equation Ax=B\n";
    // Reads the parameters:
    echo "A = ";
    $A=(double)trim(fgets(STDIN));
    echo "B = ";
    $B=(double)trim(fgets(STDIN));
    // The controlled code:
    try{
        // If the first parameter is zero:
        if($A==0){
            // If the second parameter is zero:
            if($B==0) throw new AnyNumberException();
```

319

```
        // If the second parameter is nonzero:
        else throw new NoRootsException();
    }
    // The root of the equation:
    $x=$B/$A;
    // Displays the result:
    echo "The root is \$x = $x\n";
// Handles the exceptions:
}catch(AnyNumberException $e){
    echo "Any number is a root\n";
}catch(NoRootsException $e){
    echo "There are no roots\n";
}
    echo "The problem is solved\n";
?>
```

Depending on what values for the parameters *A* and *B* are entered by the user (marked in bold), the following results of the program execution are possible. The following occurs when a nonzero value is entered for the parameter *A*, while the parameter *B* also has a nonzero value.

The output of the program (from Listing 10-4)
```
The equation Ax=B
A = 2.4
B = 12
The root is $x = 5
The problem is solved
```

The following is the result of the program execution if the parameter *A* has a nonzero value and the parameter *B* is equal to zero.

The output of the program (from Listing 10-4)

```
The equation Ax=B
A = 5
B = 0
The root is $x = 0
The problem is solved
```

If both parameters are zero, the result is as follows.

The output of the program (from Listing 10-4)

```
The equation Ax=B
A = 0
B = 0
Any number is a root
The problem is solved
```

Finally, if the parameter *A* is zero and the parameter *B* is nonzero, the result is as follows.

The output of the program (from Listing 10-4)

```
The equation Ax=B
A = 0
B = 1
There are no roots
The problem is solved
```

You have used the following strategy. The program reads the values entered by the user for the parameters and then tries to calculate the solution of the equation. But while executing the code, one of two custom class exceptions can be thrown under certain conditions. Here, you have a "general line" and two "special cases," which are handled with the help of exception catching.

321

The AnyNumberException and NoRootsException exception classes inherit the Exception class and are defined with an empty body. That means those classes duplicate the Exception class, but the classes are formally different, which is essential for us. You use the classes to throw exceptions.

You read the values of the parameters of the equation and write those values to the $A and $B variables. The main calculations are performed in the try block. You also use a conditional statement in a simplified form. It checks the $A==0 condition. If the condition is true, another (inner) conditional statement is executed. The $B==0 condition is checked there. If it is true, an AnyNumberException exception is thrown. If the condition is false, then a NoRootsException exception is thrown.

(i) **Note**   Thus, if the $A==0 condition is true, an AnyNumberException or a NoRootsException exception is thrown. In both cases, it does not reach the execution of the commands placed after the external conditional statement since handling of the thrown exception begins.

The $x=$B/$A command, which calculates the root of the equation, is executed if no exception was thrown during the execution of the conditional statement. If so, the root is calculated and displayed by the echo "The root is \$x = $x\n" instruction. The exception handling blocks placed after the try block are ignored. If an exception is thrown, then it is handled by one of the catch blocks.

The program performed the exception handling directly in the handling blocks, and the exception class was used to identify the scenario to implement. But you could act somewhat differently, "hiding" information about the scenario to implement in the exception object. Such an approach is illustrated in Listing 10-5.

Listing 10-5. One More Way to Solve the Equation

```php
<?php
   // The exception classes:
   class AnyNumberException extends Exception{
      // The constructor:
      function __construct(){
         parent::__construct("Any number is a root\n");
      }
   }
   class NoRootsException extends Exception{
      // The constructor:
      function __construct(){
         parent::__construct("There are no roots\n");
      }
   }
   echo "The equation Ax=B\n";
   echo "A = ";
   $A=(double)trim(fgets(STDIN));
   echo "B = ";
   $B=(double)trim(fgets(STDIN));
   try{
      if($A==0&&$B==0) throw new AnyNumberException();
      if($A==0&&$B!=0) throw new NoRootsException();
      $x=$B/$A;
      echo "The root is \$x = $x\n";
   }catch(AnyNumberException|NoRootsException $e){
      echo $e->getMessage();
   }
   echo "The problem is solved\n";
?>
```

The result of the program execution is the same as in the previous case. However, the execution algorithm has changed slightly. There are two main changes. First, the message displayed when an exception is generated is associated with the exception object. This message can be retrieved using the getMessage() method. Second, you combined two catch blocks into one by specifying the AnyNumberException|NoRootsE xception expression as the exception class to be handled (the exception class names are separated by the | operator). Such a block handles both AnyNumberException and NoRootsException exceptions. Also, instead of the nested conditional statements, use two consecutively placed conditional statements in a simplified form with combined conditions.

Details

The $A==0$&$B==0$ condition is true if the $A==0$ and $B==0$ conditions are both true. The $A==0$&$B!=0$ condition is true if the $A==0$ and $B!=0$ conditions are both true.

Nested try-catch Constructions and the finally Block

The try-catch constructions can be nested. If an exception thrown in the inner try-catch construction is not handled by it, then the exception is passed to the outer try-catch construction for handling. In addition, the try-catch construction can contain the finally block whose commands are executed regardless of whether an exception is thrown or not. The situation is illustrated in Listing 10-6.

Listing 10-6. Nested try-catch Constructions

```php
<?php
    // The exception classes:
    class RedException extends Exception{}
    class GreenException extends Exception{}
    class BlueException extends Exception{}
    class OtherException extends Exception{}
    // Reads the name of a color:
    echo "Your favorite color: ";
    $color=strtolower(trim(fgets(STDIN)));
    // The outer block of the controlled code:
    try{
        // The inner block of the controlled code:
        try{
            // Makes a selection:
            switch($color){
                case "red":
                    throw new RedException();
                case "green":
                    throw new GreenException();
                case "blue":
                    throw new BlueException();
                default:
                    throw new OtherException();
            } // Handles the exceptions of the inner block:
        }catch(RedException $e){
            echo "Red is beautiful\n";
        }catch(GreenException $e){
            echo "Green is wonderful\n";
        }catch(BlueException $e){
            echo "Blue is stylish\n";
```

```
    }finally{  // The block is always executed
        echo "Thank you for the answer\n";
    }
    echo "You have a good taste\n";
} // Handles the exceptions of the outer block:
catch(OtherException $e){
    echo "I don't know this color\n";
}
echo "The program is over\n";
?>
```

In this program, the user is prompted to enter the name of a color, and depending on the entered value, the program displays specific messages.

To react to different situations, use throwing and handling exceptions. The program creates four custom exception classes: RedException, GreenException, BlueException, and OtherException. Each class inherits the Exception class and is defined with an empty body.

The entered by the user name of a color is written to the $color variable. First, the symbols in the string are converted to lowercase, for which the strtolower() function is used. Next is the outer try block with the inner try-catch-finally construction inside. In the inner try block, the switch statement is executed, in which the value of the $color variable is checked. If the variable's value is "red", then an exception of the RedException class is thrown. The "green" value throws an exception of the GreenException class. If the variable's value is "blue", a BlueException exception is thrown. In all other cases, an exception of the OtherException class is thrown.

In the inner try-catch-finally construction, you handle the exceptions of the RedException, GreenException, and BlueException classes. An exception of the OtherException class is handled in the outer try-catch construction.

Let's discuss how the code is executed. First, the string the user enters is read and written to the $color variable, and the variable's value is checked in the switch statement. As a result, one of the four classes of exceptions is thrown. If it is an exception of the RedException, GreenException, or BlueException class, it is handled in one of the catch blocks of the inner try-catch-finally construction. Then, the finally block is executed, and the echo "You have a good taste\n" instruction after that block. The outer catch block is ignored, and the last instruction, echo "The program is over\n", is executed.

If an exception of the OtherException class is thrown, it is not caught by the inner catch blocks and passed to the outer catch block for handling. But before that, the finally block is executed.

The result of the program execution depends on the value entered by the user (the values entered by the user are marked in bold). Symbols in the name of a color does not matter. In particular, the result could be as follows.

The output of the program (from Listing 10-6)
```
Your favorite color: Red
Red is beautiful
Thank you for the answer
You have a good taste
The program is over
```

The result could also be as follows.

The output of the program (from Listing 10-6)
```
Your favorite color: green
Green is wonderful
Thank you for the answer
You have a good taste
The program is over
```

It could be like the following.

The output of the program (from Listing 10-6)
Your favorite color: **BLUE**
Blue is stylish
Thank you for the answer
You have a good taste
The program is over

Or it could be like the following.

The output of the program (from Listing 10-6)
Your favorite color: **yellow**
Thank you for the answer
I don't know this color
The program is over

Once again, two things are worth mentioning. First, if the inner try-catch construction does not handle an exception, it is passed to the outer try-catch construction for handling. Second, the code in the finally block is always executed, both if an exception is thrown and if no exception is thrown.

Rethrowing an Exception

An exception can be thrown after it has been thrown. In that case, the same exception object is used multiple times. Let's consider a problem that solves a linear equation once again as an example of using such an approach. The program is shown in Listing 10-7.

Listing 10-7. Rethrowing Exceptions

```php
<?php
    // The exception class:
    class MyException extends Exception{}
    echo "The equation Ax=B\n";
    // Reads the parameters:
    echo "A = ";
    $A=(double)trim(fgets(STDIN));
    echo "B = ";
    $B=(double)trim(fgets(STDIN));
    // The outer block of the controlled code:
    try{
        // The inner block of the controlled code:
        try{
            // Throws an exception:
            if($A==0) throw new MyException();
            // The root of the equation:
            $x=$B/$A;
            // Displays the result:
            echo "The root is \$x = $x\n";
        // Handles the exceptions of the inner block:
        }catch(MyException $e){
            // Rethrows the thrown exception:
            if($B==0) throw $e;
            echo "There are no roots\n";
        }
    // Handles the exceptions of the outer block:
    }catch(MyException $e){
        echo "Any number is a root\n";
    }
    echo "The problem is solved\n";
?>
```

The result of the program execution is the same as in Listing 10-4. But the code is worth analyzing.

You use the exception class `MyException`. After reading the values of the `$A` and `$B` variables, the block of the controlled code is executed. It contains the inner `try` block in which, if the condition `$A==0` is true, an exception of the `MyException` class is thrown. If the condition is false, the `$x=$B/$A` and `echo "The root is \$x = $x\n"` statements are executed. The first statement calculates the root of the equation. The second statement displays the result of the calculation. Those statements are not executed if an exception is thrown. If it is, the exception is handled in the inner `catch` block. The handling is based on checking the condition `$B==0`. If the condition is false, the `echo "There are no roots\n"` instruction is executed. If the condition is true, the `throw $e` command rethrows the previously thrown exception. Here, `$e` denotes the exception object passed to the inner `catch` block for handling. The exception is caught and handled in the outer catch block this time. In particular, the `echo "Any number is a root\n"` command is executed there. The last command to be executed is `echo "The problem is solved\n"`.

Details

It turns out that if one of the parameters of the equation is zero, a custom class exception is thrown. If, while handling this exception, it turns out that the second parameter is equal to zero, then the exception is rethrown. Rethrowing an exception means you are using the exception object thrown earlier.

The Functions for Handling Errors

Very often, errors that occur during the execution of a program are not critical and do not cause the program's termination. The typical external effect in such a case is an error or warning message. Different techniques and schemes allow you to react to such situations adequately. But even if the error is critical and is not caught in the program (using the try-catch construction), you can still "fight" against it.

Details

The basic settings (including how to respond to scripting errors) are contained in the php.ini initialization file, which is read when the PHP server starts up. To manage the mode of error monitoring, you can use the error_reporting() function. Its argument is a constant defining the error messages to be displayed. For example, the E_ERROR constant corresponds to the mode of monitoring the fatal errors leading to the termination of the program execution. The E_WARNING constant means the mode in which the non-critical warnings are monitored. The E_ALL constant specifies the mode of monitoring almost all errors (the maximum control mode).

In practice, you can use the set_exception_handler() function to handle exceptions. As an argument, it takes the function's name that is called if an unhandled exception occurs during the code execution. The code stops executing after executing the function passed to the set_ exception_handler() function. A small example is shown in Listing 10-8.

Listing 10-8. The Function for Handling Exceptions

```php
<?php
    // The function for handling exceptions:
    function handler(){
        echo "There was an error!";
    }
    // Sets the handler function for exceptions:
    set_exception_handler('handler');
    // Displays a message:
    echo "An error is about to occur...\n";
    // Throws an exception:
    throw new Exception();
```

```
    // This statement is not executed:
    echo "This message will not be displayed!";
?>
```

The following is the program's output.

The output of the program (from Listing 10-8)

```
An error is about to occur...
There was an error!
```

In this case, you describe the handler() function, and the name of the function (as a string) is passed as an argument to the set_exception_handler() function. So when an exception is thrown with the throw new Exception() statement, the handler() function is automatically called. That terminates the execution of the program.

ⓘ **Note**   There are other functions useful when dealing with errors and exceptions. For example, you can use the set_error_handler() function to define error handlers. You can throw errors using the trigger_error() function. And the list is not complete.

Another interesting feature is related to the error message disable @ operator. The operator is placed before some expression, and if an error occurs during the execution of the expression, then the corresponding message is not displayed.

⌂ **The PHP 8 Standard**

Since PHP 8, the @ operator doesn't hide fatal errors.

Summary

- You can use the `try-catch-finally` construction to handle exceptions. The controlled code is placed in the `try` block. If an exception is thrown while executing that code, it can be handled in the `catch` block. The commands in the optional `finally` block are always executed.

- To handle different exceptions, multiple `catch` blocks can be used. For each block, you specify the exception class to be handled.

- Exceptions can be thrown artificially. To do that, use the `throw` instruction followed by the object of the exception.

- You can create custom exception classes. Such classes inherit the `Exception` class. The built-in exception classes implement the `Throwable` interface.

- The `try-catch-finally` constructions can be nested, and exceptions can be rethrown. In that case, the object of the thrown exception is used multiple times.

- Special functions and utilities allow you to set the error control mode. Among them are the error message disable @ operator, the `error_reporting()` function (defines the error control mode), the `set_exception_handler()` and `set_error_handler()` functions (define an error handler), and the `trigger_error()` function (throws an error).

CHAPTER 11

Generators and Iterators

Oh, I understand. Nobody on this planet ever says what they mean.

—*ALF* (TV series)

In this chapter, you become familiar with generators and iterators. An iterator is a special object that allows you to iterate over a collection. A generator is a particular iterator. So, in any case, you deal with iterating over collections. Let's start with the more straightforward issue: the generator.

Getting Familiar with Generators

A *generator function* is a function that returns a special object as a result. That object resembles an array in its properties. But it is not really an array. Rather, it is a spectacular way to create an illusion of an array. In particular, the result of calling a generator function can be used in the foreach loop statement to iterate over a collection.

© Alex Vasilev 2024
A. Vasilev, *PHP by Example*, https://doi.org/10.1007/979-8-8688-0258-4_11

Details

Formally, a generator function returns an object of the Generator class. The class implements the Iterator interface. An object of the Generator class cannot be created using the new statement.

Let's consider the specifics of creating and using the generator functions employing small examples. You first need to know that the object returned by a generator function can be used to get a sequence of values. In particular, to get the current value, you can use the current() method, and to shift to the next value, you involve the next() method.

> **Note** Strictly speaking, "generator" is more appropriate for the object returned by a generator function. However, that term is used for the corresponding functions for convenience.

The description of a generator function has its own peculiarities. So, to include a value to the list of values to be returned when the current() method is called, use the yield statement followed by the corresponding value within the function code. An example is shown in Listing 11-1.

Listing 11-1. Getting Familiar with Generators

```php
<?php
    // A generator function:
    function colors(){
        yield "Red";
        yield "Yellow";
        yield "Green";
    }
    // Calls the generator function:
    $color=colors();
```

```
// Using the generator function:
for($k=1;$k<=3;$k++){
    // We get the current value:
    echo "[$k] ",$color->current(),"\n";
    // The shift to the next value:
    $color->next();
}
?>
```

The result of the program execution is as follows.

The output of the program (from Listing 11-1)
[1] Red
[2] Yellow
[3] Green

In this case, you describe the colors() generator function, where you use the yield "Red", yield "Yellow", and yield "Green" commands. That means that the resulting generator object (which you get when calling the colors() function) generates the values "Red", "Yellow", and "Green".

The $color=colors() command is executed in the program, which writes the result of calling the colors() function to the $color variable. Thus, the $color variable refers to an object of the Generator class. That object has, among other things, the methods current() and next(). If you call the current() method from the $color object, you get the value "Red". If, after that, you call the next() method and then the current() method again, you get the value "Yellow". Finally, another call of the next() and current() methods gives you the value "Green". All that is illustrated by the for loop statement, in which the current() and next() methods are called three times from the $color object.

Details

If you call the `current()` method after three calls to the `next()` method (that is, after all the values "written" to the `$color` object have been iterated), you get a null reference.

There would be little use for the generator functions if two methods had to be called each time to generate a new value. Listing 11-2 illustrates a better way to use a generator function.

Listing 11-2. A Generator Function and a Loop Statement

```php
<?php
    // A generator function:
    function colors(){
        $colors=["Red","Yellow","Green"];
        foreach($colors as $clr){
            yield $clr;
        }
    }
    // Using the generator function:
    foreach(colors() as $color){
        echo $color,"\n";
    }
?>
```

The program's result is almost the same as in the previous case.

The output of the program (from Listing 11-2)
Red
Yellow
Green

The code of the colors() generator function was slightly changed. The list of generated values is now implemented as an array, and the yield statement is called in the foreach loop statement in the function body. Also, you do not write the instruction with the function call into a separate variable but directly indicate it as a collection to be iterated in the foreach loop statement. The result is that instead of calling the color() function, you would specify an array with values displayed when the program is executed.

A Generator Function with Arguments

It might seem at first glance that the concept of a generator function is an unnecessary complication of the array-based approach. But it is far from being the case. The generator functions allow you to write beautiful and efficient codes. For example, Listing 11-3 uses a generator function with arguments to generate a sequence of numbers.

Listing 11-3. A Generator Function with Arguments

```php
<?php
    // A generator function with arguments:
    function numbers($count,$start,$step=1){
        for($k=1,$num=$start;$k<=$count;$k++,$num+=$step){
            yield $num;
        }
    }
    // Using the generator function:
    echo "[1]";
    foreach(numbers(5,1,2) as $n){ // Odd numbers
        echo " ".$n;
    }
```

```
    echo "\n[2]";
    foreach(numbers(7,3) as $n){ // Natural numbers
        echo " ".$n;
    }
    echo "\n[3]";
    foreach(numbers(6,10,-1) as $n){ // Reverse order
        echo " ".$n;
    }
?>
```

The output of the program is as follows.

The output of the program (from Listing 11-3)
```
[1] 1 3 5 7 9
[2] 3 4 5 6 7 8 9
[3] 10 9 8 7 6 5
```

The numbers() function is described with three arguments (the last one has a default value). The function is designed to create an object that generates a numeric sequence. The first argument $count specifies how many numbers should be in the sequence. The second argument $start specifies the first value in the sequence. The third argument, $step (with the default value 1), specifies the increment when calculating the sequence. The core of the function is the loop statement. The count of cycles is determined by the $count argument. The $num variable, used in the yield $num command, gets the initial value defined by the $start argument. For each loop, the variable's value is incremented by the value determined by the $step argument.

You call the number() function in the foreach loop statements used to display the sequence of numbers. So, the numbers(5,1,2) instruction means generating the sequence of 5 numbers, the initial value is 1, and each next number is 2 more than the previous one. The numbers(7,3) instruction is used to create the sequence of 7 numbers, starting from 3, and each number is 1 greater than the previous one. Finally, using the numbers(6,10,-1) instruction, you get the sequence of 6 numbers; the first number is 10, and each next number is 1 less than the previous one (the numbers are listed in reverse order).

An Array Based on a Generator

As noted, a generator gives the illusion of using an array. But sometimes, you must solve the more trivial task of creating an array based on a generator. In principle, the iterator_to_array() built-in function can be used for that. A generator is passed as an argument to the function, and the function returns the array created by iterating over the "contents" of the generator. Let's say you have a function described as follows:

```
function nums($n){
    for($k=1;$k<=$n;$k++){
        yield $k;
    }
}
```

Then, the following command inclusively creates the array of numbers from 1 to 5, and a reference to the array is written to the $A variable.

```
$A=iterator_to_array(nums(5));
```

Listing 11-4 creates a function that duplicates the work of the built-in iterator_to_array() function.

Listing 11-4. An Array Based on a Generator

```
<?php
    // The function to create an array based on a generator:
    function generator_to_array(Generator $gen){
```

```php
    // An empty array:
    $array=[];
    foreach($gen as $a){
        // Adds an element to the array:
        $array[]=$a;
    }
    // The function result:
    return $array;
}
// A generator function:
function nums($n){
    for($k=1;$k<=$n;$k++){
        yield $k;
    }
}
// Creates an array:
$A=generator_to_array(nums(5));
print_r($A);
?>
```

The output of the program is as follows.

The output of the program (from Listing 11-4)

```
Array
(
    [0] => 1
    [1] => 2
    [2] => 3
    [3] => 4
    [4] => 5
)
```

The generator_to_array() function is designed to create an array based on a generator. It is described with a single argument of the Generator type. That means only objects created by calling the generator function can be passed as an argument to the function. The $array=[ ] command creates an empty array in the function body. The foreach loop statement then iterates over the values produced by the $gen generator passed as an argument to the function. By the $array[ ]=$a command, the next received value of $a is added to the end of the $array array, which is eventually returned as the result of the function.

The program also describes the nums() function, which creates the generator for a sequence of natural numbers. The argument of the function determines how many numbers are in the sequence. Therefore, when the $A=generator_to_array(nums(5)) command is executed, the array of 5 elements (the natural numbers from 1 to 5 inclusively) is created, and a reference to that array is written to the $A variable.

The Generator Result

In a generator function, in addition to using the yield instruction, you can also use the return statement. Nevertheless, the result is quite the same as you could expect.

First, if the return statement is executed within the code of a generator function, that terminates the generator function execution, but at the same time, the result of the function is an object of the Generator class (that is, a generator object). If you specify a value after the return statement, then that value can be obtained through the generator object using the getReturn() method. For example, suppose you specify a number after the return statement. In that case, an object of the Generator class is returned as a result of the generator function. When the getReturn() method is called from that object, you get the number specified after the return statement. The situation is illustrated in Listing 11-5.

Listing 11-5. The Generator Result

```php
<?php
    // A generator function:
    function randoms($n){
        // The initial value for the sum:
        $sum=0;
        for($k=1;$k<=$n;$k++){
            // A random number from 1 to 9:
            $number=rand(1,9);
            yield $number;
            // Adds a new term for the sum:
            $sum+=$number;
        }
        // The result is the sum of numbers:
        return $sum;
    }
    // A generator object:
    $rnd=randoms(5);
    // Generates random numbers:
    foreach($rnd as $r){
        echo $r," ";
    }
    // Using the generator result:
    echo "\nThe sum: ",$rnd->getReturn(),"\n";
?>
```

A possible result of the program execution can be as follows.

The output of the program (from Listing 11-5)

```
4 9 4 1 5
The sum: 23
```

This program describes the randoms() generator function with a single argument that specifies how many random numbers have to be generated by the generator object. In the function's body, the $sum variable is initialized with the zero value, after which the loop statement is run. The number of iterations is determined by the $n function argument. The $number=rand(1,9) command generates a random integer in the range from 1 to 9 inclusively, and that number is written to the $number variable.

Details

The built-in rand() function generates random numbers. You call this function with two integer arguments that define the bounds of the range within which the random number is generated.

Then, use the yield $number command to include the generated value in the list of generated values. Then, due to the $sum+=$number command, the value of the $number variable is added to the current value of the $sum variable.

The last command in the function's body is the return $sum statement. That means that when the getReturn() method is called from the generator object, you get the value of the $sum variable, which is the sum of the generated random numbers.

Details

Although the return statement formally returns an integer, the randoms() generator function returns a generator object. You can call the getReturn() method from a generator object only after the object has been "worked out"— that is, after you have "looked through" the generator object in the foreach loop statement.

The `$rnd=randoms(5)` command creates a generator object (to generate five numbers), and a reference to the object is written to the `$rnd` variable. Use the object in the `foreach` loop statement. Finally, you exploit the `$rnd->getReturn()` instruction to determine the sum of the generated numbers.

Using Generators

Let's pay special attention to several issues related to using generators. Namely, let's analyze a few simple examples, starting with Listing 11-6.

Listing 11-6. Reusing a Generator Object

```php
<?php
    // A generator function:
    function nums(){
        for($k=100;$k<=300;$k+=100){
            yield $k;
        }
    }
    // Creates a generator object:
    $nums=nums();
    // The controlled code:
    try{
        // The first use of the generator object:
        echo "The first use of the generator object:\n";
        foreach($nums as $n){
            echo $n," ";
        }
        // The second use of the generator object:
        echo "\nThe second use of the generator object:\n";
        foreach($nums as $n){
```

```
        echo $n," ";
    }
}catch(Exception $e){
    echo "Something is wrong\n";
}
?>
```

The program's output is as follows.

The output of the program (from Listing 11-6)
The first use of the generator object:
100 200 300
The second use of the generator object:
Something is wrong

Everything is simple here. You need the nums() generator function to generate 100, 200, and 300. Using the $nums=nums() command, you create a generator object, and a reference to it is written to the $nums variable. The rest of the code is enclosed in the try block. There, the foreach statement executes the same block of commands twice. Each time, the $nums generator object is used. The catch block is designed to handle possible exceptions by executing the echo "Something is wrong\n" command.

What is the program's output? You get the numbers 100, 200, and 300 the first time. But then you get an exception. It happens since the generator object is an object "for a single use." It can be "iterated through" only once. After that, you must create a new generator object to generate the same sequence of values. If you try to iterate an object that has already been iterated, you get an error. Therefore, instead of writing a reference to the generator object into a variable, the generator function call instruction is used directly in practice. A small variation of the previous example is shown in Listing 11-7.

Listing 11-7. Calling a Generator Function

```php
<?php
    function nums(){
        for($k=100;$k<=300;$k+=100){
            yield $k;
        }
    }
    try{
        echo "The first use of the generator object:\n";
        foreach(nums() as $n){
            echo $n," ";
        }
        echo "\nThe second use of the generator object:\n";
        foreach(nums() as $n){
            echo $n," ";
        }
    }catch(Exception $e){
        echo "Something is wrong\n";
    }
?>
```

The output of the program is as follows.

The output of the program (from Listing 11-7)
```
The first use of the generator object:
100 200 300
The second use of the generator object:
100 200 300
```

The result of the program execution has changed. The numbers 100, 200, and 300 are displayed both times, and no exception is thrown. Changes to the program code are minimal. You no longer use a variable to store a reference to the generator object, and in the foreach statements, where the $nums variable used to be, the instruction that calls the nums() function is now placed. What does it change? Each time the nums() function is called, a new generator object is created, so, in this case, you do not reuse the generator object.

Another unexpected feature of generator objects is illustrated in Listing 11-8.

Listing 11-8. Peculiarities of Using a Generator Function

```php
<?php
    // A generator function:
    function gen(){
        echo "A generator function is executed\n";
        yield 123;
    }
    // A generator object:
    $gen=gen();
    echo "A generator object is created\n";
    // Gets the value from the generator:
    echo $gen->current(),"\n";
?>
```

Here is the result of the program execution.

The output of the program (from Listing 11-8)
A generator object is created
A generator function is executed
123

You use the very simple generator function gen(), which executes the echo "A generator function is executed\n" command followed by the yield 123 statement. That means that the message is displayed first, and then the number 123 is added to the list of the values to be generated. Iterating over the generator object returns that single value.

The $gen=gen() command creates a generator object, and then the echo "A generator object is created\n" and echo $gen->current(),"\n" statements are executed. You might expect that first, you get the A generator function is executed message, followed by the A generator object is created message. And after that, you might expect that the value 123 is displayed. However, the first two messages appear in a different order. The reason is that executing the $gen=gen() statement does not lead to executing the code described in gen(). The actual function code only starts executing when the current() method is called from the $gen object.

Objects of the Generator class have the rewind() method, which allows you to execute the part of a generator function code before the first yield instruction. A modification of the previous program where you use the rewind() method is shown in Listing 11-9.

Listing 11-9. Generator Object Methods

```php
<?php
    function gen(){
        echo "A generator function is executed\n";
        yield 123;
    }
    $gen=gen();
    // Executes the initial code of the generator function:
    $gen->rewind();
    echo "A generator object is created\n";
    echo $gen->current(),"\n";
?>
```

The program's output is as follows.

The output of the program (from Listing 11-9)
```
A generator function is executed
A generator object is created
123
```

In this case, the $gen->rewind() command is executed as soon as the generator object is created. As a result, the message A generator function is executed is displayed first. Then, the message A generator object is created is also displayed.

Passing a Value to a Generator

The yield instruction can be used to form a list of generated values and pass a value to a generator. The yield keyword is identified with the value passed to the generator object using the send() method.

Details

You can call the send() method from a generator object and pass some argument to the method. In the body of the corresponding generator function, that value (the argument of the send() method) can be accessed using the yield keyword.

An example of passing values to a generator object is shown in Listing 11-10.

Listing 11-10. Passing Values to a Generator

```php
<?php
    // A generator function:
    function nums($n){
```

```
    // The sum:
    $sum=0;
    // Gets the values:
    for($k=0;$k<$n;$k++){
        $number=yield;
        $sum+=$number;
    }
    // The result of the generator:
    return $sum;
}
// How many numbers:
$n=5;
// A generator object:
$nums=nums($n);
for($k=1;$k<=$n;$k++){
    echo "[$k] The number: ";
    // Reads a number:
    $num=(double)trim(fgets(STDIN));
    // Passes the value to the object:
    $nums->send($num);
}
// The sum:
echo "The sum: ",$nums->getReturn(),"\n";
?>
```

The result of the program is as follows (the numbers entered by the user are marked in bold).

The output of the program (from Listing 11-10)
[1] The number: **2**
[2] The number: **3**
[3] The number: **5**

```
[4] The number: 1
[5] The number: 4
The sum: 15
```

The nums() generator function has a single argument and is described as follows. You define the $sum variable with the zero initial value in the function. Then, the loop statement comes into play. The count of iterations is determined by the generator function argument $n. For each iteration, the $number=yield command is executed. It means that the value the generator receives is written to the $number variable. The $sum+=$number command then adds that value to the current value of the $sum variable.

After the loop statement is terminated, the return $sum command returns the value of the $sum variable as the result of the getReturn() method.

The generator object is created with the $nums=nums($n) command. Then, the loop statement is run. For each loop, among other things, the number entered by the user is read and written to the $num variable. Next, that value is sent to the generator object; to do that, use the $nums->send($num) command. After reading all the values, using the $nums->getReturn() instruction, you get the result for the sum of the numbers entered by the user.

Iterators

The generators discussed are a particular case of *iterators*. From a formal point of view, an iterator is an object of a class that implements the Iterator interface. The methods that must be described in the class that implements the Iterator interface are presented in Table 11-1.

Table 11-1. *Iterator Interface Methods*

Method	Description
current()	The method returns the current value of the iterator.
key()	The method returns the key/index of the current value of the iterator.
next()	The method shifts to the next value of the iterator.
rewind()	The method for setting the iterator to the state to generate the first value.
valid()	The method is designed to check the readiness of the iterator.

Note   It is not surprising that generator objects have the same methods since the Generator class implements the Iterator interface.

To create an iterator, it is enough to create a class that implements the Iterator interface and then create an object based on that class. Listing 11-11 describes the custom iterator class.

Listing 11-11. An Iterator

```php
<?php
    // The class for an iterator:
    class Fibonacci implements Iterator{
        // The last and one before the last numbers:
        private $last;
        private $previous;
        // The element numbetr:
        private $key;
        // The maximal value of the index:
        private $max;
```

```
    // The constructor:
    function __construct($max){
       $this->max=$max;
       $this->rewind();
    }
    // The methods from Iterator:
    public function rewind(){
       $this->key=1;
       $this->previous=1;
       $this->last=1;
    }
    public function current(){
       return $this->previous;
    }
    public function key(){
       return $this->key;
    }
    public function next(){
       ++$this->key;
       $this->last+=$this->previous;
       $this->previous=$this->last-$this->previous;
    }
    public function valid(){
       if($this->key<=$this->max) return true;
       else return false;
    }
    // The additional methods:
    public function resize($max){
       $this->max=$max;
    }
}
```

```php
    // Creates an iterator object:
    $fibs=new Fibonacci(10);
    // Using the iterator:
    foreach($fibs as $f){
        echo $f," ";
    }
    echo "\n";
    // Changes the number of values:
    $fibs->resize(15);
    // Using the iterator:
    foreach($fibs as $f){
        echo $f," ";
    }
?>
```

The result of the program execution is as follows.

The output of the program (from Listing 11-11)

1 1 2 3 5 8 13 21 34 55
1 1 2 3 5 8 13 21 34 55 89 144 233 377 610

🔔 **The PHP 8 Standard**   Versions higher than PHP 8 display a set of
warnings since the class methods that implement the Iterator
interface should be described with the return type (stated after braces
with the method's arguments through a colon). Namely, you should use
the following description of the Fibonacci class (the comments are
discarded, and the added blocks of code are marked in bold).

```php
class Fibonacci implements Iterator{
    private $last;
    private $previous;
```

```php
    private $key;
    private $max;
    function __construct($max){
        $this->max=$max;
        $this->rewind();
    }
    public function rewind(): void{
        $this->key=1;
        $this->previous=1;
        $this->last=1;
    }
    public function current(): mixed{
        return $this->previous;
    }
    public function key(): mixed{
        return $this->key;
    }
    public function next(): void{
        ++$this->key;
        $this->last+=$this->previous;
        $this->previous=$this->last-$this->previous;
    }
    public function valid(): bool{
        if($this->key<=$this->max) return true;
        else return false;
    }
    public function resize($max){
        $this->max=$max;
    }
}
```

Another solution is to precede each method (from the Iterator interface) with the #[\ReturnTypeWillChange] attribute.

Let's create the Fibonacci class that implements the Iterator interface. An object of the class is designed to generate a sequence of the Fibonacci numbers (the first two numbers are equal to one, and each next is equal to the sum of the previous two). The class has the private $last and $previous fields that are supposed to store the last and last but one number in the sequence. The private field $key is used to store the key of the generated number. The $max field contains the value that determines how many numbers are generated in the sequence.

The constructor has a single argument that specifies the value of the $max field. The rewind() method is called in the body of the constructor. When the method is called, the $key, $previous, and $last fields are assigned values.

When called, the current() method returns the value of the $previous field. The key() method returns the value of the $key field.

When the next() method is called, due to the ++$this->key statement, the value of the $key field is incremented by one. Next, the $this->last+=$this->previous and $this->previous=$this->last-$this->previous commands calculate the next number in the sequence and update the values of the $previous and $last fields, respectively.

The valid() method is used (automatically) to check that the iterator is ready to generate a value. The $this->key<=$this->max condition is checked in the method's body. It is true if the current number key does not exceed the maximum value set for the sequence. If so, the method returns true. Otherwise, it returns false.

Details

You need the `valid()` method to determine when the iteration of the elements in the loop statement ends.

In addition to the "required" methods from the `Iterator` interface, you describe an "additional" `resize()` method for changing the value of the `$max` field in an already created iterator object.

An iterator object is created with the `$fibs=new Fibonacci(10)` command. The object is designed to generate ten numbers in the Fibonacci sequence. That happens when you pass the `$fibs` iterator object to the `foreach` statement.

The iterator object created can be used multiple times. To do that, it is enough to put it to its original state using the `rewind()` method. Moreover, you can change the number of values generated by the iterator. So, after executing the `$fibs->resize(15)` command, the iterator object generates 15 numbers from the sequence, which is confirmed by the program output.

Summary

- An iterator is an object of a class that implements the `Iterator` interface. Iterators are used to emulate sequences, and, in particular, they are used in the `foreach` loop statements.

- If you create a class and implement methods of the `Iterator` interface in that class, then an class object can be used as a collection iterator in the `foreach` loop statement.

- You can create functions that return a generator object as a result. A generator is an object of the Generator class that implements the Iterator interface. To add a value to the list for generation, use the yield statement followed by the corresponding value.

- The current() method is used to get the current value of an iterator. To shift to the next value to generate, use the next() method. The rewind() method puts an iterator into the state to generate the first value. You can get the key of the generated element using the key() method. You can use the valid() method to check if an iterator is ready.

CHAPTER 12

Using PHP

Why must you needlessly complicate everything?

—*ALF* (TV series)

Unlike most other popular languages, PHP is not used "on its own." It is used "in a context." PHP was developed for creating web programs or scripts. Accordingly, PHP is designed for web programming. Next, let's look at some simple tasks and situations that explain how PHP code can be used in web development.

A Script in an HTML Document

Perhaps the most straightforward situation is when PHP code is included in a document with HTML markup. This approach is useful when you need to generate content for an HTML document automatically.

THE HTML BASICS

HTML (the acronym from the *Hypertext Markup Language*) is used to create web pages. That is, in fact, plain text with unique markers or descriptors, also called *tags*. Those tags are for the browser that displays the corresponding document. Namely, the tags are instructions for the browser to display the actual text in the document.

© Alex Vasilev 2024
A. Vasilev, *PHP by Example*, https://doi.org/10.1007/979-8-8688-0258-4_12

Let's explore how to create (using the PHP tools) a document that contains a list of the Fibonacci numbers (the first two numbers are equal to one, and each subsequent number is equal to the sum of the two previous numbers). In that case, instead of writing the numbers in the document explicitly, use PHP code to generate the corresponding content.

Details

Documents with HTML markup usually have the `.html` extension. For the browser, that is an indicator that the document contains hypertext markup. If you want to place PHP code in a document with HTML markup, the corresponding file should be saved with the `.php` extension.

Let's analyze the document shown in Listing 12-1.

Listing 12-1. The Fibonacci Numbers

```
<!DOCTYPE html>
<html>
<head>
<title>The Fibonacci Numbers</title>
</head>
<body>
<h1>The Fibonacci Sequence</h1>
<p>The first two numbers are equal to one, and each next number
is equal to the sum of the two previous ones. Here are the
numbers:</p>
<p>
<?php
    $n=20;
    $a=1;
    $b=1;
    echo "$a, $b";
    for($k=3;$k<=$n;$k++){
```

```
    $b=$a+$b;
    $a=$b-$a;
    echo ", $b";
  }
  echo ", and so on.";
?>
</p>
<p>Do you know what the next number is?</p>
</body>
</html>
```

Here, you deal with a document containing HTML markup; in that document, there is a block with PHP code.

Details

It is important to consider what happens when you try to open a document with HTML code. You study the most common and frequently used scheme and consider it in a very simplified form.

So, suppose that there are two computers: a client and a server. They are connected to each other. A browser is launched on the client computer, and using that browser, you try to open a document hosted on the server computer. When the client receives the document, it renders it based on the HTML markup.

If you request a PHP document on the server through the client browser, then that document is executed on the server as a script, and the result is returned to the browser. If the document contains both HTML markup and PHP code, then the already existing HTML markup remains "as it is", and instead of the PHP code, the result of its execution is substituted. The total result is a document with HTML markup designed to be displayed by the browser. You may say that you deal with dynamic documents since their contents can change due to the execution of PHP scripts directly while processing the document. That is how the preceding document is organized. It contains "static" HTML code and a block of PHP code, which "is transformed" into a block of hypertext markup during execution.

In fact, after executing the PHP code, the browser receives such a document.

```
<!DOCTYPE html>
<html>
<head>
<title>The Fibonacci Numbers</title>
</head>
<body>
<h1>The Fibonacci Sequence</h1>
<p>The first two numbers are equal to one, and each next number
is equal to the sum of the two previous ones. Here are the
numbers:</p>
<p>
1, 1, 2, 3, 5, 8, 13, 21, 34, 55, 89, 144, 233, 377, 610, 987,
1597, 2584, 4181, 6765, and so on.</p>
<p>Do you know what the next number is?</p>
</body>
</html>
```

This code differs from Listing 12-1 because the following HTML code is inserted instead of the PHP block.

```
1, 1, 2, 3, 5, 8, 13, 21, 34, 55, 89, 144, 233, 377, 610, 987,
1597, 2584, 4181, 6765, and so on.
```

That is a text, although in a general case, it could contain descriptors of hypertext markup. The text is the result of executing this code.

```
<?php
    $n=20;
    $a=1;
    $b=1;
    echo "$a, $b";
```

```
for($k=3;$k<=$n;$k++){
    $b=$a+$b;
    $a=$b-$a;
    echo ", $b";
}
echo ", and so on.";
?>
```

Anything that is displayed using the echo statement is included in the document. The code itself is simple. It calculates the first 20 Fibonacci numbers (the $n variable defines how many numbers are calculated). Namely, the last and the one before the last numbers in the sequence (two ones) are stored in the $a and $b variables. A new number is calculated for each loop. The result is displayed in the document.

ⓘ **Note** You can imagine all that as if the program prints directly into the document.

Viewing the document in the browser window shows the result shown in Figure 12-1.

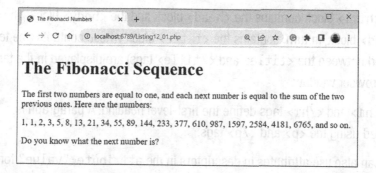

Figure 12-1. Displaying the document with PHP code in the browser window

That is, everything is more or less simple. The only thing left is figuring out how to get the result presented here.

THE HTML BASICS

To create documents with HTML markup, you must have at least a basic understanding of HTML. However, you do not intend to cover all the principles of creating HTML documents since it is not the book's primary purpose. On the other hand, it is quite difficult to understand how to use PHP scripts effectively without knowing HTML. Therefore, especially for those unfamiliar with the basics of HTML, comments are provided to explain the hypertext markup used in your code.

All descriptors in an HTML document are enclosed in angle brackets < and >. Between the angle brackets, you put the descriptor's name. Most descriptors are paired ones: there is an opening descriptor, and there is a closing descriptor. The closing descriptor contains a forward slash / in front of the descriptor name. Everything between the opening and closing descriptor is the contents of the descriptor. For example, an entire HTML document is enclosed in a block delimited by `<html>` and `</html>` tags. The beginning instruction `<!DOCTYPE html>` is a document specification.

The `<html>` block contains the `<head>` block and the `<body>` block. The `<head>` block, in turn, contains the `<title>` block whose contents (the text placed between the `<title>` and `</title>` tags) are displayed in the tab in the browser window.

The `<h1>` and `</h1>` tags define the first-level heading. A paragraph is defined using the `<p>` and `</p>` tags.

You can also use attributes in descriptors in the `attribute="value"` format inside the opening descriptor. For example, the `<html>` tag typically contains an attribute that specifies the document's language. In that case, the opening tag looks like `<html lang="en">`.

Let's consider the technical side of the issue. When dealing with the document, you suppose that the browser on the client computer makes the request, and the PHP code is executed on the server computer. Moreover, even if it is possible to place the document on the server, the debugging process is not the most pleasant in such a case. Therefore, using the same computer as the client and server during development is natural. There are several ways to do that. The following describes the one that seems to be the most simple, convenient, and understandable. It is about running a local server.

Note   Some information about the software and how to create PHP programs is provided in the *Introduction* and *Chapter 1*. You can learn how to start a local server and use the NetBeans environment there. Here, you refresh a little the knowledge gained earlier.

To start a local server, you can use the following command.

```
php -S localhost:some_port -t some_folder
```

First comes the php (or php.exe) instruction, after which you put the -S option and the localhost:some_port construction. After the localhost keyword, specify the port to communicate with the server.

Details

Different programs and services send and receive requests when the client and server interact. A unique numeric identifier matches a program and a message sent for that program. It is called a *port*. Many services choose a port automatically, but in this case, you need to specify the port explicitly. That can be almost any number, but for reliability (to not specify the port already in use), selecting a port after 5000 is recommended. For example, port 6789 is quite acceptable.

The port is followed by the -t option and a folder on the hard drive that is the server's root directory. For example, you can use the following command.

```
php -S localhost:6789 -t D:\Books\php\codes
```

In that case, files in the D:\Books\php\codes folder are treated as in the server's root directory. Interaction with the local server is carried out through the port 6789. But if you first move to the D:\Books\php\codes folder using the command line, then it is enough to use a simpler command.

```
php -S localhost:6789
```

Details

In Windows, you can use Explorer to navigate to the folder you want to use as the root directory of the local server and enter the cmd command in the address bar. The php -S localhost:6789 command is executed in the console window. You may also have to specify the full path to the php.exe file. For example, if the php.exe file is in the C:\PHP folder, the command looks like C:\PHP\php -S localhost:6789.

After starting the local server, you can view the document in a browser window. If the file is called `listing12_01.php` and is located in the D:\ Books\php\codes folder, which serves as the root directory for the local server, then you need to enter the following request in the browser address bar.

```
localhost:6789/listing12_01.php
```

If the `listing12_01.php` file contains the code as in Listing 12-1, the result should look as shown in Figure 12-1.

ⓘ **Note**   The scheme described is acceptable for testing all examples discussed next.

Handling the Request Parameters

When you enter the page's address into the browser's address bar, you can specify additional parameters and their values. That can be done quite simply. After the address, you place the question mark (?) followed by the parameter and its value in a `parameter=value` format. The & symbol is used as a separator if there are multiple parameters.

Listing 12-2 is an example.

Listing 12-2. Handling the Request Parameters

```
<!DOCTYPE html>
<html lang="en">
<head>
<title>Greetings</title>
</head>
<body>
```

```
<h1>Welcome Page</h1>
<p> We are happy to greet you, <strong>
<?php
    if(isset($_GET["name"])) $name=$_GET["name"];
    else $name="Mister X";
    echo $name;
?>
</strong>! It is a great honor for us.
</p>
</body>
</html>
```

First, let's look at the result of the code execution and then analyze it.

So, you start the local server; for example, using port 6789 (the php -S localhost:6789 command from the folder with the listing12_02.php file with the program), and enter the following request in the address bar of the browser.

`localhost:6789/listing12_02.php`

As a result, the browser window looks as shown in Figure 12-2.

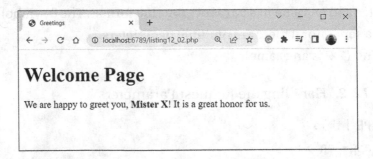

Figure 12-2. *The browser window if the name parameter is not passed in the request*

In this case, the browser renders the document with the following HTML markup.

```
<!DOCTYPE html>
<html lang="en">
<head>
<title>Greetings</title>
</head>
<body>
<h1>Welcome Page</h1>
<p> We are happy to greet you, <strong>
Mister X</strong>! It is a great honor for us.
</p>
</body>
</html>
```

The document contains a greeting with the name Mister X marked in bold.

THE HTML BASICS

A pair of the <strong> and </strong> tags were used to bold the text.

Next, in the browser's address bar, you enter another command (the important part of the command is marked in bold).

```
localhost:6789/listing12_02.php?name=Mickey Mouse
```

ⓘ Note   A space in the name parameter value in the browser's address bar is automatically replaced with the %20 instruction.

The result is shown in Figure 12-3.

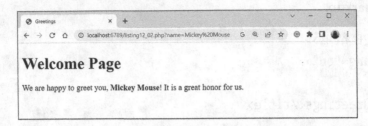

Figure 12-3. *The browser window if the name parameter is passed in the request*

In this case, specify the Mickey Mouse value for the name parameter in the request. As a result, that value is displayed on the welcome page. The document now has the following HTML markup.

```
<!DOCTYPE html>
<html lang="en">
<head>
<title>Greetings</title>
</head>
<body>
<h1>Welcome Page</h1>
<p>We are happy to greet you, <strong>
Mickey Mouse</strong>! It is a great honor for us.
</p>
</body>
</html>
```

The markup differs from the previous case only in the name (Mickey Mouse instead of Mister X). That effect is achieved using the PHP code included in the source document in Listing 12-2. The code is quite simple.

```php
<?php
    if(isset($_GET["name"])) $name=$_GET["name"];
    else $name="Mister X";
    echo $name;
?>
```

The main task is solved using the conditional statement. It checks the isset($_GET["name"]) condition. The condition is true if there is an element in the $_GET array with the key "name". Here, you need to consider that all parameters passed in the request are stored in the $_GET array. The name of the parameter is the key of the element, and the value of the parameter is the element's value. Therefore, you can use the $_GET["name"] instruction to get the name parameter value passed in the request. However, the problem is that the user may not pass a value for the name parameter in the request. Therefore, you first check if the $_GET array contains the corresponding element. If the element exists, then the $name=$_GET["name"] statement assigns the value of the name parameter to the $name variable. If the required element is not in the array, the $name variable is assigned the "Mister X" value. After that, the echo $name instruction writes the value of the $name variable to the HTML document.

Using Buttons

Often, when working with HTML documents, use *forms*. Those are special blocks with controls, such as buttons, input fields, options, radio buttons, and drop-down lists. Next, let's examine another example similar in functionality to the previous one, but you use a button and an input field this time. To understand how it works, let's start with the result.

Assume that there is an index.html file in a folder. The file must have exactly that name since a file with such a name is automatically downloaded when accessing the server (unless the file is explicitly specified in the request).

Details

When running a local server, a command like php -S localhost:6789 should be run from the folder where the index.html file is located.

After running the local server, you enter the request localhost:6789 into the browser's address bar (or specify a different port, depending on which one was indicated when running the local server). The result is shown in Figure 12-4.

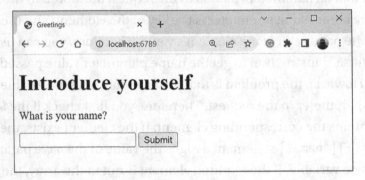

Figure 12-4. *The initial browser window*

The window contains an input field with the text What is your name? above it, as well as the **Submit** button. If you just click the button (without filling in the field), then the contents of the browser window change and is as in Figure 12-5.

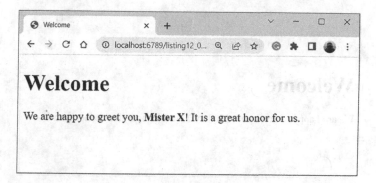

Figure 12-5. *The result of clicking the **Submit** button in the case of the empty field*

You can also do otherwise – enter a name in the field and click the **Submit** button, as shown in Figure 12-6.

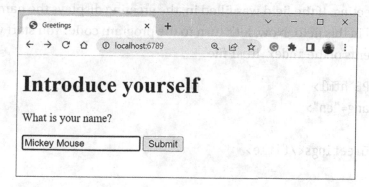

Figure 12-6. *The form with the filled field before submitting data*

After pressing the **Submit** button, you see the result shown in Figure 12-7.

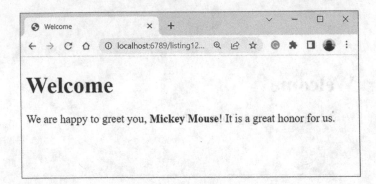

Figure 12-7. *The result of clicking the **Submit** button in the case of the filled field*

Thus, after pressing the **Submit** button, a greeting appears. If the field was empty when submitting the form data, the name Mister X is displayed in the greeting. If the field was filled in, the greeting displays the name specified in this field. Now, let's turn to the program code. You start with the contents of the index.html file.

```
<!DOCTYPE html>
<html lang="en">
<head>
<title>Greetings</title>
</head>
<body>
<h1>Introduce yourself</h1>
<p>What is your name?</p>
<form action="listing12_03.php" target="_self" method="post">
<input type="text" name="name">
<button>Submit</button>
</form>
</body>
</html>
```

In addition to the standard HTML elements already familiar to us, the document contains a form block marked with the <form> and </form> tags. Inside the form, there are two elements. That is an input field and a button. The input field is created as an <input> element.

THE HTML BASICS

It can be understood that you deal with a text field due to the type attribute whose value is "text".

A button is created using the <button> and </button> tags. The text between these tags is the name of the button.

It is crucial here which attributes are specified for the form and the input field. In particular, you use three attributes for the form. The method attribute is set to "post". It defines how the form data is submitted.

Details

There are two methods for submitting form data: GET and POST. The difference is in the way the data is transmitted. In general terms, the GET method transfers data without encoding. An example of transferring data using the GET method has already been given in the example with processing parameters passed in the request in the address bar.

The POST method transfers data more safely. In this example, you use it to transfer data to the server.

The target attribute with the value "_self" means that the response sent by the server is displayed in the same window where the form was displayed.

Details

Let's talk about the scheme. The browser on the client side makes a request to the server. The server sends a response – the page with the form. There is the **Submit** button. The form data is sent to the server when the button is clicked. The server processes the data (for doing that, a script is used that can be explicitly specified in the form description) and then sends a response (HTML code) to the browser. The document, among other things, can be displayed in the window where the document with the form was displayed initially. That is the approach you use in the example.

Finally, the `action` attribute defines the script to process the form data. The HTML code resulting from executing the program is sent back to the browser. In this example, the value of the `action` attribute is the text `"listing12_03.php"`. That means the form data is passed to the program written in the `listing12_03.php` file for processing.

Details

The `listing12_03.php` file must be in the same folder as the `index.html` file. If the file is located in another folder, then you should specify the full path to it, starting from the root directory (in this case, that is the place where the `index.html` file is located).

Submitting the form data means passing information about the state of the form's controls to the server. When processing the data, the controls need to be identified somehow. For that purpose, set the `name` attribute for the controls. In this case, there is only one control (however, it also needs to be identified). You set the input field's `name` attribute to `"name"`. Submitting the form data means that the server gets the value contained in the input field when the **Submit** button is clicked.

So, you know now what is sent to the server. The question is how the data received by the server is processed. According to the value of the form's action attribute, the program from the listing12_03.php file is responsible for processing the form data. The program code is shown in Listing 12-3.

Listing 12-3. Processing the Button Click

```
<!DOCTYPE html>
<html>
<head>
<title>Welcome</title>
</head>
<body>
<h1>Welcome</h1>
<p>We are happy to greet you, <strong>
<?php
    if(empty($_POST["name"])){
        $name="Mister X";
    }
    else{
        $name=$_POST["name"];
    }
    echo $name;
?>
</strong>! It is a great honor for us.</p>
</body>
</html>
```

You are dealing with HTML code with the following PHP block added to it.

```php
<?php
    if(empty($_POST["name"])){
        $name="Mister X";
    }
    else{
        $name=$_POST["name"];
    }
    echo $name;
?>
```

A text fragment is inserted into the document when the code is executed. But to define that text, you need to make some manipulations. The first step is to get the value entered by the user in the form's input field. As noted, you use the POST method to send the data, and the `field name attribute` from which to read the text has the value "name". Attributes that are passed by the POST method are automatically stored in the $_POST global array. The name attribute's value (enclosed in double quotes) is the element's key, and the passed value (the contents of the input field) is the array element's value.

---

i **Note**   In the example, the name attribute has the value "name". That may cause some ambiguity. Note that the "name" key of the $_POST["name"] element is associated with the "name" value of the name attribute. If the input field's name attribute had the value "newname", then the value written to the input field would be passed as the $_POST["newname"] element.

The program uses a conditional statement that checks the empty($_POST["name"]) condition. There, the $_POST["name"] element is passed as an argument to the empty() function. The function checks the text passed as an argument to define if it is empty (the user did not enter anything into the form input field). If the user left the field blank, the $name variable is set to "Mister X". If the input field is not empty, then the $name variable is assigned the value of the $_POST["name"] element – that is, the value that the user has entered in the form input field.

Once the value of the $name variable is defined, it is written to the document, and the server sends it to the browser, and thus it is displayed in the original browser window.

Using Several Buttons

Often, you have to use several buttons in the same form. When pressing different buttons, the reaction of the server should be different. The following example explains how to implement such a task using PHP. Like in the previous example, let's start with the results.

Details

As before, the local server is launched from the folder where the index.html file is located. In other words, you should place the index.html file in the folder that serves as the root directory for the local server. The code for that file is discussed later.

The initial browser window is shown in Figure 12-8.

Figure 12-8. *The initial browser window with a form and two buttons*

Details

To see the window, you should enter `localhost`, followed by a colon, and the port number specified when running the local server in the browser's address bar. For example, that could be `localhost:6789`.

The window contains a small text and two buttons named **First** and **Second**. You can click any of them. If you click the **First** button, you get the result shown in Figure 12-9.

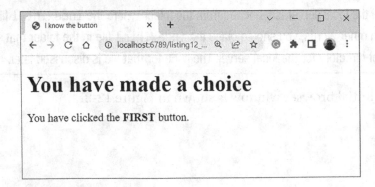

Figure 12-9. *The result after pressing the First button*

Now, the browser window contains a message with the name of the clicked button. The same happens if you click the **Second** button in the initial window (see Figure 12-8). But the button's name is different in this case, as shown in Figure 12-10.

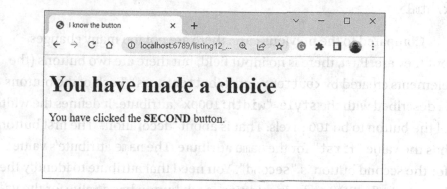

Figure 12-10. *The result after pressing the Second button*

Thus, when a button is pressed in the original window, a new document is displayed in the same window with the message containing the name of the pressed button (displayed in capital letters and in bold).

First, analyze the HTML code for the index.html file that opens when the browser starts.

```
<!DOCTYPE html>
<html lang="en">
<head>
<title>Two Buttons</title>
</head>
<body>
<h1>Two Buttons</h1>
<p>Please, select a button and click it.</p>
<form target="_self" method="post" action="listing12_04.php">
<button name="first" value="FIRST"
style="width:100px">First</button>
```

```
<button name="second" value="SECOND"
style="width:100px">Second</button>
</form>
</body>
</html>
```

Compared to the previous case, there are not too many changes, but they are. First, there is no input field, but there are two buttons (the elements created by <button> and </button> tags). Each of the buttons is described with the style="width:100px" attribute. It defines the width of the button to be 100 pixels. That is about "decoration." The first button has the value "first" for the name attribute. The name attribute's value for the second button is "second". You need that attribute to identify the buttons in the PHP code. In addition, each button has a value for the value attribute. For the first button, it is "FIRST", and for the second button, it is "SECOND". You also use those values in the PHP code.

Details

When you click a button, since, in this case, the POST method is used to send data, the element associated with the clicked button is added to the $_POST array. The key is determined by the button's name attribute, and the element's value is determined by the button's value attribute.

The form data is processed by the program from the listing12_04. php file (the value "listing12_04.php" for the form's action attribute). The code of the program is shown in Listing 12-4.

Listing 12-4. Handling a Button Click

```
<!DOCTYPE html>
<html>
<head>
<title>I know the button</title>
</head>
<body>
<h1>You have made a choice</h1>
<p>
You have clicked the <strong>
<?php
    if(isset($_POST["first"])) $button=$_POST["first"];
    else $button=$_POST["second"];
    echo $button;
?>
</strong> button.
</p>
</body>
</html>
```

That is a simple HTML code containing a small PHP block.

```
<?php
    if(isset($_POST["first"])) $button=$_POST["first"];
    else $button=$_POST["second"];
    echo $button;
?>
```

As a result of executing the code, the text (the word associated with the button's name) is determined and entered in the document. Then, the document is passed to the browser.

You use the conditional statement in which the isset($_POST["first"]) condition is tested. It is true if there is an element with the "first" key in the $_POST array. The true condition means that the user clicked the **First** button since that button's name attribute has the value "first". The element $_POST["first"] gives the value of the button's value attribute (so it is "FIRST"). That is why after executing the $button=$_POST["first"] statement, the $button variable gets the value "FIRST".

If the isset($_POST["first"]) condition is false, it means that there is no element with the key "first" in the $_POST array. That, in turn, implies that the **First** button was not clicked. If so, then you must conclude that the **Second** button was clicked. Therefore, using the $button=$_POST["second"] command, you assign the value of the element from the $_POST array with the "second" key to the $button variable. That is the value "SECOND" of the value attribute of the second button.

As a result of executing the conditional statement, the $button variable gets the value of the value attribute of the button clicked by the user. That value is written to the document the server sends to the browser.

Using Lists and Checkboxes

The following example uses PHP to process data from a form with a drop-down list and checkboxes. How the browser window looks at the initial stage is shown in Figure 12-11.

Details

You should use the previous scheme: in the root directory for the local server, you place the index.html file, which contains the form description.

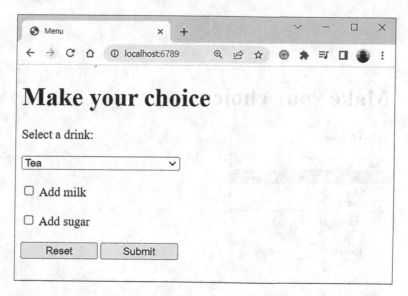

Figure 12-11. *The form with a drop-down list and checkboxes*

The window contains a form where the user is prompted to select a drink (from a drop-down list). Also, the user can select to add (or not to add) milk and sugar. The window with the expanded drop-down list is shown in Figure 12-12.

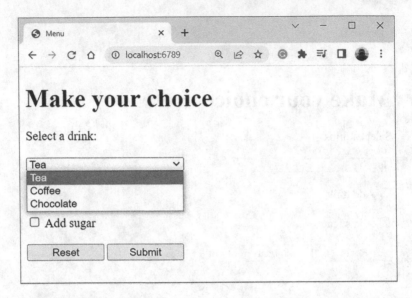

Figure 12-12. *The window with the expanded drop-down list*

There are also two buttons in the window: **Reset** and **Submit**. Clicking the **Reset** button resets the form settings. The form data is sent to the server when you click the **Submit** button. Figure 12-13 shows the window with the form settings made: the **Coffee** drink is selected in the drop-down list, the **Add milk** checkbox is checked, and the **Add sugar** checkbox is not checked.

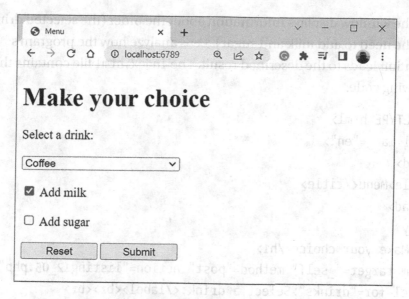

Figure 12-13. *The settings in the form*

If you send the data to the server, you get the result shown in Figure 12-14.

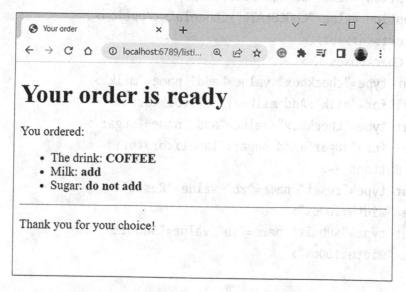

Figure 12-14. *The result of processing the form data*

The window displays information about the order (the selected drink and the need to add milk and sugar). Let's analyze how the program's execution leads to the described result. The index.html file contains the following code.

```
<!DOCTYPE html>
<html lang="en">
<head>
<title>Menu</title>
</head>
<body>
<h1>Make your choice</h1>
<form target="_self" method="post" action="listing12_05.php">
<label for="drinks">Select a drink:</label><br><br>
<!-- The drop-down list -->
<select name="drinks" style="width:205px">
    <option value="TEA">Tea</option>
    <option value="COFFEE">Coffee</option>
    <option value="CHOCOLATE">Chocolate</option>
</select><br><br>
<!-- Checkboxes -->
<input type="checkbox" value="add" name="milk">
<label for="milk">Add milk</label><br><br>
<input type="checkbox" value="add" name="sugar">
<label for="sugar">Add sugar</label><br><br>
<!-- Buttons -->
<input type="reset" name="rb" value="Reset"
style="width:100px">
<input type="submit" name="sb" value="Submit"
style="width:100px">
```

```
</form>
</body>
</html>
```

The drop-down list is an element defined by the `<select>` and `</select>` tags. And this time, you implement the buttons as `<input>` elements.

THE HTML BASICS

The element defined by the `<select>` and `</select>` tags is a drop-down list. The items of the list (you see them when expanding the list) are created by the `<option>` and `</option>` tags. The text between those descriptors is the item's content displayed in the list. You specify the value attribute for the three `<option>` elements. The `<select>` element has the value `"drinks"` for the name attribute. When the form data is submitted to the server, there is an element in the $_POST array with the key `"drinks"`, and the value of that element is determined by the value attribute of the `<option>` element selected in the drop-down list.

The checkboxes are created as `<input>` elements, with the type attribute set to `"checkbox"`. For one of the checkboxes, the value and name attributes are `"add"` and `"milk"`, respectively, and for the other – `"add"` and `"sugar"`. Suppose a checkbox is selected when submitting the form data. In that case, the $_POST array contains an element with the key determined by the value of the name attribute of that checkbox, and the value of the array element is determined by the value attribute.

The buttons are also created as `<input>` elements. The type attribute for the first button is set to `"reset"`, and for the second button, that attribute is set to `"submit"`. Therefore, the first button is a reset button. If you click it, the settings of all form elements return to their original state. The second button is a button for submitting the form data. The name attribute for buttons is equal to "rb" and "sb", respectively, but those values are not used. The value attribute determines the title displayed on the button.

The text labels are used for the list and checkboxes. The label elements are created using the <label> and </label> tags. The for attribute of those elements specifies the name (the value of the name attribute) of the element for which the text label belongs.

The <br> instruction is a command to break a line in the browser window.

The document also uses HTML comments. Comments in HTML begin with <!-- and end with -->.

As you can see from the form description, data processing is performed by the program in the listing12_05.php file. The program code is shown in Listing 12-5.

Listing 12-5. Using a List and Checkboxes

```
<!DOCTYPE html>
<html>
<head>
<title>Your order</title>
</head>
<body>
<h1>Your order is ready</h1>
<p>You ordered:</p>
<?php
    // Defines a drink:
    $drink=$_POST["drinks"];
    // Is it necessary to add milk:
    if(isset($_POST["milk"])) $milk=$_POST["milk"];
    else $milk="do not add";
```

```php
   // Is it necessary to add sugar:
   if(isset($_POST["sugar"])) $sugar=$_POST["sugar"];
   else $sugar="do not add";
   // The text to add to the document:
   $txt=<<<MYTEXT
   <ul>
   <li>The drink: <strong>$drink</strong></li>
   <li>Milk: <strong>$milk</strong></li>
   <li>Sugar: <strong>$sugar</strong></li>
   </ul>
   MYTEXT;
   // Adds the text to the document:
   echo $txt;
?>
<hr>
<p>Thank you for your choice!</p>
</body>
</html>
```

This HTML document contains a PHP code that generates text (based on the form data), and then the text is added to the document. But first, the `$drink=$_POST["drinks"]` command assigns the value attribute of the element selected in the drop-down list to the $drink variable.

ⓘ **Note**   In this case, you don't check if the $_POST array contains an element with the key "drinks" (the value of the drop-down list's name attribute) because some element in the list is always selected.

Next, two similar conditional statements follow. In the first one, the isset($_POST["milk"]) condition is checked. It is true if the $_POST array contains an element with the key "milk" (the checkbox for adding milk is checked). If so, then the $milk=$_POST["milk"] command assigns the value attribute of the corresponding checkbox to the $milk variable. Otherwise, the $milk="do not add" command is executed.

The data associated with the checkbox "responsible" for adding sugar is processed similarly. But now, the isset($_POST["sugar"]) condition is checked. If the condition is true, the $sugar=$_POST["sugar"] command is executed. If the condition is false, the $sugar="do not add" command is executed.

After the values of the $drink, $milk, and $sugar variables are defined, the $txt variable is created with a multi-line text value.

THE HTML BASICS

Use the <ul> and </ul> tags to create an unordered list. List items are defined by the <li> and </li> tags.

The <hr> instruction adds a horizontal line to the document.

The echo $txt command adds the generated text into the document, which the server returns to the browser.

A Slider and Radio Buttons

The following example continues the "culinary" theme. This time, you use controls such as a slider and radio buttons. The browser window displays the document shown in Figure 12-15 at the initial stage.

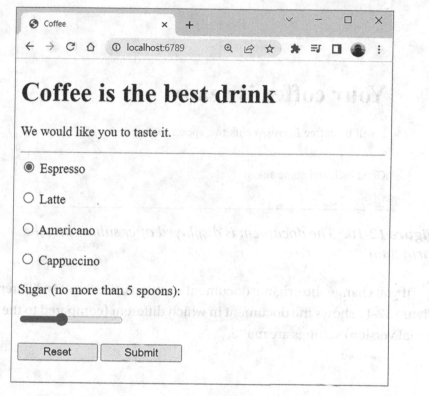

Figure 12-15. *The document with a slider and radio buttons*

In addition to text, the document contains a group of four radio buttons with the names of coffee drinks and a slider at the bottom of the form for selecting the amount of sugar to add to the drink. Two buttons in the document (**Reset** and **Submit**) allow us to clear the form (reset controls) and submit the form data to the server. The server sends a response, which depends on the form settings. For example, if the settings in the form are the same as those proposed in the initial document, the result is as in Figure 12-16.

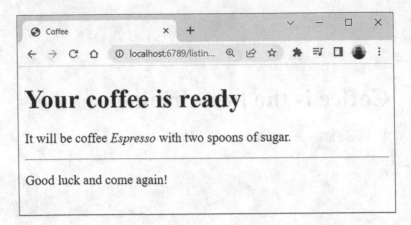

Figure 12-16. *The document is displayed after submitting the form data*

If you change the original document's settings, the result is different. Figure 12-17 shows the document in which different (compared to the initial version) settings are made.

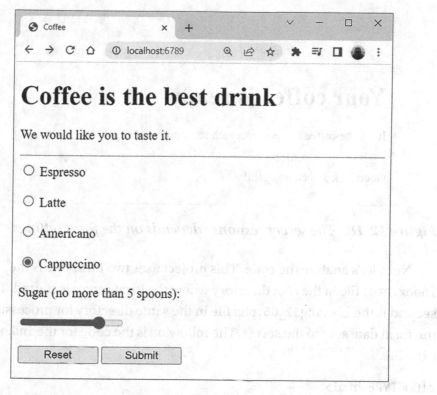

Figure 12-17. *The settings of the form are changed in the initial document*

After submitting the form data, you get the result, as shown in Figure 12-18.

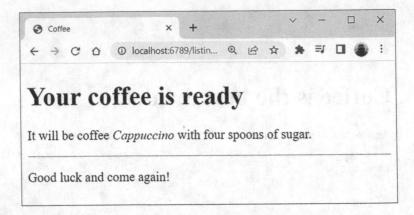

Figure 12-18. *The server response depends on the form settings*

Next, let's analyze the code. This project uses two files. One is the index.html file in the root directory where the local server is started. The second is the listing12_06.php file in the same directory for processing the form data sent to the server. The following is the code for the index. html file.

```
<!DOCTYPE html>
<html lang="en">
<head>
<title>Coffee</title>
</head>
<body>
<h1>Coffee is the best drink</h1>
<p> We would like you to taste it.</p>
<hr>
<form target="_self" method="post" action="listing12_06.php">
<!-- Radio Buttons -->
<input type="radio" id="espresso" name="coffee" checked
value="Espresso">
<label for="espresso">Espresso</lebel>
```

```
<br><br>
<input type="radio" id="latte" name="coffee" value="Latte">
<label for="latte">Latte</lebel>
<br><br>
<input type="radio" id="americano" name="coffee"
value="Americano">
<label for="americano">Americano</lebel><br><br>
<input type="radio" id="cappuccino" name="coffee"
value="Cappuccino">
<label for="cappuccino">Cappuccino</lebel><br><br>
<label for="sugar">Sugar (no more than 5 spoons):</label>
<br><br>
<!-- Slider -->
<input type="range" name="sugar" min="0" max="5" step="1"
value="2">
<br><br>
<!-- Buttons -->
<input type="reset" name="rb" value="Reset"
style="width:100px">
<input type="submit" name="sb" value="Submit"
style="width:100px">
</form>
</body>
</html>
```

The document, in general, and the form in particular, contains many familiar elements. In addition to them, there are radio buttons and a slider. The radio buttons and the slider are implemented as <input> elements.

THE HTML BASICS

For the radio buttons, the `type` attribute is set to `"radio"`, and for the slider, the `type` attribute is set to `"range"`.

In addition to the `type` attribute, the following attributes are specified for the radio buttons. The `name` attribute for all radio buttons is `"coffee"`. You use the same value for the `name` attribute since you need to group the radio buttons. One and only one radio button can be selected within a group. Group the radio buttons by giving the same value to the `name` attribute. Individual radio buttons can be identified using the `id` attribute. You use that attribute to bind a text label and a radio button. The radio buttons also have the `value` attribute. By that attribute, when processing the request, you determine which radio button was selected when submitting the form. One of the radio buttons has the `checked` attribute, which means that the corresponding radio button is selected (checked).

For the slider, the `name` attribute's value is `"sugar"`. That attribute is used when processing the form data to determine the slider. The state of the slider is defined by the `value` attribute (initially set to `"2"`). The `min` and `max` attributes are the minimum and maximum values for the slider, respectively. The `step` attribute holds the increment for the positions of the slider.

Listing 12-6 is the code used to process the form data.

Listing 12-6. Using a Slider and Radio Buttons

```
<!DOCTYPE html>
<html>
<head>
<title>Coffee</title>
</head>
<body>
```

```
<h1>Your coffee is ready</h1>
<p>
<?php
    // The function defines text with information
    // about sugar content:
    function getsugar($spoons){
        switch($spoons){
            case 1: return "with a spoon of sugar";
            case 2: return "with two spoons of sugar";
            case 3: return "with three spoons of sugar";
            case 4: return "with four spoons of sugar";
            case 5: return "with five spoons of sugar";
            default: return "no sugar";
        }
    }
    // Defines a drink:
    $coffee=$_POST["coffee"];
    // Determines the sugar content:
    $sugar=getsugar($_POST["sugar"]);
    // The text to add to the document:
    $txt="It will be coffee <em>$coffee</em> $sugar.";
    // Adding text to the document:
    echo $txt;
?>
</p>
<hr>
<p>Good luck and come again!</p>
</body>
</html>
```

The idea is quite simple. Following the form's settings, the $txt variable is formed, and its text value is inserted into the document that the server sends to the browser. The text includes the values of the $coffee and $sugar variables. The $coffee variable is determined by the $coffee=$_POST["coffee"] command. That is the value attribute of the selected radio button. The getsugar() function determines the $sugar variable. The function has a text argument (assumed to be the slider's value attribute). Depending on the argument, the function returns a string with information about how many spoons of sugar to put in coffee. The function is used in the $sugar=getsugar($_POST["sugar"]) command. Here, to get the value attribute of the slider, use the $_POST["sugar"] instruction. In all other aspects, the code should be clear.

THE HTML BASICS

The corresponding block is marked with the <em> and </em> tags to highlight a text in italics.

Summary

- PHP code can be added to HTML documents, selected by the <?php and ?> instructions. Such blocks allow us to automatically generate HTML code fragments and insert them into the final document.

- PHP scripts can be used to process requests performed through the address bar. Parameters passed in the address bar are stored in the $_GET array. The name of the parameter is the key of the element, and the value of the parameter is the element's value.

- PHP scripts are used to process form data sent to the server. Usually, data is sent using the POST method, and the parameters that the server receives are contained in the $_POST array. The name attribute of a form element specifies the element's key in the array. The value attribute of a form element is the value of the corresponding element in the array.

CHAPTER 13

Afterword: What Was and What Will Be

I'm tired. I blink with difficulty!

—*ALF* (TV series)

Programming is a field in which something new, effective, and interesting appears constantly. So, monitoring all innovations is necessary, but for objective reasons, that is not always possible. Therefore, the "minimal strategy" is to understand and assimilate the basic principles underlying this or that technology. It is important because understanding the basic concept makes it possible to quickly and easily learn new approaches and employ resources, just like new elements of a children's construction set are added to an existing framework.

The book discussed the most essential topics and issues related to learning the *PHP language*. In addition to the actual syntax rules and constructions, there is also such an aspect as the use of the language in practice. But to understand how a language "works" in real life, it is vital to know what it can do in principle. Hopefully, after reading the book and studying the examples discussed, you now have an overall picture of PHP's potential.

© Alex Vasilev 2024
A. Vasilev, *PHP by Example*, https://doi.org/10.1007/979-8-8688-0258-4_13

One more point is important to be stressed. Programming languages are studied for a variety of reasons. But the main thing, perhaps, is the desire to get a new profession, to become a programmer. That means that programming is not limited to learning a single language. Each language has its own characteristics, but certain universal programming principles are common for most languages. The presented book is to help you understand, even on an intuitive level, those principles and make it easier for them to move ahead along your professional path. And, of course, thank you for paying attention to the book.

Index

Symbols

== and != operators, 117
$A="Alpha" command, 176
$A++ command, 65
$color=colors() command, 337
$gen=gen() command, 350
$gen->rewind() command, 351
$num=func_num_args()
    command, 152
$number variable, 65
$res=power($z,$num)
    command, 136
$rnd=randoms(5) command, 346
$setNumber() method, 247

A

Abstract methods, 273
Anonymous function, 162
Array
    assignments, 111, 113, 115
    comparing, 117, 118
    concatenation, 115
    definition, 91, 125
    elements, 125
    example, 92–94, 96–98
    functions, 119–121, 123
    loop

      deleting elements, 101, 102
      elements, 104, 105
      endforeach keyword, 100
      foreach, 103, 106
      statement, 99
    multidimensional, 107, 108, 110
array_pop($C) command, 124
Assignment operators, 48, 52
Associative array, 91

B

Bitwise operations, 41

C

calc() function, 183, 184
__call() method, 226, 228, 229
catch keyword, 304
Child/derived class, 244, 271
Classes and objects
    constructor, 211, 212
    copying objects, 217–220
    creating, 203–206
    destructor, 213, 214
    fields, in constructor, 235–238
    methods, 207, 209
    OOP principles, 199–202

© Alex Vasilev 2024
A. Vasilev, *PHP by Example*, https://doi.org/10.1007/979-8-8688-0258-4

Printed in the United States
by Baker & Taylor Publisher Services

Printed in the United States
by Baker & Taylor Publisher Services